MERGERS & ACQUISITIONS

SECOND EDITION

Also from Ernst & Young

The Ernst & Young Guide to Total Cost Management
The Complete Guide to Special Event Management
The Ernst & Young Guide to Expanding in the Global Market
The Ernst & Young Resource Guide to Global Markets
Understanding and Using Financial Data:
An Ernst & Young Guide for Attorneys
The Ernst & Young Business Plan Guide, Second Edition
Managing Information Strategically
(The Ernst & Young Information Management Series)

Forthcoming from Ernst & Young
(Titles subject to change)

The Ernst & Young Almanac and Guide to U.S. Business Cities:
65 Leading Places to do Business
The Name of the Game: The Business of Sports
Privatization: Investing in Infrastructures Around the World
The Ernst & Young Guide to Financing for Growth

MERGERS & ACQUISITIONS

SECOND EDITION

ERNST & YOUNG

John Wiley & Sons, Inc.
New York • Chichester • Brisbane • Toronto • Singapore

Copyright © 1994 by Ernst & Young
Published by John Wiley & Sons, Inc.

Library of Congress Cataloging-in-Publication Data:
Mergers & acquisitions / Ernst & Young — 2nd ed.
        p.   cm.
    ISBN 0-471-57818-5 (alk. paper)
    1. Consolidation and mergers of corporations—United States.
 I. Ernst & Young.   II. Title: Mergers and acquisitions.
 HD2746.55.U5M47   1994
 658.1'6—dc20   93-7648

Printed in the United States of America

10   9   8   7

PREFACE

Mergers and acquisitions are often defining moments in a company's history. As such, these transactions are too important to leave to the experts. CEOs must be responsible for the critical decisions surrounding both overall strategy and specific acquisition transactions. At the end of the day, it is the CEO who will receive the credit for success or the blame for an ill-considered or poorly executed transaction.

Yet despite the importance of acquisitions to an organization, many otherwise well-managed companies fail to devote the necessary time and resources to this area. Countless transactions fail primarily because a company has neglected to create a strategically integrated and comprehensive acquisition program.

For this reason, the advice of qualified experts is essential. A team effort will produce the best results. Technical issues should be addressed by team members qualified in a particular field, but senior managers must assure that the strategic and operational advantages of the proposed business combination are captured in the final transaction.

This book addresses each of the components of a successful program from the vantage point of the owners and senior managers who are the organization's principal conceptual thinkers, planners, organizers, and coordinators. It attempts to strip away much of the mystique surrounding acquisitions, to identify the business issues, and to equip CEOs to make or approve judgments and decisions throughout the process. Given the fact that the M & A climate today is significantly different from the recent past, it is our hope that this book will serve as a guide for executives.

The authors are all recognized experts in their respective fields, and each has participated in numerous acquisition transactions. Equally important, having identified the issues in their particular areas about which senior managers should have a working knowledge, they have presented those issues in nontechnical language familiar to business generalists.

The mergers and acquisitions landscape has shifted since the 1980s, when the highly leveraged transaction was common. Over the past decade, the financing markets have changed dramatically and a different type of transaction has gained prominence. Today corporate buyers seeking strategic advantage are initiating fewer hostile acquisitions, and the "typical" transaction is fueled less by leverage and more by equity. In an effort to clean up their balance sheets, a growing number of companies are restructuring and selling off divisions whose debt they can no longer afford to carry. According to *Mergers & Acquisitions* magazine, "Sell-offs accounted for nearly a third of the deals in the 1980s, and it is no coincidence that they have been prominent in 1992 activity. For many companies, the best strategic bet is to sell now, even if top dollar is not achievable, and get on with a more focused game plan."

Plain vanilla is the flavor of the decade, as acquirers return to basics. CEOs now realize that they should be making acquisitions based on good corporate strategy, sound balance sheets, and more equity-based financing. Gone are the days of the quick tender offer and the approach that says, "Let's get this deal done quickly before someone else can bid up the price." Instead, acquirers are spending more time, performing more strategic due diligence work, and determining in advance precisely where a company will fit into their overall corporate strategy. And as the markets become more global, transactions must be evaluated on a more global basis as well.

Throughout the global marketplace there have been dramatic changes since the 1970s. Companies that were once flush with cash now find that if they want to remain competitive, they must consolidate, trim the fat, and become leaner and meaner operators. There is increasing recognition of the utility of strategic alliances in which two or more companies join together and pool risks, rewards, and resources to achieve specific but sometimes different strategic goals.

The ability to deal effectively with situations involving troubled companies will be a requirement for many executives in the 1990s. No longer synonymous with the term "unmarketable," in many cases these companies have fundamentally sound operations burdened by excessive debt. Spawned by the leveraged buy-out frenzy of the 1980s, these companies may present new opportunities for astute acquirers, as well as the chance to control more of the sales process than possible in a transaction involving a healthy company.

Providers of financing are receptive to cost-efficient companies and are generally willing to grant more favorable terms to a highly regarded management team. But lending standards today are more stringent than in the past. Banks have returned to the standards of the days before the highly leveraged transaction, and they examine loan requests more closely and structuring proposals more conservatively. Credit quality, which has always been the most important lending consideration, is carefully evaluated at all levels within an institution.

Successful acquisitions are usually the result of a disciplined process—a process that can be managed by a CEO in the same manner as any other major undertaking. Certainly it is essential to draw on the advice of experienced and knowledgeable specialists such as our contributing authors, but a CEO must understand the business issues and be able to assess the impact on the corporation of alternative courses of action.

BRIAN J. MILLER
New York City

ABOUT THE EDITOR

Brian J. Miller is National Director of Ernst & Young's Corporate Finance practice, based in New York. Mr. Miller is responsible for directing engagements to assist clients with corporate acquisitions and divestitures, management buyouts, strategic alliances, financial restructurings, recapitalizations, defensive strategies, and private placements of debt and equity. He also assists in the coordination of our Global Corporate Finance Network and has been an active corporate finance professional for over 14 years.

Prior to joining the firm in 1987, Mr. Miller spent nine years in commercial banking. His last position was Middle Market Regional Manager at a major New York bank. While there, Mr. Miller was instrumental in the establishment of their D.I.P. lending group, the first of its kind in a money center bank.

Mr. Miller received his B.A. from Cornell University and his M.B.A. from New York University. In addition, he has also lectured on such topics as International Acquisition Strategies, Financing Troubled Companies In and Out of Bankruptcy, Transaction Structuring, Leveraged Acquisitions and Recapitalizations, and Lending to Corporate Groups.

CONTRIBUTING AUTHORS

Stephen M. Banker is a Partner in the New York office of Skadden, Arps, Slate, Meagher & Flom. For the past 16 years his practice has focused on mergers and acquisitions and other corporate transactions, with a recent emphasis on cross-border acquisitions and joint ventures.

Richmond G. Bernhardt III is a Partner in Ernst & Young's Corporate Finance practice based in Dallas, Texas. He has responsibility for engagement activities in mergers, acquisitions, financings, and other corporate finance transactions in the Southwest Region.

Martin J. Bowne is a Partner in the Financial Services Division of Ernst & Young's New York office and is responsible for the activities of that office's Mergers and Acquisitions Due Diligence Group.

George H. Bristol is a Partner and the Regional Director of Corporate Finance-West Region of Ernst & Young. He has been an investment banker since 1974 focusing on middle market mergers, acquisitions, and financings.

Dewey B. Crawford is a Partner in the law firm of Gardner, Carton & Douglas, Chicago. He specializes in mergers and acquisitions and corporate finance and has written and spoken extensively on negotiating acquisitions.

Robert A. Del Genio is a Partner in Ernst & Young's Corporate Finance practice based in New York. He has acted as exclusive financial advisor to the board of directors and/or principal shareholders in the purchase, sale, or financing of numerous businesses in a variety of industries. He also has been active in valuing and selling troubled companies both in and outside of Chapter 11.

Dan C. Fort is a Partner in Corporate Finance for Ernst & Young based in Atlanta. He has assisted various large and middle market companies in acquisitions, divestitures, restructurings, and business strategies.

Glenn H. Gage is a Partner in the Mergers & Acquisitions Due Diligence Group of the Financial Services Division in Ernst & Young's New York office.

Janet M. Green is a Partner in Ernst & Young's Corporate Finance practice based in New York. She assists entrepreneurial companies with acquisitions, divestitures, and financial restructurings and is a frequent speaker on financing alternatives.

John S. Karls is an Ernst & Young International Tax Partner in New York City, the editor of EY's Effective Tax Strategies for International Corporate Acquisitions (2d ed., Klewer 1992), an Associate Professor at Fordham University, the Vice Chair of the American Bar Association Tax Section's Committee on Foreign Activities of U.S. Taxpayers, and an editor of the Journal of International Taxation (Warren Gorham & Lamont).

Thomas J. Kichler is a Partner and Director of Ernst & Young's Midwest Region Corporate Finance practice. He assisted numerous U.S. and European clients in planning and executing sales and divestitures, acquisitions, leveraged buyouts, and related financings. He spent two years at Ernst & Young M&A Europe, based in Geneva, Switzerland, working on cross-border transactions.

Carolyn Buck Luce is a Partner of Ernst & Young's Special Services Group, providing financial and business advisory services in the fields of Corporate Finance and Restructuring & Reorganization.

A.J. Matsuura is a Senior Manager of Ernst & Young's West Region Corporate Finance practice. He has extensive experience in structuring and financing corporate acquisitions, divestitures, and recapitalizations in standard as well as troubled company situations. In addition to having led seminars and conferences on various corporate finance topics, he has also co-authored articles and been interviewed and quoted on corporate finance issues for several national publications.

Richard P. Miller is a Principal in the Northeast Region of Ernst & Young, and a member of the Region's Technical Group. His responsibilities include assisting clients, audit partners, and senior managers in the Region on accounting, financial reporting, and SEC reporting matters.

Steven D. Oesterle is a Partner and Regional Director of Corporate Finance at Ernst & Young based in Cleveland. He also has regional responsibility for the firm's delivery of restructuring and reorganization services, valuation services, and litigation services.

Eric R. Pelander is a Partner of Ernst & Young and currently directs the firm's National Planning Group. He has consulted with numerous companies on strategic matters, including joint ventures and other strategic alliances.

Gerard B. Pompan is Director of Tax of the Ernst & Young New York Financial Services Division. A CPA and attorney, in addition to being director of tax, he heads up the Financial Services Division Tax M&A Due Diligence and Restructuring Group, which advises on acquisitions, sales, and financial restructurings. Formerly, he was with the National Office of the Internal Revenue Service in the merger and acquisitions area.

Philip D. Robers is a Partner with Ernst & Young and serves as the Area Director for Management Consulting in the Mid-Atlantic area. He has over 20 years in management consulting and has consulted with over 100 major corporations in several industries. He holds a Ph.D. in Management Science from Northwestern University.

Larry E. Senn, Ph.D. is Chairman of the Senn-Delaney Leadership Consulting Group, a firm which works with CEOs and their organizations on team building, leadership development, and reshaping corporate cultures. One of their specialties is the cultural and human resource aspects of mergers and acquisitions. Dr. Senn is a co-author of *21st Century Leadership—Dialogues with 100 Top Leaders.*

Thomas E. Shea is Regional Director of Ernst & Young's New York Actuarial, Benefits and Compensation Services practice and has provided total pay strategy and compensation consulting assistance to several hundred clients in diverse industries. He held key management positions with major corporations and consulting firms prior to joining Ernst & Young.

Michael N. Sohn is a Senior Partner in the Washington, D.C. law firm of Arnold & Porter. He is a former General Counsel of the Federal Trade Commission and currently serves as the Responsible Partner for Arnold & Porter's Antitrust Practice Group.

John E. Vaught, FSA is the Regional Director—Retirement Plan Services for the New York Metropolitan ABC practice of Ernst & Young. He is formerly of Buck Consultants and Frank B. Hall Consulting Company.

Ian P. Wilson is a Senior Manager of Ernst & Young's New York Corporate Finance practice where he specializes in cross-border mergers and acquisitions. Prior to his current position he spent several years with the firm's Corporate Finance practice in London, England.

Robert P. Wujtowicz is a Senior Manager of Ernst & Young's Midwest Region Corporate Finance practice. He previously served as a corporate banking officer for Continental Bank and in several corporate development positions.

ACKNOWLEDGMENTS

I want to express my sincere thanks to all of the authors who have given so much time to this book. They have exercised a great deal of patience through numerous iterations as we worked together to eliminate technical jargon and make the material more usable by senior managers and businesspeople generally.

From Ernst & Young, Mort Meyerson, National Director of Public Communications, was instrumental in starting the project with the publisher. His editorial suggestions were also most helpful. Bob Conway, chairman of Ernst & Young International's Global Corporate Finance Network, was instrumental in establishing the vision for this edition, and in securing the support of the many contributors both within and outside Ernst & Young. Elaine Beery, the Corporate Finance Group's creative director, was adept at helping the authors craft their contributions into a coordinated and logical progression. Finally, Marc Eiger deserves very special credit and thanks for coordinating all the frenzied activity of the final months. He was the principal liaison among the participants at that critical time.

CONTENTS

PART I

Acquisition Planning and Strategy

INTRODUCTION

An acquisition based on an underlying strategy is much more likely to succeed than one that results from an impulsive reaction to an "attractive" opportunity. Developing a strategy and implementing a proactive acquisition program is the subject of the opening chapter of this section. In the same chapter Richmond G. Bernhardt III also discusses strategic fit. An acquisition is unlikely to increase shareholder value unless opportunities exist for significant sharing of benefits that improve the competitive position of the participants.

In the second chapter of this section Dan C. Fort provides a guide to evaluating the overall attractiveness of an acquisition candidate. Products, market position, management, and other characteristics must be assessed in a comprehensive evaluation. These nonfinancial factors largely determine strategic fit. In addition, a thorough understanding of the candidate's present financial situation is a prerequisite for projecting its future performance.

Value, like beauty, is in the eye of the beholder. In an acquisition, the question is not so much "What is it worth?" as "What is it worth to us?" Steven D. Oesterle offers three valuation methodologies in the third chapter. By using these external and internal methodologies, a buyer can construct a range of values within which to negotiate. Most important, the acquirer can determine the walk-away price, the highest price at which the transaction is likely to increase shareholder value.

As Martin J. Bowne points out in the fourth chapter, no book can make a deal work if the numbers do not point toward success. The purpose of the due diligence process, which is the intense examination of a target by an objective third party, is to help investors and lenders understand the true picture behind the numbers so that they can find hidden treasures while avoiding hidden traps. As investors become increasingly selective, they place greater emphasis on due diligence to help identify high quality deals that have realistic pricing structures.

No longer synonymous with the term "unmarketable," troubled companies provide new opportunities for acquirers. Robert A. Del Genio explains in Chapter 5 that this term has also come to include businesses that are overleveraged and unable to meet their debt-service burdens—but that can still generate acceptable, or even optimal, operating cash flows. In many instances, the acquirer maintains greater control over the sales process in such businesses than in transactions involving healthy companies.

CHAPTER 1

THE ACQUISITION PROCESS: A PROGRAM FOR SUCCESS

A merger or acquisition transaction often represents a defining moment in a company's development. In spite of the importance of these transactions, the overall track record for business combinations has not been a resounding success.

Why do so many highly visible transactions fail to meet their stated objective of increasing shareholder value? How can management institute an acquisition program that avoids the most common merger and acquisition mistakes?

A long list of reasons for the mediocre record of business combinations could be given here, and a specific reason could be cited for each transaction as the principal cause of its failure. In each case, however, the acquirer probably failed to establish a compelling strategic basis for making the acquisition. And in each case the failure was related to a failure to create a strategically integrated, comprehensive acquisition program.

Typically, acquisitions have a significant impact on the overall profitability and financial health of a corporation. Thus, such transactions deserve the same thoughtful planning and execution as the introduction of a major new project, the building of a new plant, or the purchase of a major piece of equipment. Yet despite the importance of acquisitions to an organization, many otherwise well-managed companies fail to devote the necessary time and resources to this area.

Many companies simply react to acquisition opportunities. Rather than defining in advance the characteristics of a desirable candidate, CEOs often rely on their instincts and expect to recognize a good acquisition when they encounter one. Unfortunately, every investment banker can produce an acquisition candidate that sounds like a great opportunity but may not be since the acquisition characteristics are not clearly defined.

In a proactive program the acquirer is the initiator. Rather than reacting to random opportunities as they are presented, the proactive acquirer defines acquisition objectives first, then moves aggressively to achieve those objectives.

Equally important, companies executing a proactive acquisition program based on established objectives are better able to respond to auctions and other time-sensitive situations than potential buyers who must wrestle with strategic questions each time an opportunity arises. A well-organized, coordinated process increases rather than decreases flexibility.

With a proactive acquisition program, a company is far more likely to avoid costly mistakes and to make business combinations that contribute to the creation of shareholder value. Such a program also gives management considerably greater control over the company's destiny.

An acquisition program should be viewed as a dynamic process. Objectives and tactics can be modified in response to events and to the availability of relevant data, but actions are not dependent on those events. For a program to succeed it must be proactive yet under control.

A successful acquisition program must also be an integral part of a company's overall strategic plan. Acquisitions can support a number of important strategic goals including growth, diversification, product or market expansion, and access to technology. Most failed acquisitions result from permitting opportunity to drive strategy, rather than integrating acquisition decisions into an overall corporate strategy.

A comprehensive acquisition program should:

- Establish responsibility at the policy level;
- Develop an acquisition plan;
- Define acquisition criteria;
- Identify potential acquisition candidates;
- Make effective contact with candidates;
- Perform thorough due diligence;
- Negotiate terms that preserve the benefits identified; and
- Reap the benefits through effective postacquisition integration.

ESTABLISHING RESPONSIBILITY

Successful acquisition programs are positioned at the same strategic level within the company as other major functions such as finance, marketing, and manufacturing. When corporate development is the part-time responsibility of an assistant treasurer, the unfavorable results or lack of substantive activity are predictable. Given the potential impact on the corporation, the planning and execution of an acquisition program deserves the attention of a company's highest-ranking policymakers.

The tasks involved are varied and complex and must draw on different areas of expertise within the company. Calling on a multidisciplinary team of policy-level officers to act as a steering committee ensures that the views and concerns of each of the functional areas will be addressed. In addition, the involvement and commitment of these high-ranking officers assures the cooperation of their staffs.

Many middle-market companies do not have sufficient resources to dedicate senior staff members to an acquisition program. An outside financial adviser can provide a company with access to full-time corporate finance professionals to support the development and implementation of an effective acquisition program. It is critically important, however, that a financial adviser share the same long-term commitment to the company's corporate strategy as management.

DEVELOPING AN ACQUISITION PLAN

Every acquisition must contribute to a company's overall business strategy. Such a statement may seem obvious in a book directed at senior managers, but many U.S. corporations violate this principle. In many instances, acquiring companies fail to determine their strategic objectives. (Admittedly, some acquisitions fail because the execution of an individual transaction is flawed; the authors of succeeding chapters address this issue.) Some acquisitions clearly are made more to advance the self-interest of managers than to enhance shareholder value.

The mere existence of financial capability often causes management to pursue "growth for growth's sake." Utilizing excess cash flow, accumulated liquidity, and unused borrowing power to finance acquisitions simply because acquisitions are financially possible reflects dangerously flawed reasoning. The same unused liquidity and borrowing power may also attract unwanted acquirers and provide company managers with another nonstrategic incentive to acquire.

Increasing market share is frequently given as a rationale for acquiring a competitor at a high price that otherwise would be difficult to justify. If such an acquisition makes the acquirer the dominant participant in its market or otherwise creates a favorable change in market dynamics that is reflected in future profit margins, the market share rationale may be supportable. Too often, however, increasing market share or simply increasing revenues in absolute terms without evaluating the impact on shareholder value becomes a justifiable acquisition strategy in the minds of CEOs.

A sound, well-planned acquisition program will allow managers to direct their instincts—including such admirable instincts as self-preservation and the desire to manage a larger enterprise—in line with the creation of shareholder value. Only through an organized program can companies ensure that appropriate alternatives are available in a crisis. A defensive acquisition or identification of a "white knight" merger partner is far more likely to be successful if it is incorporated into an ongoing acquisition program.

How, then, can management determine whether a proposed acquisition will help a company achieve its primary objective of increasing shareholder value?

First, an acquisition should offer clear advantages over achieving the same objectives through internal growth. These advantages may include a lower level of perceived risk, time savings, reduced competition, and lower costs. The goals, however, should include definable and quantifiable benefits of one course of action over the other. Choosing between internal and external growth alternatives becomes a continuous series of "make or buy" decisions.

Second, an acquisition should meet the shared-benefits test. One of the two companies must offer cost-sharing, technological, marketing, or other benefits to the other. In the best matches, these benefits flow continuously. This happens, for example, when incremental volume is added in an acquisition and thus reduces unit costs, or when new products are added to an existing distribution system. Benefits may also be very short-lived; they may even be one-time improvements, but the opportunity to gain the advantages or to share the benefits should offer a strategic purpose for the acquisition.

Unfortunately, potential acquisition benefits may also be illusory or extremely difficult to achieve. Too often, vaguely defined benefits or synergies are offered as a rationale for making an unrewarding acquisition—or for paying too much. Overconfidence in one company's ability to manage another business is not a fundamentally sound reason to support an important investment decision.

The two strategies discussed below are similar to each other and meet the shared-benefits test, but have only limited attractiveness or utility for most acquirers.

The conglomerates of the 1970s, such as ITT, Gulf & Western, and LTV, made popular a strategy based on building a portfolio of sound, well-managed companies that were only loosely related to each other, if at all. The success of this strategy rested on management's ability to identify and acquire undervalued companies, to allocate capital between the "cash cows" and the "stars" at favorable rates, and to encourage disciplined, pragmatic, professional management by the relatively autonomous managers of the constituent companies.

Though this portfolio strategy has failed to produce added shareholder value on a lasting basis in all but a few instances, it continues to be practiced by many acquirers. Identifying and acquiring a good but undervalued company while in competition with leveraged buyout funds and similar purely financial players is difficult, to say the least. Even if the acquisition is successful, the market, which can achieve its own portfolio diversification, often penalizes the market value of the acquirer through a "conglomerate discount."

A similar strategy is to acquire companies selling at substantial discounts as a result of low earnings or actual losses. Ideal turn-around candidates are not those suffering from serious, fundamental problems. Instead, they are those companies whose performance can generally be improved by disposing of their less profitable operations, by providing capital at more favorable rates, or by exercising more pragmatic management. Such companies are difficult to identify. In addition, they may be even more difficult to acquire because of the likely competition from professional acquirers and leveraged buyout funds, who are also attracted to a target with turnaround potential.

Note that since both the portfolio and the turnaround strategies are based on the acquirer's providing benefits to the acquired company, they pass the shared-benefits test. Because such benefits are relatively short-lived, pursuing either of these strategies also requires great skill in market timing and knowing when to sell a company. Success depends as well on the ability to continue finding and acquiring attractive companies to replace those that are divested. Since most companies are not skilled in market timing, they are best served by viewing acquisitions as "keepers" and integral parts of their overall strategic plans.

The same process that helps determine a company's overall strategic plan can be used to design an acquisition program as an integral component of that plan. An integrated acquisition plan should be based on an evaluation of both internal and external factors, identifying competitive strengths on which to build, competitive disadvantages to correct, technological needs, volume-sensitive costs, and other strategic issues.

Clearly, a company's acquisitions within the same industry offer the greatest opportunity for success. Those that extend the geographic reach of distribution, increase market share (and eliminate a competitor), allow access to new technology, or add products to an existing distribution system are all likely to offer cost-sharing or other benefits.

In some cases, vertical integration may seem to be the safest departure from existing activities. This strategy should not be adopted too hastily, however. Captive suppliers have a tendency to become less efficient once the external discipline of competition is removed, and customers of the acquired company may be reluctant to be as dependent on a supplier after it becomes a subsidiary of a competitor.

Though it is often a desirable strategy, diversification through acquisition carries with it a considerably higher risk of failure. Successful diversification requires a very sophisticated analysis of existing strengths on which to build, as well as the impact on corporate culture and a host of external factors.

The ability to transfer critical skills presents a major opportunity for shared benefits in a diversification. However, identified areas of excellence are transferable to the acquisition only if they present opportunities for competitive advantage in the industry being entered. The distinctive strength of a low-cost manufacturer, for example, is of little consequence when a business is considering an acquisition in an industry where marketing excellence is the key to success.

For example, a regulated utility seeking to diversify probably should avoid industries in which sophisticated marketing and quick reaction time are the hallmarks of success. Instead, it should identify business segments where long-term planning horizons, large infrastructures, high levels of customer service, and/or sophisticated electronic systems are the keys to success.

A common error made in the diversification process is to acquire a company with a weak competitive position—usually because the acquisition price seems attractive when that company is compared with an industry leader. A sounder diversification strategy would be to build a strong position in a highly fragmented industry, or to acquire an industry leader.

Focused diversification through strong competitive positions in one or two new fields is preferable to scattered acquisitions in several areas. If the acquirer is a public company with a rational, understandable strategy—one that can be interpreted credibly by investment analysts—a "conglomerate discount" in the price of the acquirer's stock can be avoided.

Finally, an acquirer interested in diversifying must possess a keen understanding of the dynamics of the industry it is entering. Industry growth and profitability are clearly important. The demand for capital investment, the importance of technology, and other factors relating to ease of entry into an industry must also be considered. In sum, the acquirer must measure the overall attractiveness of an industry in a way that allows comparison with alternative possibilities. Being the best performer in an unattractive industry segment is likely to be unrewarding.

DEFINING CRITERIA

When an acquisition is determined to be a viable alternative to internal growth, a definition of detailed criteria for each area is a key component of the acquisition-planning process. A list of criteria should resemble a purchase order and describe the most desirable potential candidate. A typical list would include such factors as these:

- Industry or industry segment
- Method of distribution
- Size
- Geographic constraints
- Competitive strengths
- Importance of management continuation
- Preferred form of consideration (cash, stock, or other securities)
- Price range, including minimum and maximum price targets

Admittedly, it is unlikely that a perfectly ideal candidate will be identified and available, but it is important to create a benchmark against which to evaluate candidates. Weighing the importance of characteristics (such as those listed), either formally or informally, also aids in the screening process and in ascribing to candidates rankings in order of attractiveness.

An acquirer's long-term financial adviser can be helpful in completely identifying important acquisition criteria. In particular, a financial adviser can help to keep a company abreast of current developments in the markets for financing acquisitions and in creating acquisition structuring ideas.

IDENTIFYING ACQUISITION CANDIDATES

The process of identifying prospective candidates for acquisition begins with building a "universe," that is, a list of all companies that appear to meet the criteria. A variety of sources should be consulted. Easily accessible electronic data bases can generally provide 80 to 90 percent of the universe of company names, as well as limited descriptive information on the privately held companies. Other sources of information on acquisition candidates include the following:

- Trade association membership lists
- Trade publications
- Industry experts
- Government publications
- The acquirer's employees
- The public library

Clearly, the law of diminishing returns applies to the last few sources in this list. Nevertheless, one should remember that more than 95 percent of qualified acquisition candidates can be identified easily.

Screening a universe of several hundred companies to identify the most attractive candidates may appear to be a difficult and time-consuming task. In fact, through the application of specific criteria such as size or location, the company universe may be quickly narrowed down to a manageable number of candidates. Then, a comparison of the remaining companies against the remaining criteria should produce a list of fewer than 20 priority candidates. The task of gathering comprehensive information on the priority candidates is not nearly so formidable.

The prospect-identification process also gives the acquirer a feel for the dynamics of the targeted industry segment. Competitive conditions, industry growth trends, profit margins, and other important data can easily be gathered at the same time. Analyzing the characteristics that distinguish high-performing industry participants is also a useful exercise.

Once the internal universe-building process is complete, it is important to turn to external sources for prospective candidates—financial intermediaries. The research company W. T. Grimm estimates that an investment banker or broker is involved in about two-thirds of all merger transactions. An acquirer should establish contact with intermediaries in order to get an early look at as many opportunities as possible and to be plugged into the "deal flow."

It is not easy to attract and maintain the attention of a large number of the most active intermediaries. Many would-be acquirers have the same objectives, and most intermediaries have short attention spans. Major and regional investment banks, commercial banks, attorneys and other dedicated intermediaries should all be cultivated. Large business brokers are a good source for companies with sales under $50 million.

It is a good idea for the acquiring company to produce a written description or a very brief brochure. The brochure should:

- Describe the acquiring company and its products, and give at least a general idea of its size. (Public companies should enclose their latest financial statement.)
- List the company's acquisition criteria.
- Indicate the company's willingness to assume the intermediary's fee.
- Give the name, address, and phone number of the person to contact regarding opportunities.

This part of the program should be viewed as a marketing effort, with the goal of reaching as many active intermediaries as possible. Whenever feasible, contact with intermediaries should be made repeatedly and in person. If the acquirer is a public company, intermediaries should be added to the shareholder mailing list.

The goal of business brokers, and of the investment bankers whom they aggressively pursue, is to complete a transaction. They may stretch the stated criteria to include their own deals, even if the fit is marginal at best. This is not all bad. Nothing moves a candidate up the priority scale faster than the knowledge that it is, indeed, for sale. More important, intermediaries frequently do have creative ideas regarding the strategic benefits and synergies of an acquisition, and a modest enlargement of the original criteria may accommodate attractive opportunities that are presented.

MAKING EFFECTIVE CONTACT

How should contact be made with an attractive candidate that is not known to be for sale? The answer: much as one would approach a prospective customer for a very large sale.

The task is particularly challenging when the approach is made to a company's founder. His or her attachment to the company exceeds purely financial considerations. Convincing a founder to accept a reasonable proposal requires considerable selling skill, as well as good personal chemistry. The first decision is which individual to approach. Unless the candidate's CEO is also a principal owner, he or she might not be the best initial contact. An introduction made through a board member or the company's banker, lawyer, or accounting firm is usually a good strategy.

Most businesses, particularly those with annual revenues between $10 and $100 million, receive many unsolicited inquiries indicating someone's interest in buying them. An effective inquiry must differentiate itself from those other approaches. A respected financial adviser can help a company to differentiate its inquiry by demonstrating to the target that it is a serious buyer.

Except in a highly unusual situation, a straightforward approach works best. Typically, the initial contact, an introductory letter followed by a phone call, should do the following:

1. Introduce the potential acquirer's financial data, describe its history and major business lines, and provide product literature and other information.

2. Explain how the candidate was identified, how it fits the acquirer's criteria, what operating advantages are perceived, and so on. A complimentary description of the target's operation can help break through initial resistance. Even more convincing is to demonstrate a thorough understanding of the target's business and strategy; this strongly enhances the potential acquirer's credibility.

3. Request a meeting to discuss "a business combination" that will be advantageous to both parties. It is better to suggest dates that would be convenient rather than simply to ask whether the candidate is interested in discussing the proposition.

4. Obtain an appointment to continue the discussion, even in the face of a response such as, "We're not for sale." Persistence is usually worthwhile.

The acquirer should maintain contact, even when overtures are rebuffed. The candidate should be put on the acquirer's shareholder mailing list and periodic letters sent to reaffirm continued interest. It is also helpful to make calls and visits from time to time. In acquisitions, patience provides a competitive advantage.

When an indication of interest has been confirmed, quick action is important to maintain momentum. The first step is to set up a meeting with the candidate to learn about the seller's objectives and pricing expectations and the seller's operating and financial performance, and to identify any concerns or reservations the seller may have. The acquirer's goal is to obtain the information necessary to determine a preliminary price and to structure a letter of intent that outlines the key points of the proposed acquisition.

NEGOTIATING TERMS

An acquisition will take place only if agreement on a price is reached. At this juncture, an in-depth analysis of the candidate's financial position and operations will reveal how it has performed in the past and allow the acquirer to estimate how it is expected to perform in the future. A thorough assessment will include identification and quantification of the perceived shared benefits that led the acquirer to approach the candidate. It is critical that the acquirer be disciplined in assessing and quantifying the synergy of the business combination.

In any acquisition, the negotiating range is determined by quantifying the target's estimated value on a stand-alone or separate basis and its combined worth to the acquirer's business. By using a variety of valuation methods, a range of values within which to negotiate can be established. A valuation must include specific company information, a knowledge of the industry and current pricing benchmarks, a thorough understanding of valuation methods, and good business judgment.

An experienced financial adviser can be very important during this analytical process. A variety of valuation methods help to establish the ceiling and floor of the pricing parameters, as well as to determine the key factors that may affect the value. A buyer may be willing to pay a higher price if it believes the target company is key to its overall strategy. On the other hand, the acquirer may be able to pay less if the seller is under pressure to sell. Many otherwise lucrative acquisitions have not realized their potential, because of insufficient pricing analysis.

An important consideration in pricing an acquisition is an accurate understanding of the availability and cost of financing. The financial adviser can be of assistance in understanding current market conditions. A good acquisition that is poorly financed will not fully accomplish the objective of enhancing shareholder value.

Price considerations generally dominate negotiations between a buyer and a seller. Terms and conditions that provide an economic advantage for one party usually impose an economic disadvantage on the other. The give-and-take of such negotiations is rather straightforward and familiar to most business executives.

A second, sometimes equally important, consideration in negotiating acquisition agreements is the preservation of attractive non-financial characteristics of the company being acquired. These may include patents, trademarks, processes, or other proprietary assets. Most often, however, an acquirer should focus on the best way to assure the continuing services of key employees of the acquired company.

Successful acquirers identify the key success factors of acquisition candidates well in advance of negotiations. A manager's goal in negotiations should be to preserve and enhance the key success factors after the transaction has been consummated. The buyer's financial adviser and legal counsel will handle most of the details of documenting and closing the transaction.

STRUCTURING THE DEAL

Once the parties decide to move forward, a letter of intent is typically prepared. This is a three- to five-page summary of the principal terms and conditions of the transaction. The letter of intent outlines the nature of the transaction, the pricing considerations, and the intended time frame for completing the transaction. The letter frequently contains a "no shop" clause that precludes discussions with other potential acquirers. The "no shop" clause allows for an exclusive period of time for the acquirer to negotiate the agreement, conduct due diligence, obtain financing, and close the transaction. This document or a separate document should also contain a pledge by both parties to keep confidential specific business information or trade secrets learned during transaction discussions.

Letters of intent are usually not legally binding on either the buyer or the seller, except for the "no shop" clause, the confidentiality provisions and the paragraph stating that each party is responsible for its own transaction fees and expenses. A definitive purchase agreement typically creates a legally binding obligation to complete a transaction. However, a letter of intent is a serious commitment by both parties to pursue a defined transaction in "good faith." Potential acquisitions have collapsed after much time and effort because the absence of a letter of intent allowed a misunderstanding over a major element of the transaction.

PERFORMING DUE DILIGENCE

Once a letter of intent has been executed and the drafting of the purchase agreement is under way, the acquirer organizes a team of employees, lawyers, and CPAs or other specialists to conduct due diligence. Due diligence is a process that, in short, involves learning as much as possible about a seller's business, finances, and operations. The buyer needs to confirm the benefits of the acquisition and to ensure that there are no unrecorded liabilities or unidentified risks that could materially impact the business after the deal is consummated.

The depth and intensity of the due diligence process will vary depending on the time available and the acquirer's willingness to incur professional expenses. Due diligence involves many areas, including verification of asset ownership, review of customer and supplier lists, audits of financial records, and other procedures, such as reviewing all of the company's contracts and agreements. The due diligence process is described in greater detail in a later chapter.

In general, a buyer will need to re-examine the following questions more closely:

- Does the company really fit into the buyer's strategic goals?

- Is it truly as attractive as it originally appeared, or are there potential problems that could arise in the near future?

- Can the buyer manage the company successfully and achieve the benefits that have been identified?

- Will the company's management support the buyer's objectives?

- Will the buyer be able to integrate the acquisition operationally and financially into its existing company?

As additional facts become available and are analyzed, earlier conclusions may have to be modified. This may result in a lower proposed purchase price or in a decision not to proceed. It is important that an acquirer not allow the momentum of "doing a deal" to cause it to make a poor business decision.

INTEGRATING THE ACQUISITION

Part V is devoted entirely to integrating the newly acquired company into existing operations.

The only point that should be noted here is that reaping the synergies identified in the pre-acquisition analysis requires considerable planning and effort. The fact that at least part of the value of those synergies was probably included in the purchase price should be a powerful inducement.

Achieving the expected synergies requires a clear assignment of responsibility for achieving measurable goals over a defined time period within a prescribed budget. What happens all too often is that the members of the multidisciplinary team that identified and quantified all of the synergies return to their normal duties. No one is given responsibility for reaping the benefits.

SUMMARY

Whether a company expects to make a single acquisition or many acquisitions over time, a proactive and strategically integrated program to manage the process will help ensure a much greater probability of success. It will also help to prevent costly mistakes. Making acquisitions should not be an intuitive exercise. The time required to put together and execute a well-considered program is a worthwhile investment for any company.

CHAPTER 2

EVALUATING THE ACQUISITION CANDIDATE

The key to evaluating an acquisition candidate is a thorough understanding of the acquirer's business strategy. Given this fact, the evaluation process requires that information gathering be organized and that analysis of the information be done by an experienced acquisition team.

In this chapter are presented the strategic reasons for which acquisitions are generally made, a conceptual framework for evaluating an acquisition candidate, and an outline of the information required for the evaluation.

The chapter relies heavily on both the business strategy research of Harvard professor Michael Porter and the extensive empirical data developed by PIMS (profit impact of market strategy). These strategic concepts have been well utilized and tested by many companies during their acquisition evaluations.

WHY COMPANIES MAKE ACQUISITIONS

An acquisition should meet a strategic need within the acquirer's organization and, ultimately, should increase shareholder value.

Evaluating acquisition candidates, therefore, requires a thorough understanding of the acquirer's underlying business strategy. Only with such an understanding can synergies created by a potential acquisition be adequately identified, understood, and quantified. Evaluating a candidate as a stand-alone entity is somewhat routine. But the nuances involved in any created synergies can be subtle and not easily quantified. To justify the acquisition, candidate evaluation requires more than finding an opportunity where the target's economic performance outweighs the buyer's cost of capital.

Generally, an acquisition will meet one of three strategic needs—either horizontal integration, vertical integration, or diversification.

Horizontal Integration

An acquisition contemplated to meet a horizontal integration strategy is usually quite safe. Such acquisitions tend to add to product lines, eliminate competitors, or otherwise increase market share. Market share is a principal driver of profitability. PIMS* research indicates that, in general, the market share leader may be three times as profitable as the fifth-place player.

The reasons for this difference in profitability are obvious. Lower costs are afforded the market-share leader via higher volumes. Efficient capacity utilization and advantages accruing from learning curve experience drive down the market leader's relative costs. In addition, market leaders often benefit from their more effective pricing policies. Horizontal integration will also often add complimentary product lines (resulting in a more complete product line offering) and more effectively utilize product distribution channels.

---

*"The PIMS (Profit Impact of Market Strategy) research program was initiated in 1972, for the specific purpose of determining how key dimensions of strategy affect profitability and growth. Since that time, some 450 corporations have contributed annual data, for periods that range from 2 to 10 years, for their products, divisions or other strategic business units (around 3000 in total). The PIMS program is housed at the Strategic Planning Institute (SPI), whose member companies include large and small firms, North American and European, public and privately owned. Many different types of products and markets are represented in the database—among them, consumer products, heavy industrial goods, raw materials, high technology equipment, and services." Buzzel, R. D. and Gale, B. T., *The PIMS Principles*, The Free Press, A Division of MacMillan, Inc., New York, pp. VII–VIII, 1987.

Vertical Integration

Acquisitions aimed at either backward (i.e., a supplier of raw materials) or forward (i.e., a customer) integration strategies can be significantly more complex and riskier than horizontal strategies. Vertical integration often involves the management of an acquiring company in a new business. Forward integration may result in the company's competing with current or former customers, whereas backward integration can be complex and lead to increased capital intensity and reduced flexibility in sourcing. Many companies today are doing just the opposite: divesting vertically integrated businesses and moving more toward the virtual-enterprise concept. Philip Morris U.S.A., for example, recently divested its printing and packaging company, Colonial Heights Packaging, Inc., in order to secure greater flexibility, service, quality, and lower costs for its tobacco-related packaging needs.

Generally, vertical integration as an acquisition strategy can be successful if it leads to securing a supply source or distribution channel, significantly reduces supply or distribution costs without adversely affecting flexibility, improves production efficiency or working capital turnover, accesses technology, or increases entry barriers. On the negative side, vertical integration often increases capital intensity and reduces supply and/or distribution flexibility.

Diversification

As in vertical integration, acquisitions aimed at achieving diversification strategies may also be risky. Although a diversified portfolio may reduce the financial risks associated with seasonal, cyclical, or highly competitive industries, it may also increase the demands on the members of management, requiring them to understand the intricacies of different businesses, industries, and competitive forces. Diversification also minimizes the benefits arising from synergy, particularly those associated with sourcing strength, utilization of distribution channels, and shared costs.

Today there is an increasing number of signs of companies reversing their previous diversification strategies. Sears' decision to spin off its financial services business from its retail business was quite favorably received by the stock market. Other diversified companies, seeing an opportunity to enhance their market capitalization, are considering similar strategies toward de-diversification.

A thorough understanding of the acquirer's general business strategy and the role acquisitions play in that strategy enables a company to formulate more specifically defined acquisition criteria and, using these criteria, to evaluate acquisition targets more effectively.

The next section provides an analytical framework that can be used in evaluating the acquisition candidate.

ANALYTICAL FRAMEWORK

The analytical framework presented here combines Michael Porter's work on industry-competitive forces and PIMS research on the impact of various business factors on profitability. As shown in Figure 2-1, the analytical framework consists of three components, each of which includes subcomponents that affect a target acquisition's profitability.

First, industry-competitive factors include those forces that Porter so thoroughly treats in his first major work on strategy, *Competitive Strategy*. In general, neither a company's competitive position nor its operating strategies can significantly affect these forces but, rather, both must adjust accordingly. Second, a target's competitive position within the industry indicates its uniqueness among its competitors. This uniqueness is a combined result of the industry-competitive factors and the target's chosen operating strategies. Third,

FIGURE 2-1   Analytical framework

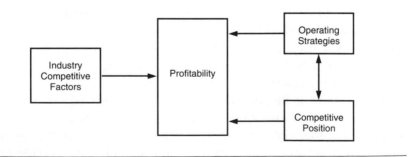

the operating strategies include the selected decisions of management, which take into account the target's overall strategy and the competitive environment.

PIMS empirical research over the years has concluded that, in general, a target's overall profitability is most affected by its management's operating strategies, followed by industry-competitive factors and the company's competitive position. About two-thirds of a target's profitability is determined by its operating strategies, and industry factors and competitive position determine the other third. The components of each of these factors are described in greater detail below. However, to properly identify and evaluate the impact on the acquisition candidate on the acquirer's profitability, it is critical to understand exactly the business segment or segments in which the target competed.

SEGMENTATION ANALYSIS

The first step in the evaluation process is to perform a segmentation analysis to determine the segments in which the target operates. Each segment has different competitive factors and, accordingly, the operating strategies and competitive position of the target within each segment will vary. Only by defining the segment can these factors be adequately understood and evaluated. The parameters that should be used in defining a business segment may vary from industry to industry. In some cases products or services may determine the segment. In other cases the determinant may be the type of customer, distribution channel, or geography. In Ernst & Young's professional services businesses there are many business segments. Some practice units are designated to deliver specific services (audit, tax, information technology, corporate finance) because of the unique resources required to deliver the services. There are also practices designated to serve different geographic areas, as well as some assigned to serve the unique needs of particular industries (health care, insurance, etc.).

TARGET INDUSTRY COMPETITIVE FACTORS

Figure 2-2 illustrates the many components of a target industry's competitive factors. Again, PIMS research has been enlightening in

FIGURE 2-2   Components of industry competitive factors

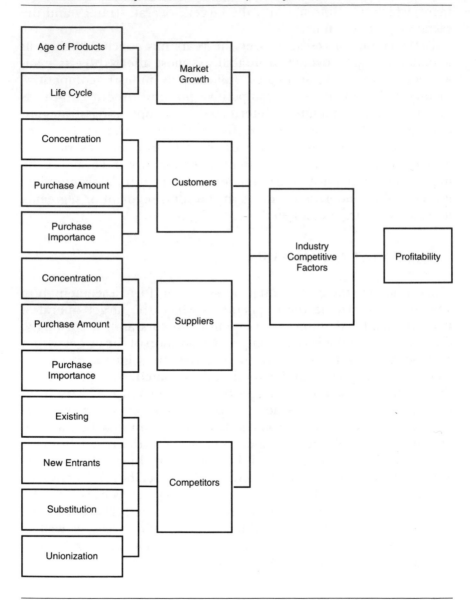

evaluating the relative importance of these factors. In most cases, the amount a customer spends has the largest impact on profitability. The larger the purchase amount to a customer, the more likely that customer will be to negotiate the price or to seek product and service alternatives from other suppliers competing with the target.

Unionization of the company and the importance of the purchase to the customer are the next most significant factors in terms of impact on profitability; together these factors generally have as great an impact as the purchase amount. Unionization can adversely affect profitability through higher labor and benefit costs and productivity issues. The importance of the purchase to a customer will possibly influence the manner in which a target approaches quality, design, technology, and so forth. As shown in Figure 2-3, the combination of these three factors may have almost a 20 percent variance in

FIGURE 2-3   Impact of industry competitive factors

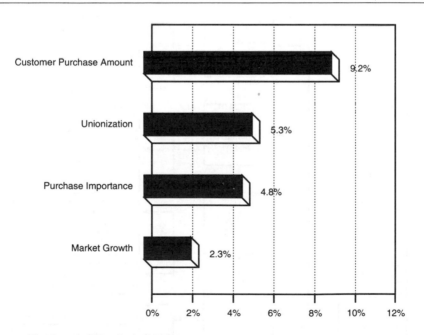

Attractive vs. unattractive businesses

profitability impact between industries in which these factors are favorable (attractive) and those in which they are unfavorable (unattractive).

OPERATING STRATEGIES

In general, the three most effective operating strategies include the pursuit of total quality management, market share enhancement, and low capital intensity. The successful combination of these strategies may result in additional benefits through productivity gains. Because a company's operating strategies account for about two-thirds of its operating performance, this component of the analytical framework provides the basis for evaluating the favorable potential of the acquisition candidate. Synergies can be identified and quantified.

FIGURE 2-4   Components of operating strategy

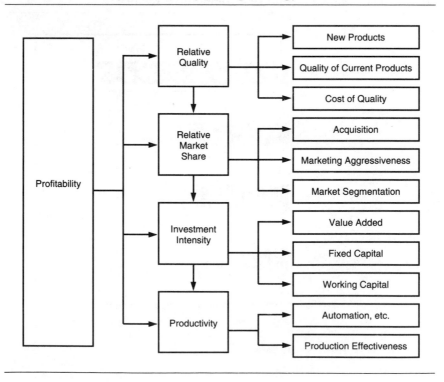

Figure 2-4 shows the various operating strategy components of the acquisition candidate that must be evaluated. Any changes in these strategies to reflect the integration of buyer and seller organizations must also be critically reviewed. These strategies are put into perspective below.

Total Quality

Total quality management (TQM) is the operating strategy that is currently gaining most attention in today's corporate world. For the acquiring company, TQM probably represented the greatest potential in the acquisition.

Evaluating an acquisition target's TQM initiatives requires focusing on two areas:

- Internal: What has the acquisition candidate done about incorporating the external customer's product and service needs in building its own marketing, manufacturing, distribution, and administrative infrastructure so as to eliminate waste? In focusing on this internal factor, companies can improve product and service quality, while simultaneously driving down operating costs by eliminating non-value-added activities and reducing cycle times.
- External: How effectively is the target meeting the product and service needs of its external customers? How does the target view its external customers? As partners? As competitors?

Evaluating the acquisition candidate's external focus on quality is relatively easy. The acquirer can directly or indirectly talk to customers and compare customer satisfaction relative to that of the candidate's competitors. What is the rate of new product introduction, the impact of technological change, product obsolescence, or substitution? Again, PIMS empirical research has determined that those companies perceived by their customers to be in the top 20th percentile, in regard to the relative quality of their products and services, are generally twice as profitable when measured against their return on investment and return on sales than competitors perceived to be in the bottom 20th percentile (see Figure 2-5). A buyer's attempts to quickly improve an acquisition candidate's rel-

FIGURE 2-5   Impact of quality on profitability

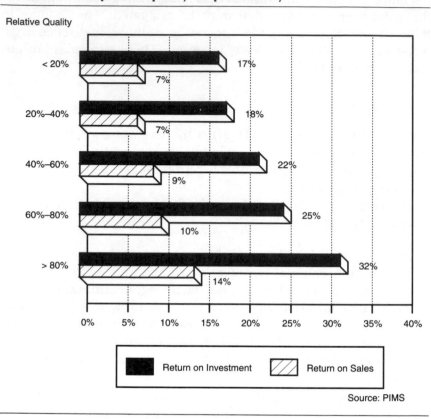

Relative Quality

< 20% — 17%, 7%
20%–40% — 18%, 7%
40%–60% — 22%, 9%
60%–80% — 25%, 10%
> 80% — 32%, 14%

Return on Investment   Return on Sales

Source: PIMS

ative quality position with its external customers can be a risky undertaking unless the buyer has an unusually high market presence that can be promptly and adequately transferred.

Evaluating an acquisition candidate's internal focus on TQM involves a determination of the candidate's cost of quality. This determination is perhaps the greatest indicator of a candidate's potential. The premise is simple. It is estimated that in American business, the cost of quality averages between 20 and 25 percent of sales. Most of these costs can be eliminated.

Figure 2-6 provides an indication of the relative costs of quality as a percentage of sales. There are four components to a company's overall cost of quality:

FIGURE 2-6   Costs of quality for manufacturers

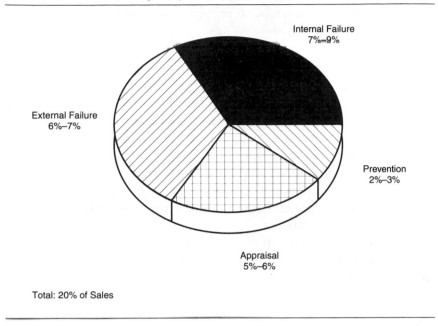

Internal Failure
7%–9%

External Failure
6%–7%

Prevention
2%–3%

Appraisal
5%–6%

Total: 20% of Sales

Internal Failure Costs.   Approximately 7 percent of a company's quality costs are accounted for by internal failure. These costs arise as the result of waste and scrap, rework, and general failure to do things right the first time.

External Failure Costs.   About 6 percent of quality cost is incurred because the customer returns the product. A defective product somehow makes it through a company's quality appraisal and inspection procedures and is eventually purchased by a customer. External failure costs include only those incurred in attempts to repair or replace the product. Because of the difficulty in quantifying future costs associated with the negative effects on customers' goodwill generated by defective products, they are not included in external failure cost. It is, however, appropriate to include the amount of lost sales in external failure costs if they can be determined accurately.

Appraisal Costs.   Five to 6 percent of quality costs arise from inspection-related activities. These appraisal costs add no value to the company's products or services. They are incurred simply to identify defects and attempt to prevent poor quality products from reaching the customer.

Prevention Costs. The "good" quality costs, which approximate 2 percent of the total, are those incurred to prevent poor quality from the outset. Typically, these costs are associated with employee training, statistically based process control activities, process optimization, and translating customer needs into measurable characteristics for management.

The obvious goal in a company's internal TQM focus is to eliminate the 18 to 22 percent of "bad" quality costs and to focus on prevention. It is clear that the potential for driving down costs in this connection is enormous.

By performing a cost-of-quality analysis, the acquirer gains significant insight into how the performance of the target company may be enhanced.

Market Share

The second most powerful operating strategy is market share expansion. Significant benefits may accrue from a larger share of the market:

- More effective utilization of fixed capital, which reduces the tendency toward "feast or famine" cycles
- Better market presence and the ability to benefit through marketing expenditures
- Lower costs through the impact of economies of scale
- Ultimately, higher profitability, which can be used to reinvest in training, technology, research and development, advertising and promotion, and so on.

PIMS research into the impact of market share on profitability clearly demonstrates the powerful effect of size. As shown in Figure 2-7, there is almost a 200 percent difference in profitability between the market-share leader and the fifth largest competitor.

FIGURE 2-7 Impact of market share on profitability
Source: Buzzell, R. D., and Gale, B.T., *The PIMS Principles*, The Free
Press, A Division of MacMillan, Inc., New York, p. VII–VII, 1987.

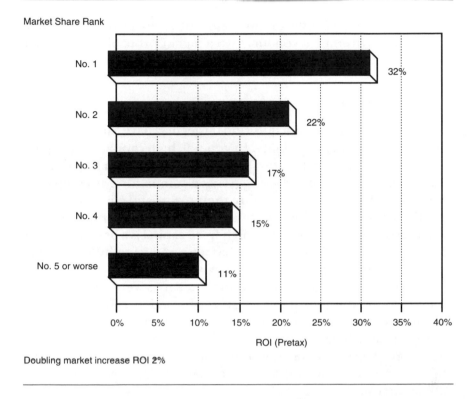

Market Share Rank

Doubling market increase ROI 2%

Evaluating an acquisition candidate relative to this strategic component obviously has a significant impact not only on the acquisition
decision but also on the future strategies employed if the acquisition
is made. For example, if the acquisition candidate is the market
leader, future strategies should focus on maximizing the impact of
economies of scale, broadening product lines and service, securing
its market image through advertising and promotion, and continuing to innovate.

If, on the other hand, the acquisition candidate is a market follower, TQM becomes enormously important as a competitive strategy. The market follower must seek out market niches—the needs
of which are not being met by the market leaders—introduce new

products, or improve the other components of its operating strategies. The future success of a market follower also depends on how industry-competitive forces respond to the follower's operating strategies. A reluctant market leader or low customer-switching costs (i.e., the buyer has little or no disincentive to charge suppliers) provide an environment conducive to a higher probability of success for the market follower's strategies.

Capital Intensity

The capital intensity of an acquisition target may have a major bearing on future costs and profitability. In general, high capital intensity adversely affects profitability for a market follower. High fixed capital can create an environment for aggressive competition as companies compete for business so as to utilize their plants and equipment. This situation can degenerate into excessive price competition and periods of depressed profitability. While high fixed capital is a barrier to entry for competitors, it also creates exit barriers, reducing future flexibility in recovering investment through exit strategies.

In evaluating an acquisition candidate, it is very important to analyze how the candidate has historically added capital intensity. Factors motivating the addition of capital intensity might include technological change in processes or products, protection against supply shortages, and vertical integration. Moreover, poor capital expenditure planning and follow-up can quickly create unwanted capital intensity.

Productivity

The fourth major component of an acquisition candidate's operating strategies involves its productivity initiatives. These initiatives are also dependent on involvement of the candidate's employees in productivity enhancements: "Do the right things right the first time and every time." Market share can help drive the efficient utilization of assets, and effective capital investment in process and product technology, automation, etc., can favorably impact productivity. Productivity may be assessed in many ways but is typically measured as a ratio of output (products) per unit of input (e.g., labor hours, machine hours, etc.).

COMPETITIVE POSITION

The interaction of a company's operating strategies and the competitive forces of the industry in which the company competes determine the company's competitive position. That competitive position will dictate future operating strategies for the buyer.

Competitive position can be quantified by the interrelationship of a company's cost of capital, its actual profitability, and its expected profitability. The relationship between a company's actual profitability and its cost of capital determines future changes in shareholder value. As long as actual profitability and expected profitability exceed the cost of capital, shareholder value is created. The reverse situation calls for a turnaround strategy.

The relationship between a company's actual profitability and the profitability expected in the company's specific industry determines the sustainability and future course of operating strategies. If a company's actual profitability exceeds its expected profitability, sustaining that performance will be very challenging and may call for defensive strategies. On the other hand, a company with actual profitability lower than expected could be a bargain purchase for a buyer if appropriate revisions in operating strategies can be effectively implemented. Over time, there is a general tendency for actual and expected profitability to converge.

Charting a company's competitive position can be quite enlightening to a buyer and can have a favorable impact on purchase negotiations as well as on future operating strategies. It can also help to prevent costly mistakes.

INFORMATION REQUIREMENTS

The following list of categories should be helpful in developing the necessary information about a target company for the evaluation process. The actual information required will obviously vary, depending on individual circumstances. This list, however, should provoke some thought as to what should be included.

Market Served
- Location of market served
- Geographic coverage relative to competition

- Size of market served
- Growth rate of market served

Products
- Stage of product life cycle
- Scope of product line relative to competition
- Product standardization
- Customization of products relative to competition
- Variety within product line relative to competition
- Product concentration
- Frequency of product change
- Shelf life
- Delivery time

Customers
- Number of customers
- End customer types relative to competition
- Distribution channels to end customer
- Direct relationship to end customer relative to competition
- Immediate customer concentration
- Immediate customers shared with competition or with other business units within company
- Relative size of largest immediate customer
- Customer purchase frequency
- Customer purchase amount
- Purchase importance for customers
- Customer-switching cost
- Percentage of sales to internal customers (e.g., subsidiaries, divisions, etc.)
- Sales to internal customers compared with competitors' sales to internal customers

Suppliers

- Number of suppliers
- Supplier concentration
- Suppliers shared with competition or other business units within company
- Relative size of largest supplier
- Relative profitability of largest supplier
- Importance of the target company's business to supplier
- Cost of switching from largest supplier
- Company backward integration
- Backward integration relative to competition
- Rate of change in purchase prices
- Purchase prices relative to competitors' purchase prices for same items

Operations

- Cost of quality
- Proportion of production process in small, large, and/or continuous runs relative to competition
- Run size of process relative to competition
- Automation of process relative to competition
- Future factors likely to change production process
- Number of employees
- Functional allocation of employees
- Strengths and weaknesses relative to competition
- Number of business units
- Unionization
- Labor disruption
- Wage cost change
- Wage rates relative to competition
- Salary levels relative to competition

- Distribution cost relative to competition
- Standard capacity
- Standard capacity relative to competition
- Capacity utilization
- Capacity utilization relative to competition
- Capacity increments
- General and administrative cost relative to competition
- Working capital relative to competition
- Fixed capital relative to competition
- Capital budgeting (methods, hurdle rates, postimplementation audits)
- Incentives and compensation
- Profitability relative to competition

Market Position
- Market share and market-share trends relative to competition
- Price relative to competition
- Importance of quality for product, service, reputation
- Cost of quality relative to competition
- Importance of price versus quality to customer
- Trends in returns and allowance relative to competition
- Trends in late deliveries relative to competition
- Trends in new-product sales
- Areas of new-product sales (e.g., new markets, product change, etc.)
- New-product introduction relative to competition
- R & D
- R & D relative to competition
- Sales and marketing expenditures relative to competition

Competitive Behavior
- Operating strategies relative to competition
- Areas of leadership for target versus competition

Market Boundaries
- Barriers to entry
- Number of competitors
- Number of new entrants
- Number of new entrants in supply channel
- Number of new entrants in customer channel
- Origin of entry (e.g., foreign, supplier/customer vertical integration, competitor, new business, etc.)
- Market success of entry
- Basis for success of new entrant (e.g., product superiority, service, marketing, etc.)
- Number of exits
- Number of exits in supply channel
- Number of exits in customer channel
- Anticipate number of future entrants
- Anticipate number of future exits

Financial Measures
- Balance sheets
- Balance sheet levels and ratios relative to competition
- Income statements
- Expense levels and profit margins relative to competition

CHAPTER 3

VALUING THE POTENTIAL ACQUISITION

Evaluating a potential acquisition, which includes determining a fair price for it, is an integral part of a well-run corporate development campaign. The purpose of this chapter is not to provide an exhaustive "how-to" manual for performing a valuation, but rather to pinpoint the approaches and key issues that will enable readers to understand the valuation process and the chief executive's role in it. The chapter will:

- Define value;
- Discuss the integration of the valuation process with the target evaluation process and due diligence efforts; and
- Describe and compare valuation techniques.

VALUE—WHAT IS IT?

Publius defined value in the first century B.C.: "Everything is worth what its purchaser will pay for it." The IRS, in Revenue Ruling 59–60, states that fair market value is "the price at which the property would change hands between a willing buyer and willing seller, neither being under any compulsion to buy or to sell and both having reasonable knowledge of the relevant facts." Both of these definitions imply that what a purchaser will pay is often determined by who he is, what information he possesses, and the process by which value is determined.

For instance, value can change dramatically depending on the assumptions made by a potential purchaser about the expected future earnings performance and cash flow from an acquisition. Different potential purchasers may have very different ideas about appropriate value. For example, a management group whose projections and calculations support one price for a business may find themselves outbid by a corporate buyer that relies on comparable projections, but that is already in the acquisition target's industry. Because of its ability to eliminate overhead or to benefit in some other way from combining similar businesses, the latter firm will be able to pay a higher price.

INTEGRATION OF THE VALUATION PROCESS

The valuation process is a critical component of both the target evaluation and due diligence processes. A great deal of financial, operational, and other information is gathered during the target evaluation process and is used as a basis for determining a preliminary range of values for the acquisition candidate. Later, as part of the due diligence process, more detailed information is gathered to confirm or challenge the information and assumptions used in the preliminary assessment of value. As the financial information and assumptions are refined in the due diligence process, the range of values for the acquisition candidate are also refined to reflect the updated assumptions and other new information.

The acquiring company's senior management must feel comfortable about the results of the target evaluation and due diligence processes. These results are crucial in helping to establish ranges of value and parameters for negotiation. In particular, the following data should be gathered during the target evaluation and due diligence processes to provide a basis for effective valuation:

Products/Markets

- Breakdowns of volumes/margins by product lines, as a basis for determining future sales growth (existing and new products)
- Requirements/costs for future sales and marketing
- Trends for pricing/margins; future constraints/opportunities

Operations/Organization

- Cost structure components, current and expected
- Key staff requirements/costs
- Labor costs/expected requirements/relationships

Financial

- Capital expenditure requirements
- Working capital relationships and the impact of growth
- Costs that stay/grow/decline after the acquisition
- Synergies that may reduce costs

Industry/Competition

- Competitor actions as they may affect pricing or unit demand
- General industry trends as they may affect revenues or costs

Although specific questions should be asked and answered during each phase of the target evaluation and due diligence processes, they will have a common underlying theme. The end result should be a clear understanding of the potential acquisition. With this knowledge, a potential acquirer will have the necessary information to make an educated judgment about whether the company's reported historical earnings and cash flows are the correct basis on which to value the business, or whether adjustments must be made to those numbers to fairly assess value.

These processes should also result in understanding the target's markets and industry accurately enough to model several alternative future-performance scenarios. The various components of costs should be understood sufficiently to create models for selling and administrative costs under different revenue assumptions. Changing cost relationships could significantly increase or decrease the cash flows generated by the business. The working capital and fixed capital requirements projected for the future are also critical, inasmuch as these will have an impact on the cash flows generated or on those required to achieve sales and earnings targets.

VALUATION TECHNIQUES

Techniques for valuing a potential acquisition include the following:

- Discounted cash flow analysis
- Comparable transactions analysis
- Comparable companies analysis
- Other methods

Each technique will be described in turn.

Discounted Cash Flow Analysis

Discounted cash flow analysis is a very common approach. Alfred Rappaport, professor emeritus of Accounting and Information Systems at Northwestern University's Kellogg Graduate School of Management, has suggested that as many as half of the major acquisition-minded companies rely exclusively on the discounted cash flow technique to analyze acquisitions. The same methodology used to make internal development decisions about plant or equipment additions is often applied to an acquisition decision.

The discounted cash flow technique takes into account that a dollar received today is worth more than a dollar received a year from now because today's dollar can be invested to earn a return during the intervening time. Another important aspect of the discounted cash flow technique is that it is "future oriented." The focus of the discounted cash flow technique is to assign a value in today's dollars to the cash flows that are expected to occur in the future. This future orientation is critical, inasmuch as the buyer of a company will be able to realize the value only of future cash flows, regardless of the target company's performance in the past.

As diagrammed in Figure 3-1, the discounted cash flow technique

FIGURE 3-1   The discounted cash flow technique

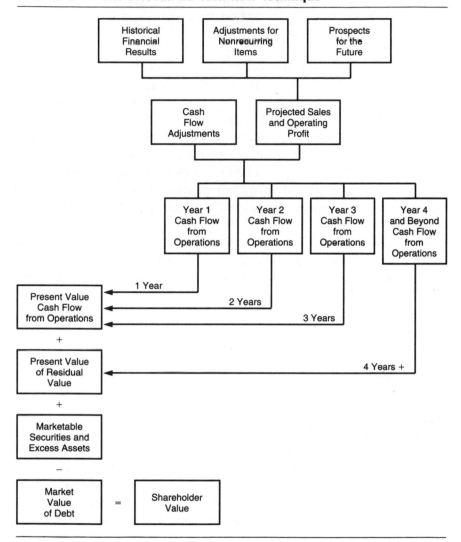

*The discounted cash flow value (or what the total capital employed in the business is worth) has been calculated based on operating profits that do not consider financing costs (for example, interest expense) or income from nonoperating assets. As a result, the net value of the equity is derived by subtracting the market value of debt and adding the market value of nonoperating assets.

begins with a projection of sales and operating profit. These projected financial results are based on an assessment of the company's recent historical financial performance, adjusted for nonrecurring and nonoperating income and expense items, as well as on certain assumptions regarding the company's prospects for the future.

The projected operating profit estimates (after taxes) are then adjusted by adding back depreciation and deducting net investments in working capital and capital expenditures. The projected free cash flows from operations and residual value are discounted back to the current period using an appropriate discount rate to compute the total value of the company for debt holders and stockholders. The net equity value is then determined by deducting the market value of interest-bearing debt and adding the market value of any excess assets.

Obviously, the usefulness of this technique depends on the extent to which the underlying assumptions are appropriate. In addition to the income statement, four other components of this modeling technique can affect the result:

- Length of the projection period
- Reinvestment requirements
- Residual value
- Discount rate

Length of the Projection Period.   The period to be considered for the analysis ideally should be the natural business cycle. Whether this is a two, five, or ten-year period may vary by industry, or it may be determined by the purchaser's own strategic planning cycle. In common practice, the discounted cash flow period is generally considered to be three to seven years. A period that includes both peaks and valleys should be modeled to help the purchaser understand how cost/working capital relationships can change at different operating levels.

Reinvestment Requirements.   In any cash flow projection, after-tax profits are not an accurate representation of available cash flow. Adjustments should be made to consider the reinvestment required to make the business grow. Specifically, this reinvestment can take the form of working capital, fixed capital investment, or both. The determination of projected working capital requirements should consider the historical relationship of sales to receivables, inventory, and payables—modified for appropriate changes in business policies and industry practices.

With regard to fixed asset expenditures, the relationship between past depreciation and past capital expenditures to sales growth helps one understand how business growth (or lack of growth) has been related to investment.

Based on past trends, as well as management's input regarding likely future capital expenditure levels, a realistic forecast should be developed. The analysis must be sensitive to the strategic timing of capital expenditures. For instance, significant capital expenditures in the early years may provide substantial benefit to the company's overall value in later years.

Residual Value.   At the end of the projection period, the acquired business will have remaining value. In current literature, various suggestions have been made as to what this residual value may be. The Kellogg School's Rappaport has addressed this concept as being connected to a company's strategy.

In his essay "Coming to Grips with Residual Value" (*ALCAReview*, Fall 1986), Philip J. Eynon, executive vice president of Alcar and an associate of Rappaport, writes:

> Residual value and the method you choose to estimate it are strongly affected by two factors, the strategy being pursued during the forecast period and the competitive position of the firm.
>
> For a company pursuing growth, which is therefore investing heavily during the forecast period in order to achieve superior returns in the future, the residual value often represents 60–90 percent of its total value. Conversely, this percentage can be much smaller for a business that is pursuing a harvest strategy designed to maximize short-term returns at the expense of future competitiveness. Thus, while residual value reflects the value beyond the forecast period, its size is directly related to the strategy pursued during the forecast period.

Mechanically, residual value can be calculated in several ways. Two of the most common are the perpetuity method and the multiplier approach. The perpetuity method capitalizes the final year's projected cash flow/income by the discount rate, as if it were an annuity. From a theoretical perspective, this method assumes that any company able to generate returns greater than its cost of capital will eventually attract competitors. These competitors will drive the returns of all companies in the industry down to the minimum acceptable cost of capital rate.

The multiplier approach applies a multiple of earnings before interest and income taxes (EBIT) to the final year's EBIT. The higher the discount rate, the lower the effective EBIT multiple.

Because the residual value may be a large part of the potential acquisition's overall value, the underlying assumptions and approach must be adopted on a situation-by-situation basis and the sensitivities understood.

Discount Rate.   The discount rate (also called the cost of capital) used to calculate the present value of each year's cash flow may be derived from several sources. These include a company's own strategic plan, which may identify required hurdle rates for any investment, or an analysis of rates of return for the industry. The calculation process for cost of capital will not be elaborated here. However, one of the most important issues a chief executive officer must understand is how the discount rate is being applied and whether that rate of return can reasonably be expected for an acquisition in the target industry.

An important point to remember is that the proper cost of capital is that of the potential acquisition, not of the potential acquirer. The reasoning behind this view is that the potential acquisition's cost of capital is the price it must pay to the suppliers of capital, given its industry and operational risks, to motivate them to invest in the company. If one uses the acquirer's cost of capital to construct a discount rate, the emphasis will be focused on the wrong bundle of risks.

Figure 3-2 shows how the discounted cash flow method was used to analyze a potential acquisition candidate with $28 million in sales in the most recent year, net earnings of $538,000, and a net worth at the end of the fiscal year equal to $4.7 million. The example candidate is a custom metalworking company that machines a wide range of castings to high tolerances for a variety of end markets,

FIGURE 3-2   Discounted cash flow valuation of a company ($ thousands)

	Next Year	Year 2	Year 3	Year 4	Year 5	Terminal Value
Sales	$34,723	$45,000	$50,850	$57,461	$64,930	
EBIT margin	9.4%	8.5%	8.5%	8.5%	8.5%	
EBIT	3,264	3,825	4,322	4,884	5,519	
Income taxes (cash basis)	1,110	1,301	1,469	1,661	1,876	
Net operating income	2,154	2,524	2,853	3,223	3,643	30,358
Cash flow adjustments						
Plus: Depreciation	1,392	1,800	2,034	2,298	2,597	
Less: Net change in working capital	(505)	(831)	(268)	(304)	(344)	
Capital expenditures	(1,866)	(3,575)	(4,061)	(4,298)	(4,597)	
Free cash flows	1,175	(82)	558	919	1,299	
Net present value at 12.0%	1,049	(65)	397	584	737	17,226
				Total corporate value		19,928
				Less: market value of debt		(13,348)
				Shareholder value		$6,580

including the automotive, agricultural machinery, and electronic component industries. The figure illustrates the projection process that models the company's income statements, as well as a determination of working capital and fixed capital requirements in future periods.

Once the initial model has been developed, iterations are also appropriate to test the sensitivity of value to certain assumptions used in the first projection. Figure 3-3 illustrates how the value changes according to variations in the assumptions for the discount rate and EBIT margin. Tests of sensitivity to changes in sales growth, expense relationships, and capital requirements are not shown, but should be considered when analyzing potential value. This is especially important when the projected sales, earnings, or capital structure differs significantly from historical trends.

The analysis of sensitivities is particularly relevant in a negotiation because it gives the buyer an idea of price ranges within which any negotiation can occur. It further helps to establish a "walk away"

FIGURE 3-3   Testing the sensitivity of assumptions used in the discounted cash flow analysis ($ thousands)

	EBIT Margin (Held Constant from Year 2–Year 5)		
	8.0%	8.5%	9.0%
10.0%	10,280	12,126	13,965
Discount rate 12.0%	5,084	6,580	8,073
14.0%	1,481	2,731	3,977

price, above which any transaction would not achieve a satisfactory return under any of the buyer's assumptions.

Finally, the discounted cash flow approach provides a vehicle whereby the operating management can make a number of "what if" assumptions that take into account planned changes to the potential acquisition's operations and can determine the effect of these changes on the value. However, the increased value that the buyer will contribute will not necessarily translate into a proportionate increase in the purchase price. In fact, many negotiations focus on the buyer and seller sharing the amount of estimated value to be generated by the buyer.

Comparable Transactions Analysis

The marketplace often provides examples of transactions consummated within the industry of the potential acquisition. Although numerous private transactions are rarely recorded in the press, a variety of published sources and computer data bases now available will give the buyer some sense of how the real world values companies that are similar to the potential acquisition.

The overall objective of the comparable transactions approach is to identify some pricing relationships: ideally, price/earnings ratios, EBIT multiples, and/or market/book value premiums for transactions consummated. Seldom is there a transaction with a company that is truly comparable in all major respects. Extensive research is important to identify those situations that are most similar. A number of data sources can be used, including the following:

- *Mergerstat Review,* an annual publication of merger and acquisition transactions published by Merrill Lynch Business Brokerage & Valuation.
- *National Review of Corporate Acquisitions.*
- *Mergers and Acquisitions* (newsletter).
- Annual reports of companies within the potential acquisition's industry (some of these companies may have made acquisitions and may also have disclosed sufficient information regarding pricing).
- Lotus One Source—U.S. M & A data base (a CD ROM–based computer data base containing information from the IDD U.S. Mergers and Acquisitions and Compustat Research data bases).
- Securities Data Company's Mergers & Corporate Transactions on-line computer data base.

For the example of the custom metalworking company, consider the data reported for transactions by *Mergerstat Review* regarding the fabricated metal products industry, as shown in Figure 3-4.

Based on this data, the value of the potential acquisition can be calculated as follows:

Current year reported earnings	$538,000	
Current year reported net worth		$4,700,000
Average P/E ratio	14×	
Average market/book value multiple		1.4 ×
Estimated value	$7,532,000	$6,580,000

In general, when using the comparable transactions methodology the buyer should be aware of the following key issues:

FIGURE 3-4 Data reported for a recent year's transactions by *Mergerstat Review*

Announce Date Close Date	Buyer Name Seller Name Business (Unit Sold)	Annual Sales (Millions)	Price Offered (Millions)	Method of Payment	P/E Paid	Buyer's P/E	Premium	Multiple to Book
	19 Fabricated Metal Products							
06/06/9X 08/24/9X	Tomkins Pic Phillips Industries Inc. Manufactures metal doors, sash, trim	$942.0	$527.5	N/A	13.6		32.1	2.7
02/21/9X 06/08/9X	Danaher Corp. Easco Hand Tools Inc. Manufactures specialized hand tools	$206.8	$83.2	STOCK	NEG	8.4	5.7	1.6
03/28/9X 07/18/9X	Illinois Tool Works Inc. Buell Industries Inc. Manufactures fasteners and metal parts	$86.8	$39.1	STOCK	NEG	15.8	16.9	0.9
06/01/9X 06/29/9X	Okabena Partnership V-6 Explosive Fabricators Inc.– 13% Explosive metal workings and metal fabricate	$11.0	$1.0	N/A	14.4		15.0	0.5

50

- The research used to develop the multiples must be understood. Multiples may distort the noncash elements of any transaction. Company-specific factors such as market share, intangible assets, and technical competence may have an impact on multiples yet may not be reflected in summary statistics.

- Companies that make up the sample from which multiples are derived may not match the potential acquisition exactly.

The buyer must be comfortable with the earnings and book value given for the potential acquisition. Although the due diligence process will most likely reveal whether reported earnings and/or book value are meaningful, any valuation should likewise use the most meaningful numbers. For example, if a privately held company has significant salary expenses that would not continue once the buyer purchased the company, an adjustment would be reasonable—and should be made—to assess the potential acquisition's true earning power.

Comparable Companies Analysis

An additional point of reference for the buyer can be provided by the buyer's making some assessment of how the value of the potential acquisition compares with market prices of publicly traded companies subject to similar economic trends and risks. This approach is similar to the comparable transactions method in that it identifies a pricing relationship and then applies it to the potential acquisition's earnings or book value. Although details of the process will not be elaborated here, sources of company-specific statistics include Value-Line Investment Surveys, Standard & Poor's Corporation Records, Moody's Industrial Manual, and computer data bases such as Lotus One Source.

For the example of the custom metalworking company, the following is a summary of data regarding selected public companies that appear to be comparable:

Company	Market	Description	*Current Year P/E Ratio*
Simpson Industries	NASDAQ	A manufacturer of machined components, assemblies, and cutting tools, selling its products to OEMs of automobiles, trucks, diesel engines, and heavy equipment. Recent sales approximated $192 million.	25
Intermet Corp.	NASDAQ	A manufacturer of a variety of ductile and gray iron castings and machined components for OEM manufacturers of automobiles, light and heavy trucks, construction equipment, and other industrial products. Recent sales approximated $320 million.	16
Newcor, Inc.	NASDAQ	A designer and manufacturer of special-purpose machinery and equipment and a manufacturer of precision machined components for automotive and industrial users. Recent sales approximated $99 million.	6
Modine Manufacturing	NASDAQ	A developer and manufacturer of vehicular heat-transfer products. The company markets and distributes its products to OEM manufacturers, the automotive aftermarket, and the nonresidential building market. Recent sales approximated $482 million.	11

In using the value of comparable public companies as a valuation benchmark, it is often necessary to consider certain factors. The comparable companies' multiples were calculated based on the stock for a minority interest in publicly or freely traded companies. Adjustments for control premiums and privately held discounts may be necessary.

Control premiums represent the amount an investor would be willing to pay in excess of the minority interest value in order to exercise control over the company. The following theories explain why a premium may be paid:

- An investor who has control has the ability to alter the company's capital structure.

- The controlling investor can change the compensation structure of the company, including his or her own compensation level.

- The controlling investor has the ability to set the company's dividend policy.

- An investor who has control has, in some cases, the ability to liquidate the company.

Privately held discounts represent reductions to value for privately held companies, based on their lack of access to public debt and equity markets, exposure to financing risks, and other factors. These discounts may also reflect a marketability discount based on the extent to which the investor's interest in the company can be converted into cash at the owner's discretion.

For the purposes of our valuation example, it is assumed that the investment will remain liquid and that the privately held factors do not apply to the target. Therefore, no privately held discount was applied. However, a control premium was used to adjust the value of the target. *Mergerstat*'s research includes control premiums and shows that they vary by industry and that they have changed over time. For our example, the data in Figure 3-4 were used to develop the control premium by averaging the premiums paid on transactions that *Mergerstat* analyzed. Points to remember when using comparable companies analysis include the following:

1. For purposes of comparison, pure-play companies are better than conglomerates. To the extent that a conglomerate is a potential acquisition, each business unit may need to be valued separately.

2. Outlying P/E multiples (given a poor earnings history) may not be meaningful in developing comparable data.

3. Always determine where current multiples stand in relation to history. P/E and other earnings multiples fluctuate, and using this method requires an understanding of whether the averages used are at the high end or the low end of the historical range.

4. Determine which are the best and worst performers in the list of comparable companies and compare the potential acquisition to each of the extreme examples.

Based on the comparable companies' data, the value of the potential acquisition can be calculated as follows:

Current year reported earnings:	$ 538,000
Average P/E ratio	14×
Control premium	17%
Estimated value	$8,812,000

Other Methods

In approaching valuation, two other methods can provide points of reference, but it is important to remember that they are appropriate only under certain specific circumstances. These methods are (1) book value or adjusted book value and (2) liquidation analysis.

Book Value or Adjusted Book Value.   This method can provide a starting point for the valuation discussion. However, this is an accounting-based concept that does not necessarily reflect earning power. Generally accepted accounting principles (GAAP) may permit the use of alternative depreciation or inventory methods which result in book values that may not reflect the true market value or value in use of those assets. Similarly, the value of intangible assets such as customer lists, patents, and an entrenched sales force may not be reflected on a company's balance sheet but may contribute to a superior earnings performance for a business. Further, book value, adjusted for anticipated purchase-price accounting adjustments, will help to provide an initial estimate of the goodwill to be recorded in the transaction. Although such an amount does not affect the theoretical value of the target, it may affect the perception of certain buyers, particularly of publicly traded companies. In addition, acquirers should analyze how much it would cost to build a company from scratch as opposed to buying an existing one, the standard "make versus buy" analysis.

Liquidation Analysis. If the business has relatively little value as a going concern, an appropriate analysis may be to consider what individual assets would be worth if they were sold at auction or in a 60- to 90-day liquidation. At a minimum, this establishes a floor for valuation.

SUMMARY OF VALUATION TECHNIQUES

The advantages and disadvantages of each valuation technique can be summarized as follows:

Method	Advantages	Disadvantages
Discounted cash flow	Provides a method to model expected performance and to understand sensitivities.	May not reflect the reality of pricing trends in the markets.
	Aids understanding of performance, cash flow, and balance sheet relationships.	Methodology may be cumbersome and may involve "soft" numbers relative to residual values.
Comparable transactions	Provides a comparison with actual acquisitions—what other people are paying.	Transaction data may be incomplete; the most similar deals may not be published; the published deals may not be similar; every deal is unique.
	Reveals who other buyers are and may offer insights into potential competitive bidders.	

Continued

Method	Advantages	Disadvantages
Comparable companies	Provides a benchmark of how the public markets view particular industries.	May ignore the reality of expected future performance.
Adjusted book value/ liquidation analysis	May be most relevant if a business is being acquired for its underlying assets as opposed to going-concern value.	May not reflect economic value of the business, especially if the target generates strong earnings.

For the example of the metalworking company, the three most often used valuation techniques yield the following estimated values:

Discounted cash flow: $6,580,000
Comparable transactions: $6,580,000 to $7,532,000
Comparable companies: $8,812,000

In this particular example, the discounted cash flow method results in a figure lower than the market-based approaches. To some extent, this is due to the significant capital expenditures that are expected to be required in the near future. Of all the methods, discounted cash flow is, in most cases, the most useful because it can be tailored to fit the facts of each specific situation. Business judgment must be applied to determine the willingness of a buyer to pay a higher price (and potentially to accept a lower return) in order to make the purchase. Further, these valuation methods may not adequately reflect other strategic reasons to complete the acquisition. The buyer should, however, guard against including illusory synergies in the analysis to justify bidding more.

It cannot be sufficiently stressed that valuation must include research, understanding, and judgment. Doing one's homework is often the best way to avoid the problem of paying too much.

Once completed, the valuation result must be folded into the buyer's own planning process and compared with the indicated price to determine whether the desired return on equity, return on assets, earnings per share, or threshold can be met. These valuation processes are tools used to set ceilings and floors for the pricing decision. They are also necessary to help assess the key levers that may change the valuation.

A valuation should never be done in a vacuum. It should evolve naturally from a thorough due diligence process, and should be an integral part of any negotiation strategy.

CHAPTER 4

DUE DILIGENCE

After the roaring decade of the 1980s, merger and acquisition activity has entered a new phase. Buyers and lenders are becoming more selective. There is increasing emphasis on high quality deals that have realistic pricing. Investors are placing greater importance on due diligence—the intense examination of a target by an objective third party.

No book can make a deal work if the numbers do not point toward success. Buyers and lenders will not be able to decide whether to pursue an acquisition unless they have a full and detailed knowledge of the financial affairs of the target company. This discussion can help buyers and lenders understand the true picture behind the numbers so that they can find hidden treasures while avoiding potential hidden traps.

FINANCIAL CONSIDERATIONS

Buyers have a number of sources available to them when undertaking an evaluation of a target. For public companies, Securities and Exchange Commission filings such as Forms 8-K, 10-K, 10-Q, and proxy materials provide historical financial statements. External and internal auditors' work papers and management letters, operating budgets, and cash flow projects are also fruitful sources of information. Reports from consultants, contracts and agreements such as leases, compensation and employee benefit agreements, and previous acquisition agreements will help round out the picture.

A key area for due diligence is the uncovering of undervalued, overvalued, and unrecorded assets and liabilities. Judgments are required in determining the appropriate carrying value of assets or in the measurement of certain liabilities. Judgments may well differ when made through the eyes of an acquirer rather than through the eyes of a seller. Further, mistakes may occur in the preparation of financial statements prepared according to GAAP. Each of these is considered in turn. Assets may be carried at below their market or appraised values because financial statements prepared according to GAAP generally measure assets at historical costs or depreciated historical costs. The following are examples of undervalued and unrecognized assets on a balance sheet:

1. Property, plant, and equipment are carried at depreciated historical cost: This may be below market or appraised value.

2. Inventories: In cases where the LIFO cost method is employed, balances are generally understated in comparison with their current replacement costs.

3. Investments in joint ventures and unconsolidated subsidiaries: Because of "cost" and "equity" conventions, these investments may be understated as compared with their current market value.

4. Marketable equity securities: Portfolios are generally reported at the lower of cost or market, in which case cost may be lower than present market value.

5. Computer software: The costs of software that was developed for the company's internal use may be written off as incurred and may therefore be an unrecorded asset.

6. Excess pension plan assets: In a single-employer pension plan, the full excess of the fair value of the plan's assets over liabilities is usually not reflected in the balance sheet.

7. Net operating loss and tax credit carryforwards: These are generally not recognized as assets unless stringent criteria are met.

8. Debt or leases at favorable rates: If obligations have a lower than market value interest rate, this reduces the company's effective liability. This equates to an unrecorded asset.

9. Intangibles: These include licenses, franchises, trademarks, customer lists, and unpatented technology. Intangibles that are purchased from others are carried at depreciated historical cost, which may be below fair value. Internally developed intangibles are generally written off as costs are incurred, and may constitute unrecorded assets.

The following are a number of assets in a balance sheet that may be overvalued:

1. Obsolete and slow-moving inventories.

2. Uncollected receivables or receivables not currently due, that bear no interest or below market-rate interest.

3. Property, plant, and equipment that is being held for future sale or that is currently being used at levels that will not allow for the recovery of the carrying cost.

4. Single-employer pension plan assets in excess of pension obligations recognized in a prior business combination where a subsequent decline in the market value of the assets has occurred.

5. Investments in consolidated or unconsolidated subsidiaries that may not be realizable: For example, restriction on the transfer of foreign funds may mean that the carrying value of foreign subsidiaries may not be fully realizable.

6. Intangibles: The recorded values may have diminished in comparison with current revenue, as compared with the values on the date when the assets were first recorded.

7. Assets currently being constructed when the costs are not recoverable: This may occur because the project will not be finished, or because future operations will not be adequate to cover the carrying costs.

Some liabilities may not be fully reflected, or reflected at all, in the target's balance sheet. This is because generally accepted accounting principles do not require that some contingent liabilities be recognized in a company's financial statements. Further, certain liabilities such as postretirement medical benefits require the use of estimates, which may differ between a buyer and seller. Here are some examples of these types of liabilities:

1. Threatened or pending litigation.

2. Obligations to employees, including severance, unfunded benefit plans, incentive contracts, and employment agreements.

3. Unfunded health and life insurance or other welfare benefit obligations for active and retired employees.

4. Obligations to an underfunded multiemployer pension plan.

5. Penalties for noncompliance with governmental agency reporting requirements.

6. Guarantees of third-party indebtedness.

7. Potential and actual claims for product and environmental liability.

8. Obligations relating to product warranties and product defects.

9. Deficiencies in federal, state, and foreign tax payments. These include income taxes, personal property taxes, sales taxes, payroll taxes, and excise taxes.

10. Obligations for product returns and discounts.

11. Contract obligations for sales, supplies, and purchases.

EVALUATION OF A CORPORATE DIVISION OR SUBSIDIARY

In cases in which the target is a corporate division or a subsidiary that previously was neither accounted for nor operated on a "stand-alone" basis, a number of special issues arise. Foremost among these, a determination must be made as to whether operating results for the division or subsidiary reflect actual costs. The question is whether the financial information properly reflects the cost of stand-alone operations and whether the entity has the quality of management required to operate the stand-alone business successfully. Was the earlier success of the division or subsidiary attributable to management skills within the entity, or was it the result of management by the corporate parent?

It is often difficult to calculate accurately the costs for a corporate division or subsidiary, because it frequently benefits from services provided by affiliates. Sometimes the division is charged for those services, but often it is not. Although in some cases those costs were calculated as though they were provided by an unrelated third party, they are sometimes calculated on some other basis. Examples of these kinds of services include such support functions as tax, legal, treasury, benefits administration, accounting, general management, internal audit, and information processing.

Corporate divisions and subsidiaries may also benefit by being included in programs that would have a much higher cost if they had to be obtained on a stand-alone basis. These include benefits such as a medical plan, property and casualty insurance program, pension plan, transportation program, and advertising services.

In general, the due diligence process must seek to determine whether transactions between the division or subsidiary and its corporate affiliates have taken place at terms that would prevail between unrelated parties. Some examples of such transactions include product sales, sale or lease of facilities and equipment, and borrowing or lending of funds. Moreover, in cases in which the division or subsidiary derives a significant portion of its revenues from a corporate affiliate or purchases substantial amounts of raw materials or component parts from affiliates, it is essential to know whether those relationships will continue (and at what values) once the target entity is sold.

WARNING SIGNS

Historical trends are critical indicators of potential future results. But the evaluator must also be able to identify warning signs that may indicate "soft" items that were generated outside normal operations.

Unusual one-time occurrences may misleadingly inflate income. In such cases, it is crucial that those events be identified so that the evaluator does not draw inaccurate conclusions about future performance. Such items include the following:

1. Gains and losses from the sale of productive assets and nonstrategic businesses.

2. Litigation and insurance claim recoveries.

3. Reversals of accounting reserves, such as those for bad debts, restructuring, litigation, and inventory obsolescence.

4. Costs and losses that are netted against revenues and revenues netted against costs. One example would be a nonrecurring cooperative advertising allowance received by a distributor from a franchiser that is netted against advertising expenses.

5. Facility closings and realignments.

6. Single-employer pension plan terminations.

7. Recent changes in health insurance financing.

8. Significant year-end account adjustments. Large adjustments to the year-end inventory accounts that result from the taking and pricing of inventory may indicate that the interim period sales margins are not reliable.

Changes in accounting methods may also have a direct impact on the quality of earnings and make it difficult to compare reported results, because similar or identical transactions may be recorded differently in historical financial statements. The following are examples of such changes:

1. New professional accounting standards that require changes in methods, particularly FAS 106, "Employer's Accounting for Post Retirement Benefits Other Than Pensions."

2. Changes among alternative accounting methods.

3. Changes in the estimated number of years for asset depreciation or amortization.

4. A change in the company's philosophy in applying accounting principles. Applications may become more conservative or more aggressive, and both will have an impact on the company's earnings.

Financial statements must disclose material extraordinary and nonrecurring items, changes in accounting methodology, and transactions with related parties; however, in practice, materiality is a matter of judgment which may differ between accountants. In addition, all related party transactions may not be disclosed in financial statements, and separate audited financial statements for divisions or subsidiaries are not always available.

How can a due diligence team identify nonrecurring events or related-party transactions when they are not disclosed in a financial statement? Generally, this can be done by conducting comparative reviews of a company's historical income statements, talking with management, and reviewing fluctuations in balance sheet reserve accounts. Other analytical procedures include comparing actual versus budgeted results, reviewing the work papers of the target company's auditors, and reviewing agreements and legal correspondence.

INVOLVEMENT OF ACCOUNTANTS IN M & A TRANSACTIONS

Outside accountants' assignments include the following:

- Consulting with investors or lenders early in the decision-making process to evaluate potential tax consequences, deal structures, cash flows, SEC and other regulatory reporting consequences, and economic aspects of a particular industry.

- Participating as a member of the due diligence review team. The accountant is often the principal financial expert on this team. Responsibilities include the evaluation of a target company's historical financial statements and quality of earnings; the identification of undervalued, overvalued, or unrecorded assets and liabilities; the preparation and assessment of a target company's prospective operating results and cash flows; and the consultation on structuring the transaction.

- Reviewing filings with the SEC (i.e., Forms 8-K, 10-K, and 10-Q, and registration statements, including merger proxies) and monitoring compliance with the SEC's rules and regulations.

- Tax planning with the focus on the target company's potential tax problems, and the maximization of tax benefits both through the transaction's structure and after completion of the deal.
- Evaluating the target company's forecasts or projections.
- Valuing the target company's business for the purpose of assisting the buyer in allocating the purchase price for both income tax and accounting purposes.
- Valuing the existing qualified and nonqualified pension and deferred compensation obligations and retiree medical and life insurance obligations.
- Evaluating the adequacy of the target company's management, computerized systems, and accounting systems and procedures.
- Performing traditional accounting and auditing services, including acquisition and post-acquisition audits.

Sometimes an audit of the target company's historical financial statements is called for. This generally happens when the final purchase price or credit approval depends on the carrying value of the target company's net assets or its operating results. In addition, an audit may be appropriate if due diligence suggests that net assets or earnings may be overstated, or if historical financial statements have been subjected to procedures that are less comprehensive than an audit. An audit may also be required if the target company's historical financial statements must be included in SEC filings.

Forecasts and projections are other tools that accountants can help provide to supplement historical financial statements. These are particularly crucial, because an ongoing business may have a different financial and operating structure than its predecessor. For example, servicing the acquisition debt could have a critical impact on future cash flows.

Forecasts and projections differ. A forecast is based on assumptions that reflect conditions that the management expects to exist, in order to present the best estimate of expected financial results. A projection uses hypothetical assumptions to present an estimate of what would happen if those assumptions were to materialize. Forecasts present the financial effect of what the management expects to happen, whereas projections answer the question "What would happen if . . . ?"

An outside accountant can report on a projection only if (1) its use is expected to be "limited" or (2) it is presented in combination with a forecast that also is being reported on by the accountant. The first condition is defined as a situation in which projections are distributed only to people who are in a position to negotiate directly with the target's management. One or more projections presented in combination with a forecast may help potential investors better understand downside risk, as well as present them with profit projections that are more optimistic than the results suggested by the forecast.

When outside accountants report on forecasts and projections they can perform three different services: an examination, a compilation, and the application of agreed-upon procedures.

An examination is similar to an audit of historical financial statements. Although professional standards prohibit an accountant from guaranteeing that a forecasted or projected result will be achieved, the accountant can assure the client that the underlying assumptions are appropriately supported, that the key factors have been addressed, and that they provide a reasonable basis for the forecast or projection. An examination is the highest level of service that an outside accountant can provide for a forecast or projection.

In a compilation, the accountant performs limited procedures similar to those performed in a compilation of historical financial statements. That is, a compilation of a forecast or projection involves assembling (to the extent necessary) the prospective financial information based on management's assumptions and performing certain other procedures with respect to the forecast or projection without evaluating the support for it, or expressing an opinion or any other form of assurance in regard to the underlying assumptions.

Finally, in the report on the application of agreed-upon procedures, the accountant can provide assurance concerning only the results of the procedures that are performed, and distribution of this report is restricted to those parties who have agreed to the procedures performed.

When prospective financial information is provided for an SEC filing, the SEC will not accept compilation reports. In addition, the SEC does not allow an accountant to examine prospective financial information included in a public filing if the accountant has helped to prepare the information.

CHAPTER **5**

ACQUIRING TROUBLED COMPANIES

Historically, the business community has not associated companies involved in formal Chapter 11 proceedings or in near-bankrupt "workout" situations with opportunities for maximizing value. The conventional wisdom held that such companies were "damaged goods." Shareholders, boards of directors, and management teams routinely abandoned such companies to firms and individuals who specialized in workouts, that is, salvaging the value that was presumed to be left in them. A workout, although an honest effort, invariably represented one more futile step on the road to the inevitable bankruptcy filing. It was no surprise, then, that businesses and workout specialists came to use the terms "bankruptcy" and "liquidation" synonymously.

But the merger mania of the 1980s fundamentally altered the way the general business community evaluated the situations of troubled companies. The pervasive use of the highly leveraged transaction (HLT) expanded the profile of financially troubled companies.

The definition of "financially troubled company" expanded as well. The term came to include businesses that were overleveraged and unable to meet their debt-service burdens, but could still generate acceptable, or even optimal, operating cash flows, given their internal resources and market opportunities. This "good company/ bad capital structure" profile fits a growing number of companies in the United States, most of which are substantially smaller than the Revco- and Campeau-sized transactions that have received a significant amount of publicity.

TO SELL OR NOT TO SELL

Whether a company is in trouble or not, the most important criterion used in determining the viability of an acquisition is the company's marketability. The more of the following criteria a troubled company meets, the more marketable it will be:

- Is a manufacturing rather than a distribution operation.
- Fills a unique product niche rather than produces a commodity item.
- Has a well-known brand name or trademark that is undamaged by its current situation.
- Sustains a strong, defensible market share.
- Has well-maintained facilities and equipment.

Determining whether there is a market for a company requires a thorough analysis of the firm's primary business. This analysis should also reveal the nature of the company's problems. Problems can be broadly characterized as operational or financial in nature.

The ideal situation for a sale exists when a company's problems are primarily financial and do not directly affect its ability to generate operating cash flows. In such cases, sellers can more easily package and market the deal. And buyers can respond more quickly because the key operating factors—sales, cost of goods, and operating expenses—are in good order, identifiable, and, perhaps most crucial, separable from the financial issues.

When a company's problems are primarily operational in nature— poor overhead cost-control, inefficient production methods, or obsolete products—the choice to sell or reorganize and continue to operate a company may not be as clear.

Corporate executives must consider their business's strengths and weaknesses in relation to the universe of likely buyers. Despite operational problems, a sale may still be very viable, especially if a name brand or a trademark product is involved or if the potential buyers are direct industry participants. In these cases, buyers usually have the means and wherewithal to correct or eliminate many of the purchased company's operational problems.

When there is a great deal of interaction between financial and operational problems, company executives must exercise greater diligence before making a decision to sell. For example, in the working-capital-intensive retail industry, the loss of liquidity brought on by an excessive long-term debt burden can lead a company into an overaggressive management policy on working capital. This change in policy could have a profoundly negative impact on the company's relationships with suppliers and customers alike, thereby affecting key operating factors.

Delaying payments for merchandise (e.g., stretching days in accounts payable) could prompt suppliers to alter their trade-credit policies as well as the flow of goods. Reducing inventory could result in increased shortages and empty shelves. The need for cash could force a premium retailer to hold more sales, thereby transforming itself into a discounter. And, if an interim period is required to properly position the company for sale by isolating and remedying operating problems, the timing advantage of a sale could be lost.

Ideally, the advantage of selling a company over reorganizing and operating it is that a sale can be executed much faster—in a year or less. In addition, the realized values are certain and quantifiable to the various constituencies, including the board of directors, management, shareholders, and creditors.

In comparison, a rigorous workout or "bootstrap" plan of reorganization, in which the funding needed to satisfy the requirements of the plan are internally generated, usually requires more than a year. Thus, the values that could be realized by the various constituencies are likely to be less certain.

When a company involved in a reorganization has multiple lines of business that can be rationally separated into stand-alone units, executives should assess each unit on its individual merits.

SALES: A GAME OF FOUR-DIMENSIONAL CHESS

Who makes the decision to sell a troubled company and how the sale will be executed are two critically important questions in the sales process. When a healthy company is sold, the shareholders, board of directors, and management all participate in decisions about the timing and methods of sale. Although the individual parties may have differing views and priorities, they share the opinion that the goal of a sale is to maximize shareholder value. The sale process and, consequently, the sale strategy should be conducted in two dimensions—between the seller and the various buyers.

In the case of a troubled company, however, the relative power of the shareholders, board of directors, and management will be tempered by the secured and unsecured creditors. As a result, corporate executives must take into account a third sales dimension: creditors' objectives.

Although all parties will support the general objective of "maximizing value," their individual views will differ on what those values should be and how they will be best realized. The differences will depend on the parties' positions in the hierarchy of priority, and on how their rights have or have not been protected by the various legal documents, contracts, and agreements. The closer a company is to a Chapter 11 filing, the more important creditors' objectives become in making the decision to sell and, subsequently, in designing the sales process.

Once a company files for protection under Chapter 11, the decision to sell becomes inexorably linked with the Bankruptcy Code. Now a company must add a fourth dimension—the court—to the sale process. In the end, the court will be the final arbiter mediating the common and conflicting objectives of the constituencies involved.

At this point, all constituencies will likely retain legal counsel specializing in bankruptcy law. Throughout the process, intense negotiations over the sale and its execution will invariably continue between the various parties. Underlying the debates that will rage over the structure of the formal sale process are the following considerations:

- Who will be retained as the financial advisor;
- How the financial advisor will be controlled;

- Who will be included or excluded from a buyers' list;
- Whether a sealed-bid auction or a limited auction will be conducted;
- Who will conduct due diligence;
- Who will write the contract; and
- Which parties will enter into a definitive sale agreement.

Should the various parties fail to reach a consensus on the formal sale process, the final decision will rest with the court. Even if a consensus is reached, the respective bankruptcy counsels should consult the judge hearing the case before a motion describing the sale process is submitted to the court for approval.

Traditionally, companies or assets in Chapter 11 filings are sold pursuant to a plan of reorganization, which is a time-consuming process that may take several years. After it is developed, the plan and a disclosure statement are filed with the court.

Subsequent to filing, there is a minimum 25-day waiting period before a disclosure statement hearing. At the hearing, the various involved parties have an opportunity to raise their objections to the statement, and if there are significant objections, additional time must be spent in redrafting it.

If and when the disclosure statement is approved, the court must then confirm the plan of reorganization. A confirmation hearing usually occurs after a minimum 30-day-notice period. The sale of the company or its assets is not final until the court confirms the plan of reorganization at this hearing. The transaction, however, typically does not close until a further 10-day approval period has lapsed.

Because of the lengthy time requirements associated with completing a sale via the traditional Chapter 11 processes, many companies are now turning to sales as part of "prepackaged bankruptcy" and "363 asset sales" options. In a prepackaged bankruptcy, the company files a plan of reorganization with the court that has already been approved by creditors representing at least one-half their number and two-thirds of the amount of debt. With support from its creditors, the company hopes that it can significantly shorten the time period between filing and confirmation. Consequently, proceeds from a sale of this type would be available sooner than they would in a traditional Chapter 11 process.

An asset sale using Section 363 of the Bankruptcy Code often permits assets of a bankrupt estate to be sold before the formal reorganization process is completed. The proceeds from the asset sale are included in the estate and then become available for distribution through a plan of reorganization. The 363 asset sale can significantly reduce the time between finalizing the purchase agreement and the actual closing.

Once a purchase agreement is signed, the company submits it to the court. The agreement then becomes subject to higher and better offers for a period typically lasting anywhere from 30 to 60 days. If interested parties appear during that period, the court sponsors an auction where all bidders have a final opportunity to outbid the contracted party, subject to qualifying guidelines such as the minimum increase in purchase price over the previous offer (i.e., minimum incremental bids) and proven financial wherewithal.

The objective of the court-sponsored auction is to ensure that the contracted party for the company has indeed made the highest and best offer. It is not unusual, then, that the presumed buyer going into court with a definitive purchase agreement may not be the party that walks away from the process owning the company.

Figures 5-1 to 5-3 are examples illustrating the steps involved in selling a company out of Chapter 11. Figure 5-1 outlines the initial stages of the marketing process. (These stages do not differ from the approach used in a sale of a healthy company.) Figures 5-2 and 5-3 outline two different paths that companies may follow after the court receives revised expressions of interest.

A 363 asset sale is outlined in Figure 5-2, and a sale pursuant to a plan of reorganization is depicted in Figure 5-3. Figures 5-2 and 5-3 illustrate that the sale of a company out of Chapter 11 may result in an auction.

All transactions, therefore, are subject to public scrutiny, and numerous opportunities exist to reopen the sales process. As shown in Figure 5-2, the 363 asset sale is not final until approved by the bankruptcy court. As in Figure 5-3, the sale pursuant to a plan of reorganization is not final until the court confirms the plan of reorganization and all appeals are exhausted.

FIGURE 5-1 Initial stages of the marketing process

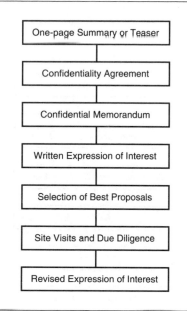

```
┌─────────────────────────────────┐
│  One-page Summary or Teaser     │
└─────────────────────────────────┘
                │
┌─────────────────────────────────┐
│   Confidentiality Agreement     │
└─────────────────────────────────┘
                │
┌─────────────────────────────────┐
│    Confidential Memorandum      │
└─────────────────────────────────┘
                │
┌─────────────────────────────────┐
│  Written Expression of Interest │
└─────────────────────────────────┘
                │
┌─────────────────────────────────┐
│   Selection of Best Proposals   │
└─────────────────────────────────┘
                │
┌─────────────────────────────────┐
│  Site Visits and Due Diligence  │
└─────────────────────────────────┘
                │
┌─────────────────────────────────┐
│  Revised Expression of Interest │
└─────────────────────────────────┘
```

THE BUYER'S ROLE: LEVERAGING HIGH ANXIETY

When a healthy company is sold, buyers exercise little control over the actual sale process. But in the sale of a troubled company, buyers play significant roles. A seller should be aware that when more than one constituency is involved in the sale of a troubled company, astute buyers will have some power to manipulate the process to their advantage by leveraging the anxiety of one constituency against the interests of another.

For example, the selling company (management team, shareholders, and board of directors) may have decided, in order to protect proprietary technology, not to include direct competitors in the sale process. The secured creditors may be comfortable with this decision if they have fully collateralized positions—even in the event of liquidation. However, because the direct competitors are the buyers most likely to pay the highest price for the troubled company, the unsecured creditors may not feel that the company's decision is in their best interests. These unsecured creditors may

FIGURE 5-2   Outline of a 363 asset sale

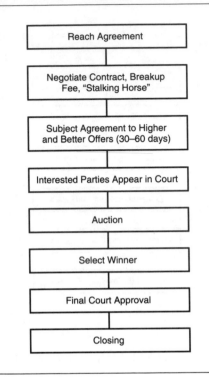

believe that marketing the company to direct competitors is worth the risk—especially because it may be their only opportunity for any monetary recovery.

In the sale of a healthy company, this decision by the seller would stand. However, in the sale of a troubled company, the seller may not have the final word. An interested competitor that the troubled company excluded from participating in the sale could align itself with the unsecured creditors and try to force its way into the process. In a workout situation, the unsecured creditors could put up road-blocks, such as threatening to change trade credit terms until a favorable reconsideration is made. In a Chapter 11 filing, the unsecured creditors could petition the court to allow the competitor into the process as a matter of a fiduciary responsibility to obtain the highest and best offer for the company.

FIGURE 5-3   Outline of a sale pursuant to a plan of reorganization

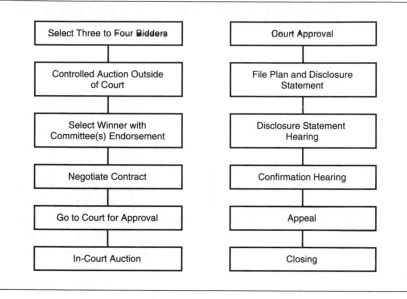

Because buyers in Chapter 11 sales can continuously influence the selling process—even after one buyer successfully navigates the formal sale process and signs a purchase agreement with the seller, the contracted buyer or "stalking horse" is likely to expect or demand some form of protection, i.e., a "topping fee" or "breakup fee." A topping fee is a fee payable to the contracted buyer or stalking horse if an agreement is reached with another buyer. A breakup fee is a fee payable to the contracted buyer or stalking horse if the sale is not consummated because of circumstances beyond the contracted buyer's control. The contracted buyer desires this protection to stabilize its position as a buyer in the event of a court-sponsored auction. Excluded buyers, on the other hand, may try to destabilize the process by playing on the anxieties of the constituency that has the most to gain by blocking any protection clauses. For example, although a breakup or topping fee acts to protect the leading bidder, it can also deter higher competing bids in court. The outcome of these conflicts will likely be a court-negotiated settlement.

Because troubled companies are no longer synonymous with "unmarketable," it is advantageous to play on the anxiety among the various constituencies rather than on the company's troubled situation. Leveraging high constituency anxiety can give buyers of troubled companies increased power in the selling process.

CONCLUSION

Based on the daily reports of companies that suspend debt payments, renegotiate credit terms with lenders, or file for protection under Chapter 11, it is apparent that the ability to deal effectively with situations that involve troubled companies will be a requirement for many executives in the 1990s. In many cases, such companies have fundamentally sound operations burdened by excessive debt. These are the new breed of troubled companies, spawned by the leveraged buy-out (LBO) frenzy of the 1980s. In other cases, any number of traditional operating problems may impair the fundamental operations of a company.

Other situations may involve a combination of both problems—weak operations and weak financial conditions. However, in all cases those executives responsible for managing troubled companies will face increasing pressure to seek more timely alternatives to reorganizing and operating such companies. The sale of a troubled company is one alternative—viable, proactive, and timely—to maximizing values under these less than optimal circumstances.

PART II

Financing Alternatives

INTRODUCTION

In the first chapter of this section, Robert Wujtowicz discusses structuring the acquisition transaction. Second only to accurate assessment of the strategic fit of a proposed acquisition, the most important decision facing a CEO is likely to concern the method of financing for the proposed deal. Clearly, the impact of the acquisition on future earnings and on shareholder value will be influenced by both how much is paid and how it is paid.

In Chapter 7, on bank financing, Janet Green examines the current lending climate, in which tougher standards are the norm. In the 1990s banks have returned to basics and, to a great extent, to lending as it was before the days of the highly leveraged transaction. The exception to the rule is the asset-based transaction with a commercial finance lender or the commercial-finance affiliate of a bank or other multiline lender. In such a case, the lending institutions closely monitor the borrower's underlying assets and are therefore not as quick to demand repayment.

George Bristol discusses mezzanine financing in Chapter 8. Mezzanine financing acts as an important facilitator in an acquisition or sale transaction and can provide benefits to both the buyer and the seller. A buyer can make a more competitive offer for a business with mezzanine capital because it provides additional funds above the sum of the buyer's available equity and the available senior debt financing. A seller may realize greater proceeds through the sale because mezzanine capital can sometimes provide more dollars to the buyer without unacceptably reducing his or her return on investment. The availability of mezzanine capital has been the greatest determinant of financial buyers' pricing of acquisitions in the last ten years.

CHAPTER **6**

STRUCTURING ACQUISITION FINANCING

Instead of receiving primary attention, financing is often left as a final detail in structuring an acquisition. Yet many business failures are attributable to inappropriate capitalization rather than operational problems.

In structuring acquisition financing, the acquirer must assess both his own financial position and expectations and those of the acquisition target. These analyses should be future oriented and based on financial statement projections and sensitivity analyses. Also, financial structure ultimately must consider the suitability of financing products available in the market. The structuring objective should be to meet both the buyer's and the seller's needs at the lowest cost with a suitable level of risk. This chapter outlines the major steps and issues to be considered.

STEP 1: COMPLETE A SELF-ASSESSMENT

Before initiating any acquisition program, management should review its financial position and capitalization. This review includes examination of its targeted capital structure, its liquid asset position, unused borrowing capacity, and projected cash flow.

By completing a self-review before initiating an acquisition program, management can avoid potential problems. Acquisition objectives must be consistent with financial capacity. The self-assessment may help reveal that there are no attractive acquisitions possible within the buyer's financial parameters. In industries where scale economies, high-cost capital equipment, or extensive information systems are critical to achieve sufficient profitability, companies that are candidates for acquisition can be quite large, and financing requirements substantial. If acquisition criteria and financial capacity are inconsistent, a potential buyer must either revise its criteria or increase its capital base prior to embarking on an acquisition program.

In addition, demonstrating strong financial capacity makes the buyer more attractive to prospective sellers. An acquirer's ability to react quickly may be critical to being the winning bidder in an auction. Should a bidder pause to reflect upon financing capabilities during the bidding process, it may lose a valuable acquisition opportunity.

In establishing the appropriate long-term capital structure for the business, the buyer should attempt to minimize the average cost of capital while balancing business and financial risk. Companies that have cyclical earnings, products tied to commodities with fluctuating prices, rapid growth prospects, or businesses in start-up phases will be financed primarily by equity funding. Companies with large tangible asset bases, stable operating profits, and proprietary products will often have higher debt-to-equity ratios.

The buyer should conduct a survey of capital structures of companies operating within the same industry. This comparison will demonstrate the capital structure of competitors, plus provide insight on the public market's views on an appropriate capital structure. This exercise can provide comparisons for smaller, privately held companies, even though targeted capital structures should have lower debt-to-equity ratios than those competitors in the public market. Because a smaller company lacks a large capital base and has limited access to public markets, a larger proportional equity base provides a safety buffer during cyclical downturns.

Owners of privately held businesses must balance their cost of capital objectives with their appetite for risk. Regardless of industry standards and analyses that indicate the capacity for financial leverage, shareholders must also reflect on their own personal risk tolerance.

Because no financial position is static, the corporate self-assessment should be future oriented. Financial and operating management should work to prepare financial statement projections (i.e., income statement, balance sheet, and cash flow) for a three to seven-year period, depending on industry characteristics. Consideration should be given to industry cyclicality, including sensitivity to key assumptions and "what if" scenarios.

If balance sheet projections demonstrate future requirements for a substantial infusion of new capital, an attempted acquisition could stifle a company's internal growth prospects. Conversely, although a company's financial position may not reflect its "targeted" capital structure, future cash flows could show financial capacity for substantial growth by acquisition.

Buyers must appreciate that an acquisition may temporarily divert a company from its targeted capital structure. As a good rule of thumb, the combined company should be able to reasonably achieve its targeted capital structure in a five to seven-year period following the acquisition through either internal cash flow or refinancing.

In analyzing unused borrowing capacity, management can apply standard lending ratios to its unsecured assets and operating cash flow. Appropriate ratios vary widely depending on the business, industry characteristics, and the current state of financial markets. Debt service (e.g., interest and principal payments) should be covered by a comfortable margin from cash flow generated by operations, whether the financing is secured by assets or by operating cash flow. Asset-based advance rates and coverage ratios are detailed later in this chapter.

STEP 2: PREPARE TARGET ASSESSMENT

Detailed due diligence is a key exercise in any acquisition review. Several specific actions should be added to customary due diligence procedures when outside financing will be sought. For structuring acquisition financing, a detailed forecast of income statements, balance sheets, and cash flow of the target is a critical analytic tool. Ordinary due diligence may or may not produce a detailed financial statement forecasts for the target company. Where the target company has already prepared such analysis, acquirers must seriously challenge key assumptions and adjust for anticipated changes in the operating environment. If the acquirer must prepare its own financial statement projections, assumptions and forecasted results should be reviewed with target company management when possible.

After the target has been analyzed as a stand-alone entity, the target and the acquiring company should be analyzed as a combined entity. Financing sources will review the proposed combined company, even if security interests and liens are expected to be applied only to the target company's assets. Financing sources want assurances that the combined company will not suffer distress that forces disposition or nonoptimal handling of the target company's assets.

In reviewing the combined company, one cannot simply add the two companies' operating results together. Capital investments or severance payments may be required to integrate two companies. In some cases, redundant or nonstrategic assets or businesses may be divested. A conservative approach should be used in estimating both net sale proceeds and the divestiture timetable. Several companies currently operating in bankruptcy had grossly erred in their projections of asset disposition. As a result, financial institutions are now quite conservative in lending to companies whose cash flows are expected to be generated by dispositions.

Operating synergies and cost savings may result from the combination of the two companies. Financing sources recognize the difficulty in realizing operating synergies and cost savings, and borrowers should expect financing sources to take a conservative view with regard to the amount of savings to be achieved and the time required. Supporting documentation should be provided when available.

Although financial and quantitative reviews are important, a company's qualitative review is critical to structuring acquisition financing. Management should determine whether the merged entity would have fundamentally different risk characteristics (e.g., technology-obsolescence risk, cyclical risk, risk of change in customer concentration or external factors) than the companies as stand-alone entities. If so, perhaps the combined company's targeted capital structure should be reviewed further.

STEP 3: REVIEW FINANCIAL OPTIONS

Acquisition financing can take an infinite number of forms, but all combinations involve the same principal elements. Acquisitions can be financed through cash, secured debt, unsecured debt, debentures, or stock.

The inverted triangle in Figure 6-1 provides a view of acquisition financing mechanisms. This triangle may have substantially more layers for larger companies with complex financings. For example, a company may have several layers of senior (or "first priority") debt, varying by term, maturity, and collateral. Likewise, certain securities may blur between levels, such as convertible debentures or bonds with warrants.

From the top to the bottom of the triangle acquisition financing typically becomes more expensive. Although dividend payout rates on preferred or common stock may seem inexpensive, the total after-tax cost, including dilution of ownership interests, renders it far more expensive than debt. The high cost of equity is readily

FIGURE 6-1   Acquisition financing mechanisms

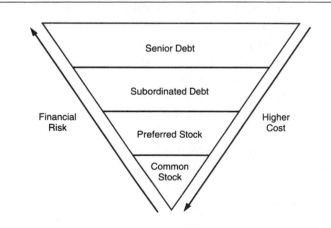

apparent for those companies that have raised additional equity
capital through public offerings or private placements. Institutional
investors and venture capitalists making common stock investments
often seek annual rates of return in excess of 35 percent per year.

The sources higher in the inverted triangle provide increased
financial leverage and, therefore, produce a higher overall financial
risk for the company. In evaluating financing options, the acquirer
should keep in mind its self-assessment and the realities of the marketplace.

In structuring any transaction, the objective is to maximize the
satisfaction of the conflicting needs of the buyer and the seller. For
buyers, acquisitions utilizing their stock as consideration typically
provide a performance incentive, conserve cash, and create the lowest risk for an enterprise. However, most sellers prefer some type
of cash payment or combination of cash and notes. In transactions
involving publicly traded companies, cash or combinations of cash
and note payments have accounted for more than 60 percent of
purchase considerations every year since 1989, according to Merrill
Lynch's *Mergerstat Review*. For companies whose common stock is
not actively traded, stock consideration is much more rare.

Sellers may be willing to consider some type of contingent payment or seller financing to facilitate completion of the transaction.
Contingent payments, or "earn outs," are often a useful mechanism
to balance risk between the buyer and seller for unproven operations. For example, if an unproven new product line or distribution
system is expected to yield highly profitable results, buyers may be
reluctant to pay until results are demonstrated. Outside financing
based on unproven potential cash flows is very difficult to obtain.

The structuring of contingent payments can be based on the
occurrence of some specified events (e.g., successful defense in litigation, continuing employment of key personnel over a period of
time, or retention of key customer accounts for a defined period)
or on various measured financial results (e.g., sales, profits, cash
flow, or return on capital employed). Contingent payments are most
effective when:

• The entity to be acquired will remain separable and measurable;

• The sellers will remain actively involved in the business; and

- Future contingencies are clearly defined and measurable.

To an acquirer, seller financing may represent a simple and low-cost method of acquisition financing. An acquirer should be prepared to demonstrate strong financial stability to reassure the seller of its capability to service the debt. Low-rate seller financing can be used to bridge a purchase price gap. Buyers may be willing to pay a higher price in consideration for low-cost seller financing.

Often, however, one of the seller's major objectives in divesting is liquidity for estate planning or other purposes. In that case, the purchase price must be financed by the acquirer's available cash reserves or by outside financing. Cash availability for acquisitions will be limited to existing cash reserves and cash readily generated through the sale of existing assets. For example, home office properties or other fixed assets may generate cash through a sale-lease-back transaction. However, such transactions should be considered in the menu of options for senior financing, as relative after-tax financing costs may be higher than traditional secured debt.

Debt financings vary in form by seniority and term. As demonstrated in Figure 6-1, the greater the seniority of the debt instrument, the lower the interest cost. In providing seniority, the borrower does sacrifice future flexibility. Covenant restrictions should be balanced to provide protection for the lender without sacrificing the borrower's growth and other strategic objectives.

Although commercial paper and senior notes issued in the public market may offer low-cost financing, these securities are generally unavailable for debt requests of less than $50 million. Other senior financings include revolving lines of credit, asset-based senior debt, senior notes, and leasing.

Rates and fees will vary on asset-based senior loans depending on the size of the debt financing, the collateral, the liquidity of the assets used as security, and the financial condition and overall risk of the borrower. Asset-based senior loans are typically written based on advance rates of 65 to 90 percent of net accounts receivable, 25 to 70 percent of inventory (typically excluding work in progress), 50 to 80 percent of the liquidation value of property, plant, and equipment, and 50 to 70 percent of the fair market value on real estate.

Advance rates vary, depending not only on business risk, but also on the banking environment at the time. Following a period of high credit loan losses in the late 1980s and early 1990s and increased scrutiny by regulatory agencies of highly leveraged transactions (HLTs) and real estate lending, financial institutions reduced their lending appetites. At the same time, financial institutions increased their demands for personal guarantees, raised collateral requirements, and shortened average loan maturities.

Interest rates are usually quoted as a percentage in excess of banks' base lending rates, typically the Prime rate or the London Interbank Offering Rate. Although the interest-rate environment has been relatively stable for several years, it may still be prudent to obtain a rate cap to limit interest rate risk. Fees should be considered as an integral part of the total financing cost. These may include a commitment fee, agent's fee, collateral management fee, syndication and placement fee, and audit fee.

Cash flow–based financing is also available in senior and subordinated forms. In these borrowings, the lender looks to the acquirer's postacquisition cash flows as security for repayment, although a primary or subordinated lien on assets is often demanded. Cash flow–based financing may be difficult to obtain for smaller lending commitments.

In evaluating appropriate cash flow coverage, lenders will review and revise the acquirer's pro forma operating results to ensure that cash flows will cover required payments by a comfortable margin. As of this writing, lenders generally require interest coverage ratios to exceed 1.5 to 2.5 in the first year, and free cash flow to debt-service coverage ratios to exceed 1.5 to 2.0. Even on asset-based loans, financing sources will examine relevant coverage ratios to gain comfort with credit risks. Such coverage ratios will typically be integrated into restrictive covenants in loan documents.

STEP 4: APPROACH FINANCING SOURCES

Unless a transaction can be readily financed with internal cash, seller financing, or unused borrowing commitments, an acquirer must be prepared to present the proposed financing structure to the outside market. The key to successfully raising financing for an acquisition is to communicate effectively the funding needs, the ability to repay, and the value of the collateral offered.

Depending on the size and complexity of the transaction, it may be appropriate to prepare a financing memorandum which explains the proposed financing and the company's ability to service it. Whether or not the information is formalized in a financing memorandum, the acquirer should prepare written information in the following areas:

- Executive summary
- Proposed financing structure
- Products/services
- Competitive market
- Management and organization
- Operations and facilities
- Regulatory, environmental, or other key risks
- Historical financial statements
- Prospective financial statements

Although this information may be similar in form to a prospectus used to sell securities, the emphasis here is to demonstrate the buyer's recognition of and ability to manage the risk of the credit. Assistance of an outside financial adviser can be particularly helpful in preparing this information. An adviser can provide an experienced approach and lend credibility to the documentation.

Although a proposed financing structure should reflect considerations discussed earlier in this chapter, the acquirer should be flexible to modifications proposed by financing sources. Because market conditions are continually changing, any proposed structure must be tested against the current outlook of financing sources. Selection of the appropriate financing source to approach will substantially influence the response.

Financing sources include commercial banks, foreign bank branches, finance companies, "hybrid" lenders, insurance companies, and private investment companies. The choice of parties to approach depends on the size and type of financing requirements.

Asset-based lending groups of commercial banks, specialized as-set-based lenders, and commercial finance companies may provide the most competitive packages on asset-based loans, whereas foreign banks' U.S. branches may provide more competitive cash flow–based senior loans. Certain "hybrid" lenders, such as GE Capital or Heller Financial, may be more expensive for senior financing, but may be able to provide a senior and subordinated package that satisfies all borrowing needs at the lowest cost. A commercial bank with a local presence would generally be the most competitive for small acqui-sition financing needs.

Personal and prior relationships with financial institutions may have some influence on the selection of financing sources. Lenders should be considered as long-term financial partners. Financing packages should be evaluated not only from a cost perspective, but also from the perspective of an ongoing relationship. As with any financial partner, some due diligence and reference checking may be appropriate to determine compatibility. Bank lending officers move frequently within and among financial institutions. Establish-ing good contacts with several people within a financial institution can be helpful for future relations.

CONCLUSION

Structuring acquisition financing requires a constant balance of risk and return trade-offs. Financial structure can significantly affect a company's future growth, profitability, and options. Although a company's financial staff and its advisers are generally responsible for formulating financing alternatives, senior management must play a key role in the process. During the flurry of activities sur-rounding a transaction closing, the strategic implications of financ-ing alternatives must remain in focus. Clearly, rates, fees, covenants, and other financing terms are important, but management and fi-nancial advisors must also consider future capital needs, long-term shareholder objectives, and the balance of business and financial risks.

Acquirers must carefully analyze and communicate their objectives and plans for the future to their financial advisers and financing providers. They must keep in mind that financing structures must harmonize with long-term plans. In the 1990s, companies can ill afford to allow poorly planned financings to jeopardize corporate strategies.

CHAPTER 7

BANK FINANCING

Companies are finding that in the 1990s it is more difficult to convince banks to finance acquisitions than it was in the 1980s. What caused the apparent loss of lending appetite?

A combination of greater scrutiny by regulatory agencies, the competitive pressures of eroding market share and margins, and substantial credit-loan losses have forced banks to concentrate on preserving their capital and minimizing risks. Tougher lending standards are now the norm. Deals are being made, but today they are being evaluated in a much harsher light than in the recent past. Banks have returned to basics—that is, to a large degree, to lending as it was before the days of the highly leveraged transaction.

Banks react to the current environment by examining loan requests more closely and structuring proposals more conservatively. Credit quality, which has always been the most important lending consideration, is carefully evaluated at all levels within an institution. To minimize their exposure to risk, banks are now attempting to increase collateral, make covenants more restrictive, obtain personal and/or parent-company guarantees, and shorten the time term of loans. In addition, banks attempt to syndicate many credits by selling off a substantial portion of a loan to other banks—thus further minimizing their risk exposure in any given credit. The banking community's aggressiveness in minimizing its exposure to risk has made the financing process thornier and more difficult to navigate.

A company seeking bank financing for an acquisition should take a proactive approach to facilitate the financing process. If the company makes its banker's job easier, it will ultimately make its own job easier.

The process begins with communication. Keeping the banker apprised of its intention to make an acquisition will help a company to expedite the process. Before beginning the acquisition search, the would-be acquirer should discuss its strategy with its banker. The banker will then be able to indicate the bank's financing parameters; this is extremely useful information that can help to determine the price the acquirer can afford to pay.

The first step in obtaining financing is to prepare a plan that emphasizes the company's key strengths and highlights the strategic elements of the acquisition. It should also address operational and financial elements of the transaction. A plan provides the banker with a road map; it will be a valuable tool in the credit-review process when key credit decision makers (often unknown to the company's management) determine whether to provide funding. At that time it is important for the company to present the bank with well-thought-out ideas and alternatives. In addition, a contingency plan that addresses a worst-case scenario and that demonstrates protection for the bank can greatly enhance the bank's comfort level and the company's chance of getting the financing. It is also important to keep options open: the company's current banker may not be the appropriate financing source, because of size limitations or lack of expertise.

This chapter deals primarily with acquisitions of a size or complexity that produces significantly new and different financing needs for the acquirer, either to finance the purchase itself or to finance the ongoing operations of the new company after the acquisition. The chapter addresses three major areas: bank loan structures, the way a banker evaluates a transaction, and suggested criteria for evaluating bank financing sources.

BANK LOAN STRUCTURES

Commercial banks offer a wide variety of loan products. However, virtually every loan can be classified as one of three basic types:

- Demand loans
- Short-term notes
- Term loans

Each of the three basic loan structures deals with unforeseen risks differently. With a demand loan, the lender has a high degree of leverage to demand repayment at any time or to insist on basic changes in terms. The bank's ability to demand payment is somewhat more limited with a short-term note, which typically can be called in advance of maturity only in the event of nonpayment of principal or interest. With a term loan, the ability of the lender to act, and the ability of the borrower to deviate from the plan without having to be inordinately concerned about how the lender may respond, are usually tightly controlled by a well-defined set of covenants negotiated at the time the loan is made.

Demand Loans

The demand loan, as its name implies, is payable on the demand of the bank. Demand loans may be couched in terms that make their essential (demand) nature difficult to discern, and the borrower needs to review closely the bank's proposal. With a demand loan the borrower is dependent on the continued good faith of the lender—that the lender will not take unfair advantage—and on the continuance of lending policies that may affect the loan.

Most traditional acquisition loans made by banks are not demand loans. By its very nature, an acquisition presents a range of uncertainties, and the acquisition loan must be viewed as a long-term proposition. Using a demand loan to finance an acquisition can only compound those uncertainties. The exception to this rule is an asset-based transaction with a commercial finance lender or the commercial-finance affiliate of a bank or other multiline lender. In such a case the lending institution closely monitors the borrower's underlying assets and is therefore not likely to demand quick repayment.

Short-Term Notes

In an acquisition, a short-term note is only slightly preferable to a demand loan. Commonly, a short-term note has a stated maturity of 90 days and may be renewed at maturity. Short-term notes are most often used to advance money under lines of credit. The continued willingness to lend at the maturity of each note is left to the discretion of the bank.

Term Loans

From the point of view of the borrower, the ideal way to finance all or at least the bank-debt portion of an acquisition is with one or more term loans.

There are two basic types of term loans: revolving credit loans and straight term loans. With a revolving credit loan all or any part of the total amount committed by the bank can be borrowed, repaid, and reborrowed any reasonable number of times during the commitment period. A straight or conventional term loan is an amount borrowed once to be repaid according to an agreed-upon amortization schedule. It is quite common for an acquisition to be financed with both a conventional term loan and a revolving credit loan; the revolving credit loan is designed to finance seasonal or other peak borrowing, and the conventional loan is used to finance the company's more permanent credit needs.

Term loans are not unique to banks but are also available from insurance companies and pension funds, the public markets, asset-based lenders, and a variety of specialized lending sources. Although term loans by banks usually have somewhat lower interest rates, their maturity schedules typically are not as long as those of insurance company loans and are often at variable rather than fixed rates.

Pricing.   Given the almost unlimited array of corporate risk profiles and financial structures used in acquisitions, it is difficult to generalize about the rates a bank will charge for acquisition loans. As a general rule, any term loan will carry a rate at least ½ percent higher than a short-term note, and the rate for a highly leveraged acquisition may be in the range of 1 to 2 percent above that. In addition, banks will charge various up-front fees ranging from ½ to 3 percent.

Collateral.   Term loans can be secured, and on small and middle market acquisitions, generally are, by either specific assets or stock of the company or its subsidiaries, or both. The distinction between a bank loan and an asset-based loan does not depend on the type of collateral but on the greater frequency in monitoring and verifying of collateral values by asset-based or commercial finance lenders. The types of assets most often used as collateral are receivables, inventory, and various types of fixed assets. The most sensitive of these may be inventory, inasmuch as a bank lien on inventory may have implications for the level of trade credit the company will be given.

Term.   Different banks have strikingly different attitudes about the appropriate duration of term loans. Some have policies requiring repayment in less than five years. Few banks will extend an acquisition loan beyond seven years. The loan amortization schedule is as important a consideration as the life of the loan. Depending on circumstances, a four-year loan repaid on a seven-year schedule with a "balloon" at the end of the fourth year may be more appealing than a five-year loan with equal amortization.

Forecasts.   Whatever the ultimate maturity date, banks want the borrower to provide financial forecasts showing the ability to repay the acquisition debt, in accordance with its proposed terms, and a detailed, written explanation of the assumptions that underlie the numbers. At the very least, the period covered by the forecasts must be one during which the term-loan portion is paid down to such a level that the remaining amount merely represents normal working-capital financing, or is an amount that will not be difficult to refinance.

Bankers have identified three common weaknesses in forecasts used to support an acquisition financing request. They have found that a would-be acquirer may:

- Assume that all the anticipated efficiencies will be realized easily or quickly;
- Ignore business cycles and project "hockey stick" growth (growth that is unreasonable based on past performance or not predicated by a significant change in operating assumptions); or
- Ignore the possibility that interest rates will rise significantly during the term of the loan.

Forecasts can and should reflect awareness of each of these real-world risks. Usually, a bank will want to consider both a base-case scenario, representing what can be agreed upon as likely to occur, and a downside or pessimistic case.

Guarantees or Nonrecourse Financing.   The acquiring company is often motivated to structure a transaction so that lenders have access for repayment only to the assets and business prospects of the acquired entity, thereby protecting the acquirer and ensuring that the target company retains a high degree of autonomy. An important element of that autonomy is maintaining the confidence and morale of key operating and finance personnel to ensure their retention after the acquisition.

However, the lending institution will often push for a full guarantee from the acquiring company (and, in the case of privately owned acquirers, from the primary shareholders) or will suggest a limited-recourse transaction, in which the parent company gives some support but not necessarily a 100 percent guarantee or a cosignature. Limited recourse may take the form of a "comfort letter" which expresses the intent of the acquiring company to see that the target company makes good on its obligations and has adequate capital to operate.

Even with no written support, and even in some cases with no verbal support, the bank may view the parent company's name on the door of the acquired company as a promise of substantive direct support. Although the parent company or the borrower is in no way responsible for what the bank may hope is a degree of support that was never intended, the bank may well ask just what support the acquirer intends to provide under difficult circumstances. This is an appropriate inquiry and should be welcomed. If the intent really is for the bank to have no recourse, that should be clearly stated and stressed.

Loan Covenants.   The covenants of an acquisition loan, that is, the terms of agreement between the two parties, are instrumental in enhancing a banker's comfort with and commitment to a decision to make a loan to an acquiring company. The covenants in term loan agreements associated with mergers or acquisitions may vary from those in other corporate finance transactions largely in the definition of and limitations on merger-accounting treatment and in provisions that protect the bank from unforeseen liabilities. Covenants typically relate to financial performance, measured by a series of liquidity, leverage, and cash flow tests; business issues such as existing liens and contracts; the duties and responsibilities of the acquirer and target, such as continuing existing lines of business, providing timely financial statements, etc.; and contingent liabilities, such as lawsuits, environmental claims, and ERISA (Employee Retirement Income Security Act) claims—particularly those associated with termination of plans or with multiemployer pension plans.

HOW A BANKER EVALUATES THE TRANSACTION

The banker's view of an acquisition differs from that of the company contemplating an acquisition. From the point of view of the company, an acquisition must strike an appropriate balance between risk and return before it is seriously considered. A bank looks at the risks and rewards both to the borrower's business and to its own. Banks operate at slim gross margins, by the standards of a manufacturer or wholesaler, with leverage of between 12 and 15 to 1, and can ill afford mistakes that could lead to major write-offs. From the bank's point of view, large acquisitions financed primarily with debt represent an unknown and potentially large risk at what may be a less than commensurate return.

In the absence of external support to help the bank become comfortable with the acquisition, the borrower must demonstrate a historical track record that supports the future success reflected in the projections, and an ability to provide at least three "comfort factors": interest and principal coverage, sensible balance sheet leverage, and a second way out (an alternative way to repay the loan if future projected cash flows do not materialize). In a well-crafted loan agreement, each of these three factors will be required in the form of covenants to which the borrower agrees. A violation of any of these covenants could put the loan in default, and this may result in either a waiver or amendment to the original loan agreement, a significant renegotiation, or even acceleration and demand for payment of the loan.

Historical Financial Performance

Historical financial performance is the primary basis for a bank's analysis of a company's ability to service its acquisition debt. Historical financial performance also demonstrates the borrower's performance against the market and its management's skill in navigating the peaks and troughs of industrial and economic cycles. Banks generally request three to five years of the target's historical financial statements and spend a great deal of time exploring the reasons for changes in key revenue, expense, and balance sheet items.

Interest and Principal Coverage

A bank's first comfort factor is strong projected interest coverage, often expressed as the ratio of earnings before interest and taxes to interest (EBIT/interest). Sometimes the bank may add depreciation and amortization to EBIT (EBITDA) so that it more closely mirrors anticipated cash flow. The bank looks for projected interest coverage to be consistent with the industry and size of the new company.

The specific level of interest coverage a banker expects to see varies. However, the minimum is at least 1.25 to 1 times at closing; even this level is acceptable only for a company with a strong balance sheet and a strong presence in a key and stable market that has very little business cycle sensitivity. The interest coverage norm ranges between 1.5 and 2.5 times.

Similarly, banks look at cash flow coverage—the ratio of the operating cash flow (after interest payments) of the target company to fixed charges, typically, capital expenditures and principal payments. Coverage of 1.2 or higher is almost always expected.

Balance-Sheet Leverage and Other Key Ratios

A bank's second comfort factor is balance-sheet leverage, which may be represented by the ratio of total liabilities to equity. Banks expect that this leverage ratio will stay at a normal industry level following a merger, or that it will return quickly to a normal level. The outer horizon is three to four years in most cases.

What is normal for this ratio is difficult to specify and may vary significantly by industry. Historically, a maximum ratio (for total liabilities to equity) of 2 to 1 was a common target for manufacturing companies. For a distribution company, 3 to 1 was common, and a ratio of 10 to 1 might be common for a finance company. However, regulatory pressure on banks regarding highly leveraged transactions has moved many banks to reduce their leverage standards by 25 to 40 percent from prior levels. An association of credit professionals, Robert Morris Associates, publishes a series of standard ratios by size of company in various industry classes that can serve as a useful barometer for a bank's expectations.

A Safety Net

The third comfort factor a bank consistently seeks is a company's alternative way out of a bank loan. Interest and principal coverage are necessary but depend on projections which, by their very nature, are uncertain. Balance-sheet leverage is important in analyzing the potential for additional leverage or for a comparison with competitors, but balance sheets do not repay debts. Historical performance gives some comfort in that it demonstrates how a company has performed in the past. An alternative means of repayment offers a bank a safety net if projections are not met. This second way out may be provided by a guarantee, by the liquidation value of corporate assets, or by the breakup or ongoing business value of subsidiaries or divisions. Typically, the weaker the interest and principal coverages projected, the stronger the second way out must be.

The bank wants to protect its loan advances in the event that the company's operations deteriorate to the point where interest or other ongoing expenses cannot be met in a timely fashion. The bank will almost always design a safety net in the form of loan covenants constructed to provide the banker with the opportunity to act—or at least to consider acting—long before a situation degrades to the point where liabilities cannot be paid.

Another Term Loan Option: Asset-Based Financing

A secured, or asset-based acquisition financing, although it can be just as complex as an unsecured one, focuses more on the underlying collateral value of the accounts receivable, inventory, and fixed assets of the acquired company, and relatively less on its cash flow.

The structure and amount of financing available is, therefore, closely related to the estimated liquidation value of the underlying assets. Because the lender is afforded a greater level of comfort when the loan is collateralized, often significantly more leverage is available—either to pay a higher purchase price or, more important, to lower the amount of equity capital needed—to maximize returns to investors and managers. Loan terms are also generally more flexible, although the lender's monitoring of collateral values will generally make asset-based loans more expensive than other forms of senior financing. It is also important to note that although collateral is taken as security to protect the lender against default, the projected cash flow is still considered by lenders as the primary source of repayment.

A typical asset-based loan package consists of a revolving loan tied to the current assets, and a term loan supported by fixed assets. The amount of the loan package is usually limited to percentages of the assets that support it. Over the years, lenders have developed standard percentage norms for different industries and collateral. In general, the following percentages are typical of asset-based financing:

- 70% to 85% of *eligible* accounts receivable
- Up to 60% of *eligible* inventory
- 50%+ of the *liquidation value* of property, plant, and equipment

The Revolver

The revolving loan portion of a financing package may have no amortization schedule, but the amount outstanding at any time is limited to certain percentages of accounts receivable and inventory. Accounts receivable are the most liquid assets, and, as a result, lenders are willing to lend as much as 85 percent of eligible receivables. Ineligible receivables are generally those that are 60 days past due, poor credit risks, and accounts that are subject to offset for any reason.

Inventory advance rates vary widely, coinciding with the liquidity of the goods. Advances against inventory, however, normally carry a maximum of 50 to 60 percent of manufactured costs for raw materials and finished products. Work in process is usually considered ineligible.

Because the levels of current assets are constantly changing, the lender requires periodic reports from the borrower, usually weekly, to ensure that the loan stays within the established limits. (This more intensive monitoring of asset-based loans also makes such loans more expensive.) In effect, the revolving portion of the loan serves as a substitute for some initial equity capital and, to a great extent, future capital as a business grows. The borrower has substantial flexibility because the revolving loan limit actually grows as asset values increase with increased business activity.

The Term Loan

Term loans are, for the most part, generally amortized over five to seven years, although some lenders agree to ten years, depending on the marketability and useful life of the underlying fixed assets. The machinery, equipment, and real estate supporting a term loan usually warrant much lower rates of advance than the current assets, because of their illiquidity and the dependence on future cash flows to amortize the debt. The asset-based lender almost always requires a current appraisal prepared on a liquidation or quick-sale basis. The rates of advance vary from as low as 50 percent to 100 percent (in rare cases) of liquidation value.

Establishing Advance Rates and Collateral Levels

The process of establishing the percentage of inventory and receivables on which the financing source will lend is part art and part science and takes into consideration all aspects of a company's profile, as well as lender comfort factors. Typically, a lender sends a field audit team to visit both the acquirer and the company to be acquired to review the books and records and the collateral, as part of the process of setting these terms.

The greater the dependence on term debt, the more emphasis the lender places on cash flow. As a general rule, the more consistent the cash flows have been, the more aggressive the rates of advance will be. Conversely, an inconsistent or weaker cash flow will prompt a lender to use conservative rates of advance.

In some instances, particularly when cash flows are very strong, asset-based lenders lend more than the advance rates against the collateral would otherwise dictate. In these cases, however, because of the greater incremental risk, the lender expects to receive more rapid principal payments, usually over one to two years, and a significantly greater return than just the rent for the use of funds. The lender considers the "overadvance" (above the normal percentage of collateral) to be a higher risk loan, and may expect to be compensated with additional fees and/or a percentage of future earnings or cash flow.

There are significant advantages for buyers in dealing with a lender willing to take this approach, because it generally means that the buyer will not be required to provide as much equity. On the other hand, both the lender and the buyer must take into consideration the stark fact that too little equity or capital in a financing could turn out to be punitive to both parties if things do not go as planned.

Pricing and Covenants

Pricing of asset-based loans varies greatly, but customarily involves a closing fee of ¾ to 2½ percent, and an interest rate of anywhere from 1 to 3 percent over the prime rate. Pricing is a function of overhead, the cost of monitoring the collateral and perceived risk for the lender. The closing fee is used by a lender to compensate for its up-front work and to enhance yield in the first year of the loan, which is usually the riskiest. For the most part, the asset-based lender attempts to limit risk to zero by carefully determining rates of advance, collateral coverage, and predictability of cash flows. In effect, rent is charged for the use of the money, because the risk has been somewhat modified. Covenants on asset-based loans are generally of the same form as those for standard term loans.

EVALUATING BANKING SOURCES

The company should choose its banks as carefully as it does other suppliers of key products. The process of choosing banks too often breaks down when major acquisitions or mergers must be consummated quickly. Banks may then be approached hastily, with less than appropriate attention given to their selection. Banks with the lowest prices, weakest terms, and greatest commitments are appealing in the heat of the deal, but may not be the best choices. A company using the services of a commercial banker in financing a merger or acquisition should at a minimum insist upon and require four elements to make the process work: money, deal structure, speed of response, and confidentiality.

Money

The primary role of a commercial bank in the acquisition arena is to provide much or all of the money needed to make the purchase a reality. The timeworn adage in banking is that there is always money for good deals. However, banks have consistently experienced cycles of aggressiveness and retrenchment in their lending practices. Soft corporate earnings in the late 1980s and early 1990s reduced the available cash flow coverage needed to make banks comfortable with many loans and severely limited the banks' pool of "good deals." In addition, federal legislation and regulations on highly leveraged transactions and risk-based capital further increased banks' reluctance to finance marginal deals.

Deal Structure

Money plus a good deal structure is worth more than money alone. A loan that is sufficient to make a deal but is poorly structured will almost certainly present problems down the road—if not with the deal, then with the relationship with the bank. It is critical to an acquirer that the loan agreement allow sufficient operating flexibility. The acquirer and its advisors should work with the bank to negotiate in the context of an overall agreement—not point by point—and the bank should be encouraged to consider the sensitive trade-offs between operating flexibility for the company and appropriate risk controls for the bank. At the end of the day, if a comfortable deal structure cannot be negotiated, the acquirer must reevaluate the deal itself. Because banks are in the business of making loans prudently, the problem may be the deal itself and not the banks.

Speed of Response

The bank must offer a quick response to a credit request. Every deal has moments when it can fall apart or come together, and at those moments an acquirer may need funds very quickly.

How long it takes a bank to make a decision depends in part on the personality and practices of the bank and of the individual banker. But the time period also depends on the quality and organization of the information presented as the basis for that decision. Working closely with the bank(s) or with a corporate finance professional acting as an agent and adviser should ensure a good financing package. Ideally, the package should provide a self-initiating credit analysis to which the bank needs only to add its own credit approval form.

Confidentiality

A process that takes place over time, that includes many people and deals with confidential information, is inherently unstable. Acquiring companies do not want their competitors to know what they are doing until the deal is done, and sellers do not want their competitors to know they are for sale. The list of people who have to be "in the know" about an acquisition can be extensive: senior management, the board of directors, financial advisers, accountants and lawyers (times two—one set on each side), and the bankers. The acquirer desires—and has every right to require—that the bank respond, with effort and with speed, so as to minimize the number of people that need to be involved in the process.

INHERITED BANKS

It is often the case that with an acquisition an acquirer inherits lending institutions. One commonly mentioned reason for retaining them is the necessity of maintaining the morale of the financial staff of the acquired company. The rationale in this case is that because the target's financial staff had certain favored banks, those banks should be retained in the interest of demonstrating that the acquired company will continue to have a measure of autonomy. Multinational companies often retain banks in an acquisition, because international operations require banks that can provide local currency facilities. Inherited banks certainly know the target better than a new bank does initially, and this could be an advantage to the acquirer. Therefore, retaining some of the acquired company's banks may be appropriate. However, each bank relationship should be evaluated individually and in the context of the total company's needs.

CHAPTER 8

MEZZANINE FINANCING

Although *mezzanine capital* is difficult to define, one easily recognizes it when it appears. Mezzanine capital is not the same as senior debt, which often comes from banks or, in large transactions, insurance companies. It is also not equity, which has a return based almost entirely on future results. Mezzanine capital finances that portion of a purchase price which relates to the cash flow of the business that appears predictable—but is in excess of assets which satisfy senior lenders.

Mezzanine financing has a pivotal role and can be an important facilitator in an acquisition or sale transaction. When it is available, a buyer can pay more for a business because mezzanine capital will provide additional funds above the sum of the buyer's equity investment and the amount of available senior debt financing. A seller can realize greater proceeds through the sale, because mezzanine capital provides more dollars to the buyer without dramatically reducing his or her return on investment. In fact, when taken together with the required equity investment, the availability of mezzanine capital has been the greatest determinant of financial buyer's pricing of acquisitions since the early 1980s.

In the 1980s, when mezzanine capital was readily available, financial buyers paid higher multiples of earnings or cash flow and put up less equity for acquisitions. Many of these acquisitions became the headline-making troubled companies of the early 1990s. The financial structures of acquisitions today reflect the negative experience caused by the structures of the previous decade. Today, although a greater portion of equity must finance an acquisition, mezzanine financing retains an important role in helping to create prices that satisfy a seller while allowing a financial or leveraged buyer to compete for an acquisition.

Most acquisition financings consider total interest coverage at levels that vary according to the volatility or predictability of the business. In a typical acquisition of today, financing may support a loan structure that has an earnings coverage of 1.5 times the total interest. The mezzanine capital may be subordinated debt with a fixed interest rate that is included in the calculation for this coverage. If the subordinated debt interest causes the coverage ratio to fall below one that satisfies senior lenders, the mezzanine capital may be structured as a preferred stock with a fixed dividend. The key consideration in the use of mezzanine capital is that the structure must satisfy the requirements of the senior capital source.

Stated or fixed returns on mezzanine capital very rarely provide returns satisfactory to the capital source, considering the level of risk. Accordingly, a portion of return for mezzanine capital is almost always contingent on future performance. This can be either contingent additional interest or, most typically, equity in the ownership of the company. The equity is often in the form of warrants to purchase common stock for some extended period of time. These warrants may come with an unlimited number of additional features, such as a demand buyback at a guaranteed price. Nonetheless, mezzanine capital is less risky to the investor than pure equity because of its contractual return and its seniority in the capital structure.

In the 1980s, when very little equity was invested in many acquisitions, this seniority feature was worth very little. Now that seems to have changed, as most capital structures have a more significant equity investment.

HOW MEZZANINE CAPITAL CAN BE USED

As mentioned earlier, mezzanine capital is neither senior debt nor equity. It requires higher returns than senior debt but significantly lower returns than equity. The following hypothetical situation illustrates the manner in which mezzanine capital is used:

A financial buyer has identified a company in a stable industry which has $50 million in revenues and $5 million in earnings before interest and taxes. The seller would like $35 million in cash for the company, or 7 times EBIT. The buyer presents the opportunity to a bank which agrees to a combination of a revolving credit and five year term loan totaling $20 million, secured by all of the assets of the company. The loans carry a blended interest rate of 8 percent, and the term loan requires principal payments of $1.8 million per year. The buyer is willing to invest $7 million in equity, and requires a 30 percent rate of return.

To satisfy the seller, the shortfall of $8 million must be filled by mezzanine capital. The buyer calculates that it can pay a current coupon of 11.25 percent on this subordinated debt while maintaining 2.0 times interest coverage in the first year. As is typical in these transactions, the subordinated debt does not require principal payments for five years. However, to compensate for risk of lending in a subordinate position to a fully secured senior lender, the mezzanine capital provider requires a 20 percent total return on its investment. Therefore, it mandates an equity participation, or ownership position in the company, to bridge the gap between the current coupon and the total return requirement. The buyer offers the mezzanine investor 17.5 percent of the equity, payable upon refinancing the transaction in five years.

The buyer expects the company to achieve sales growth of 7 percent per year, and to maintain its existing EBIT margin of 10 percent. The buyer further expects to use the majority of the company's excess cash flow (after taxes, required loan repayments, capital expenditures, and working capital requirements) to further reduce the senior debt outstanding. If the business performs as predicted, at the end of five years the bank debt will be reduced to $7.5 million, based on $9 million in required payments and $3.5 million in prepayments. Estimating value at the same 7 times EBIT, the company will be valued at approximately $47.3 million. After subtracting the senior debt of $7.5 million and the mezzanine debt of $8 million, the value of the equity is $31.8 million.

The mezzanine investor would receive approximately $5.2 million from the sale of its 15 percent of the equity. This yields a return on equity to the buyer of 31 percent, slightly above its target of 30 percent. The buyer will also want to determine if it is possible to receive additional returns—either by improving profitability, reducing the selling price, squeezing more leverage out of the bank, or finding a cheaper mezzanine source.

Even if additional returns cannot be achieved, the buyer is still much better off with the mezzanine capital than without it. Using the same operating assumptions as above (growth, profitability, prepayment of senior debt with excess cash and method of estimating future enterprise value), but assuming a $15 million equity investment and no mezzanine, the buyer could not expect a return on equity of more than 21–22 percent.

Such an example illustrates how a financial buyer structures its financings, and how mezzanine capital can stretch the buyer's resources.

SOURCES OF MEZZANINE CAPITAL

Because of the value of mezzanine capital to the success of financial buyers, the sources of mezzanine capital are extremely popular with this group of acquirers. In the 1980s the public high-yield market was extensively utilized because it could provide extremely large amounts of money, most often at fixed rates. The market was so strong that it allowed instruments that didn't pay any current interest (pay-in-kind or PIK) but compounded at high (16 percent) rates, which seemed too good to be true (and were).

Huge amounts were invested in mezzanine capital by bond funds, insurance companies, savings and loans, and industrial companies with excess cash. Many smaller financings were handled privately with all sorts of lenders, including insurance companies, savings and loans, and nontraditional sources. These sources have largely dried up for all but a handful of large financings.

Many new mezzanine funds have sprung up to fill the vacuum in this market. These funds typically invest $5 to $15 million in a transaction with required rates of return of 18 to 30 percent. They usually prefer subordinated debt with common-stock purchase warrants. One of the difficulties in using these funds is that senior lenders often have problems with the loan-agreement language of the mezzanine lender. These problems are solved with extensive, expensive negotiations.

In certain circumstances large finance companies prove willing to provide both the senior and mezzanine capital for a transaction. Obviously, such willingness can cut through the intercreditor problems, because the companies are the sole source of capital. These "one-stop shops" are good sources for many deals under $50 million.

In the past few years insurance companies have been pulling out of the mezzanine market, especially when it comes to committing their own funds. Yet every now and then a highly visible mezzanine investment is made by an insurance company.

Another good source of mezzanine capital is the seller, who provides the capital in the form of seller notes. These are similar to funds from independent suppliers, but the seller, likely having greater confidence in the business, may be willing to provide more capital or to require a lower return on investment.

In the end, experience says that a well-structured deal will find an appropriate capital source.

PART III

Legal and Regulatory Issues

INTRODUCTION

The legal documents that transfer the ownership of a corporation in an acquisition or merger transaction are necessarily complex, and a company will retain a qualified expert to represent and advise it. Nevertheless, the success of a transaction may rest on how well the CEO of the acquiring company understands the provisions of the agreements and their implications.

As Dewey B. Crawford explains in Chapter 9 of this section, there are many complex issues to consider when negotiating an acquisition agreement. Each acquisition agreement must be tailored to the specific circumstances of the transaction, but the essential features of any acquisition agreement are representations and warranties, covenants, conditions precedent to closing the acquisition, and indemnification.

Special legal and regulatory concerns are added when securities of either the acquirer or the company being acquired are held by the public. Carolyn Buck Luce presents some of the tactical alternatives in acquiring and merging public companies in Chapter 10 of this section. The sequence of events and choice of structure in such acquisitions are guided largely by applicable law and regulations.

In Chapter 11, Stephen M. Banker continues the discussion of the legal and regulatory constraints and advantages that accompany proposed business combinations between companies when at least one of them has publicly held securities.

All sizable acquisitions are subject to antitrust law and practice. In Chapter 12 of this section, Michael N. Sohn provides insights into how antitrust laws affect mergers and acquisitions and how the Department of Justice currently administers those laws.

CHAPTER 9

THE ACQUISITION AGREEMENT

Negotiating an agreement for an acquisition is usually a long and complicated task. At each step along the way the parties involved must cooperate to ensure that even as they preserve their own best interests, they preserve the best interests of their negotiating partners. The acquisition agreement is the formal, legal version of the sum of all discussions that businesspeople have had about an acquisition; it is the articulation of the often oversimplified ideas of the parties as to the terms of the transaction.

Businesspeople experienced in this area recognize that an extraordinarily large number of issues must be addressed, even after the handshake stage has been reached. Newcomers to the acquisition arena are often surprised by the complexities of working out a formal acquisition agreement. The agreement is intended to answer in advance questions that might otherwise lead to confusion, differing interpretations, dispute, and, ultimately, litigation. In its purest form, it accurately and unambiguously sets forth all the rights and obligations of the parties to the agreement.

The four most critical features of this agreement are representations and warranties, covenants, conditions precedent to closing the acquisition, and indemnification. This chapter focuses primarily on those features. It should be remembered, however, that each acquisition agreement is specific to its own particular transaction.

Although other provisions of an agreement are also important, experience has shown that a failure by the parties and their counsel to fully understand and appreciate the interplay of these four provisions has, more than any other factor, caused the failure of transactions that could otherwise have succeeded, as well as undue acrimony between the parties. Not surprisingly, these are also the issues on which the businesspeople should focus in a proposed acquisition transaction. Together, they assure that the acquirer has sufficient information to make informed judgments and that the information is correct; they also determine which party will suffer the adverse consequences of liabilities unknown or indeterminable at the time of closing.

Customarily, the purchaser drafts the acquisition agreement. This enables the purchaser to control the terms and conditions of the acquisition.

THE AGREEMENT IN PRINCIPLE

Just as an *acquisition agreement* represents the culmination of an acquisition, the start of negotiations is marked by an *agreement in principle*, often called a letter of intent or memorandum of understanding. A letter of intent may set forth little more than a brief sketch of the principal points of agreement; however, it can serve three useful purposes:

1. Although generally not legally binding, the letter of intent does represent a moral obligation that is normally taken very seriously by the parties.

2. The letter of intent memorializes the basic terms of the transaction, which helps to prevent subsequent misunderstandings, both intentional and unintentional.

3. The letter of intent can form the basis of a filing under the Hart-Scott-Rodino Antitrust Improvement Act of 1986 (see Chapter 12 for a more complete discussion of antitrust considerations) and begin the waiting period under that law while the parties negotiate the definitive acquisition agreement. Under the provisions of the Act, a notice must be filed for all transactions that involve commerce in the United States and that satisfy certain requirements regarding the size of the parties involved in the transaction, as well as the size of the transaction. Depending on the nature of the transaction and whether there is any need for further investigation following the filing of the notice, the length of the waiting period varies.

There are good reasons not to have a letter of intent. The parties may not wish to make the public announcement that is generally required of public companies. The seller may also be negotiating with other parties and may want to avoid alienating them. If important points remain open, a letter of intent may weaken one party's bargaining position. Finally, much energy can be wasted in negotiating an agreement in principle that might be better spent in negotiating the definitive agreement.

Generally, the agreement in principle is in the form of a letter addressed to the seller, or to the seller's stockholders if they are to be the parties to the transaction. It is signed by the purchaser, and countersigned by the seller or the stockholders. This agreement is not normally intended to be legally binding, although portions of the letter, such as an agreement to maintain confidentiality or not to negotiate with others, may be binding.

A letter of intent should cover the following points:

- A description of the form of transaction—merger, stock purchase, or asset purchase—if known at the time of signing.

- Details of consideration for the purchase. If stock is to be used, the stock exchange ratio or other method of valuation should be set forth. If other securities are to be used, basic terms should be described. Essential terms of contingent or deferred payment are also included.

- Significant protective provisions, such as an escrow or pledge. Escrow provisions are often used when there is a possibility that the target company's future earnings may not meet certain expectations or that potential liability could arise at some time following the closing. Therefore, a portion of the purchase price may be set aside for a specified period of time in an escrow account. If breaches of representations or warranties are discovered after the closing, all or a portion of these funds is returned to the purchaser; the balance goes to the seller. If the purchaser issues a promissory note as part of the consideration, the seller may want all or a portion of the assets or stocks acquired by the purchaser to be pledged as security for the note's payment.

- Special arrangements, such as employment contracts with the seller's directors, officers, or employees.

- Brokers' and finders' fees.

- An outline of any registration rights if stock is to be used. Registration rights are the contractual rights of the holders of restricted stock (stock that has not been registered under the Securities Act of 1933) to have such stock registered under the Securities Act so that it may be freely sold or transferred.

- Any restrictions on the seller's business pending the closing.

- A "no-shop" clause that commits the seller not to solicit other offers or provide information to or negotiate with other interested parties.

- A "bust-up" fee to be paid to the purchaser in the event the seller is acquired by a third party.

Finally, the major conditions to consummation of the transaction, such as (1) execution of a definitive agreement containing representations, warranties, covenants, conditions, and indemnifications appropriate to such a transaction and (2) any other particular conditions that have been discussed, such as tax rulings, financial performance, off-balance-sheet conditions, or consents of third parties that need to be worked out before the transaction can be completed.

STRUCTURE OF THE ACQUISITION AGREEMENT

The structure of an acquisition agreement depends on the nature of the acquisition, that is, whether it is an acquisition of the stock or of the assets of the target company. In an assets transaction, it is critical to identify, as specifically as possible, the assets and liabilities that are being transferred.

Most acquisition agreements are similar in structure and share a number of principal features, including the following:

- The operative terms of the transaction, which include identification of the assets or stock to be acquired, the consideration to be paid, and the mechanics of the transaction.

- Other ancillary or related terms of the principal transaction, such as earn-out or financing provisions. An earn-out provision is a provision calling for future payment by the purchaser of additional consideration in the event that certain contingencies are met, such as the acquired business's attaining designated levels of earnings. A financing provision is one that makes clear that the purchaser's ability to pay for the seller's business is subject to its ability to obtain financing from a third party; it also defines the parameters of such financing:

  — The seller's representations and warranties
  — The purchaser's representations and warranties
  — The seller's covenants pending the closing
  — The purchaser's covenants pending the closing
  — Conditions to be met by the seller in order to close
  — Closing and termination provisions
  — Indemnification provisions
  — Miscellaneous matters, such as finders' fees, expenses, and particular laws governing the transaction

Indemnification provisions are especially crucial in an acquisition. Because of the potentially high costs of certain contingent liabilities such as taxes, environmental matters, product liability, litigation, and employee benefits, indemnification is the means by which the purchaser is protected against such liabilities. With respect to these contingent liabilities, indemnification should cover inaccurate or incomplete representations and warranties, as well as liability to third parties. In the case of environmental liability, the indemnity should also cover liability for natural resource damage and cleanup costs, when such damage and/or costs result from activities prior to the closing (even if the cleanup is not required until well after the closing).

The discussion of representations and warranties, covenants, conditions precedent to closing, and indemnification presented in this chapter addresses the agreement from the purchaser's point of view and assumes that there will be a deferred closing—one in which the transfer of assets or stock and payment of the consideration occur only after a lapse of time following execution of the acquisition agreement. Except in the smallest of acquisitions, a deferred closing is by far the rule. This is principally due to the need for one or both parties to take certain actions, such as to make the proper filings under Hart-Scott-Rodino, to obtain third-party consents, to obtain financing or shareholder approval, or to allow for the requisite passage of time under applicable laws. A simultaneous signing and closing is easier in many respects, inasmuch as there is no need to address changes or events that may occur between signing the closing or to negotiate restrictions on the seller's conduct of the business prior to the closing.

The representations and warranties and the provisions for indemnification are usually the most substantive and therefore involve the heaviest negotiations. The covenants and deal-specific closing conditions interrelate with the other provisions and must be considered in any discussion of the flow of an acquisition agreement.

REPRESENTATIONS AND WARRANTIES

The representations and warranties of an agreement serve three important functions:

1. Informational: Prior to execution of the definitive acquisition agreement, representations and warranties provide the means by which the purchaser is able to learn as much as possible about the seller's business.

2. Protective: Between signing and closing, they provide a mechanism for the purchaser to be relieved of its obligations to consummate the transaction if adverse facts are discovered.

3. Supportive: These features of an agreement provide the framework for the seller's indemnification of the purchaser following the closing.

Although some practitioners and commentators make legal distinctions between *representations* and *warranties*, in common practice the terms are used interchangeably.

The seller's representations and warranties normally account for the largest part of the acquisition agreement. Their scope is limited in number only by the seller's negotiating ability and the purchaser's attorney's imagination. However, the most common and most important representations and warranties fall into a few broad categories, including financial statements, assets, taxes, contracts, employee matters, environmental protection, product liability litigation, corporate organizations, and existing restrictions.

The informational aspect of representations is served by forcing the seller to formally impart important information about its business to the purchaser to a degree and in a manner it probably has never before attempted. Not only does this help to educate the purchaser, but it may also, through the focus of the representations, alert the purchaser to troublesome areas requiring more detailed investigation.

The purchaser normally performs the definitive investigation of the seller's business after execution of the definitive agreement, although an earlier preliminary investigation is usually made. A standard condition of the purchaser's obligation to consummate the acquisition is that at the closing the seller's representations be true not only when they are actually made at the time of the signing of the agreement, but also at the time of the closing. If adverse facts are discovered during the detailed investigation, the seller will be unable to reaffirm its representations at closing, and the condition to the purchaser's obligations to close the transactions will not have been satisfied. This is the protective aspect of representations and warranties.

If, notwithstanding the purchaser's detailed investigation, it develops after the closing that a representation was untrue or materially inaccurate, the normal indemnification by the seller gives the purchaser an indemnifiable claim—a claim for which the seller will have to compensate the purchaser—supported by this breach of a representation.

The information about the seller and its business generated by the representations is normally provided through the use of schedules and lists—the so-called disclosure schedule. For example, the seller typically represents that it has no real property, except for the property listed on the disclosure schedule. The representation then goes on to confirm that the disclosure schedule contains a description of the buildings and other improvements on the property and a legal description of the property, and that there are no liens or defects in the seller's title except as disclosed in the disclosure schedule.

The parties can agree on the length of time that certain representations and warranties survive the closing. In areas where potential liability exists but is likely to take longer to arise or to be discovered, such as environmental issues and product liability, the applicable representations and warranties generally survive longer than other commercial representations and warranties. Generally, representations and warranties relating to matters such as taxes and employee benefits last until the expiration of the applicable statute of limitations, whereas matters such as capitalization and stock holdings usually survive indefinitely.

The representations are the skeleton. The disclosure schedule, which appears as an appendix to the agreement, is the flesh. This arrangement streamlines the actual agreement. In addition, if the seller is a public company it often tries to disclose information only in the disclosure schedule so that it can keep the information out of subsequent proxy statements.

Preparation of disclosure schedules may be very intimidating to the seller, and the process often causes friction between the buyer and the seller. Yet because of the importance of disclosure schedules in protecting the purchaser, considerable care must be exercised before the purchaser agrees to reduce or eliminate required disclosures.

The seller can be expected to raise the dual issues of materiality and knowledge in negotiating the representations and warranties— that is, the seller will want to limit disclosure to material items and then only to items of which it has knowledge. The buyer's businesspeople must have a clear view of how these terms may limit the company's ability to recover future damages.

In acquisitions of public companies it is fairly common to employ the term *material* in the representations and warranties, as in this context representations and warranties usually do not survive the closing and therefore do not set the parameters for indemnification.

Where an objective standard of what is material can be established, the likelihood of misunderstandings or applications of different standards is minimized. Agreeing on a dollar standard for materiality—for instance, contracts involving payments in excess of $25,000—may answer the concerns of both sides. Although the purchaser wants to learn everything it can about the seller, listing every contract and commitment may be truly burdensome to the seller and may merely bog down the purchaser. Establishing a dollar standard limits the seller's disclosure to items that are truly material and may make the purchaser's analysis easier as well. On the other hand, it may be important for the purchaser to learn about every item of litigation, not just those that are material, and thus no materiality standard should be established for these items.

A knowledge qualification involves somewhat different problems. Initially, it is easy to be sympathetic to a seller that wants to be held responsible for only those things about which it has knowledge. However, if a major claim exists but is unknown to the seller, the purchaser will not want to be saddled with the risks associated with that claim. Responsibility is the essential ingredient in determining whether a knowledge qualification is appropriate. A knowledge qualification shifts responsibility from the seller to the purchaser.

Financial Statements

The single most important representation covers the seller's financial statements. If the purchaser were limited to receiving one representation, this is the one for which its counsel would recommend holding out. The financial statements provide the most comprehensive picture of the seller's business and, when coupled with the representation, provide an excellent framework for the three functions served by representations.

The representation typically is to the effect that the seller has provided the purchaser with financial statements as of certain dates and for particular periods, some or all of which have been prepared in accordance with GAAP, and that they fairly present the seller's financial condition as of the dates of the balance sheets, as well as the results of the seller's operations and cash flows for the periods covered by the income statements and cash flow statements.

To bridge the gap between the date of the balance sheet and the date of execution of the acquisition agreement, there is usually a representation either that no material adverse change has occurred in the seller's operation or financial condition or that, except as set forth in the disclosure schedule, no events of certain kinds—such as losses, dividends, and asset dispositions—have occurred since the date of the most recent financial statements.

The seller usually makes a representation that it has no liabilities except those reflected or reserved against in the balance sheet or as set forth in the disclosure schedule, and that since the date of the balance sheet the seller has incurred no liabilities other than in the ordinary course of business and consistent with past practices. It is normal for there to be a representation that the seller has filed all required tax returns and paid all taxes due, and that adequate tax reserves are reflected in the balance sheet.

Assets

Representations normally cover the seller's various assets: real property, machinery and equipment, patents, trademarks, trade names, intellectual property, and other intangibles. These representations relate to title to the assets, their condition, and similar matters.

Depending on the nature of the target company's business, intellectual property could be a very important asset. Therefore, if the intellectual property is a major asset to the business, a separate representation and warranty should specifically address intellectual property matters. The intellectual property representation and warranty should provide that the seller has full and clear title to the property, that the registrations or patents are valid and subsisting, in full force and effect, and that the registrations or patents have not been claimed to be invalid or unenforceable in whole or in part and that they are not infringing the intellectual property rights of others.

Taxes

In a stock acquisition, the purchaser inherits the tax liabilities of the target company. Therefore, to protect the purchaser, a tax representation and warranty is very important. Because the target company's tax returns should completely and accurately reflect its financial condition and status, the tax representation and warranty also serves as a means of checking the information contained in the target company's financial statements. In assessing the purchaser's potential liability, it is important to determine which tax years remain "open" (those years in which the target company's tax returns may still be examined). In addition to stating which tax years are open, a typical tax representation and warranty should provide, among other things, that all tax returns were timely filed, that all taxes were paid when due, that there are no liens for any taxes against the target company's assets, and that there are no actions, suits, or claims with respect to any taxes relating to the target company.

Leases, Contracts, and Commitments

Representations disclosing leases, contracts, and commitments are required to have enough descriptive material to enable the purchaser to determine how much effort to spend on examining the actual documents. There should also be a representation that the leases and contracts are in full force and effect and that no party to them is in default.

Ascertaining the important and material documents through this representation and warranty also alerts the purchaser as to whether consents are required to transfer such leases, contracts, or commitments prior to consummating the transaction. A representation and warranty by the seller discussing necessary consents should also be included in the acquisition agreement.

Employee Matters

Representations covering employee matters include employee benefit plans, compensation, employment contracts, collective bargaining agreements, and similar issues. Representations regarding employee benefit plans and their funding and compliance with the Employee Retirement Income Security Act of 1972 (ERISA) often run several pages.

This is a particularly important representation and warranty for the purchaser because the liability for inadequately funded plans or unforeseen termination of defined benefit plans could be costly. In addition, provisions with respect to transferring benefit plan assets and liabilities and providing that employees are treated fairly need to be included and are often quite extensive.

Environmental Protection

Because environmental liabilities may be imposed by statute on the purchaser, and as such may be extremely costly, comprehensive representations and warranties (and indemnities) regarding environmental matters should be included in an acquisition agreement. Such costs are difficult to ascertain and often cannot be determined until well after the closing. Therefore, to get some idea of the potential liability to the purchaser, an environmental audit should be conducted by a team of environmental engineers and attorneys prior to signing a definitive agreement.

A standard environmental representation and warranty should provide, among other things, that the seller has obtained and is in compliance with all terms in all permits, licenses, and authorizations, as well as with the provisions of all environmental laws, decrees, judgments, and notices; that there is no pending or threatened litigation or compliance order; that there have been no reportable discharges or releases of hazardous substances; and that there are no known conditions that may prevent future compliance with applicable laws or give rise to environmental liability.

Product Liability

Because product liability is assumed upon the acquisition of the stock of a company, the purchaser should insist on a representation and warranty covering exposure to potential product liability.

Litigation and Compliance with Laws

Invariably, an acquisition agreement contains representations concerning the seller's existing or threatened litigation, compliance with laws, and the absence of defaults under other agreements. Such representations also guarantee that the transactions contemplated by the acquisition agreement will not result in a breach or default under any applicable laws or regulations or under any agreements. Because of the significant dollar amounts that may be involved, as discussed above, compliance with environmental laws and regulations is addressed specifically and at great length.

Corporate Organization and Capitalization

Representations are made concerning the organization of the seller and its subsidiaries; capitalization, including outstanding capital stock and ownership of subsidiaries' capital stock; the seller's corporate powers and authorization; and approval of the acquisition agreement and transactions contemplated by the acquisition agreement.

Existing Restrictions

The acquisition agreement should include a representation and warranty by the seller that the transaction will not violate the target company's charter documents or any law or statute, and that it will not conflict with or result in a default under any agreement or result in the creation of a lien or encumbrance.

Other Representations

In addition to these standard representations, other representations usually cover a variety of different matters dictated by the particular transaction and the special concerns of the purchaser and its counsel. These items range from the location of bank accounts to a guarantee that there are no misstatements or omissions in the seller's proxy statement.

If the seller is walking away from the transaction with cash, the seller's concerns are narrowly focused on the purchaser's ability to pay, and the purchaser's representations need cover only corporate authorization and the ability to consummate the transaction—the purchaser's financial condition. If a continuing relationship is contemplated because the purchaser will be issuing securities, or a contingent or delayed payout is involved, the seller will want representations of greater scope, covering the purchaser's financial statements, published filings with the SEC, and any items of particular concern.

COVENANTS

Covenants cover the period between signing and closing and consist of (1) negative covenants, which restrict the seller from taking certain actions without the purchaser's consent, and (2) affirmative covenants, which obligate one or both parties to take certain actions prior to closing.

Negative covenants are intended to protect the purchaser against the seller's taking actions that will change the nature of what the purchaser expects to acquire at the closing. The purchaser normally does not want the seller to take cash out of its business through dividends, bonuses, or other distributions. Nor does the purchaser want the seller to increase its debt, increase salaries, or enter into substantial commitments.

The number and breadth of negative covenants depends in part on the purchaser's level of comfort with the seller. It may be that a simple covenant to the effect that the seller will operate its business only in the ordinary course consistent with past practice will suffice. On the other hand, the purchaser may wish to cover every conceivable act. Such provisions would include all or some of the following:

- Not to change accounting methods or practices
- Not to enter into transactions that are not in the ordinary course of business
- Not to amend the charter or bylaws
- Not to change the capitalization, or issue or agree to issue any new shares of capital stock
- Not to make dividends or distributions on or to repurchase any shares of capital stock
- Not to enter into contracts or commitments in excess of a certain amount or extending beyond a relatively short period of time
- Not to terminate or modify leases or contracts
- Not to make any capital expenditures
- Not to transfer property outside the ordinary course of business
- Not to make loans to directors, officers, or employees
- Not to release claims or waive rights
- Not to discharge liens or prepay debts
- Not to do, either by commission or omission, anything that would cause the seller's representations to be untrue.

If the purchaser will be issuing securities in the acquisition there may be similar negative covenants against it, although typically these covenants cover only changes that would materially alter or affect the securities to be issued or their value.

Affirmative covenants, which cover those things that must be done in order for the closing to take place, frequently obligate both the seller and the purchaser. For example, if Hart-Scott-Rodino must be made, each party must prepare and make the requisite filings.

Other typical affirmative covenants obligating the seller include the following:

- To allow the purchaser full access to the seller's books, records, and properties for purposes of evaluation and inspection
- To call and hold a meeting of stockholders if required and to use the seller's "reasonable efforts" to obtain shareholder approval
- To make any required filings with governmental agencies and to obtain any consents required of governmental agencies or third parties

Anything required of the purchaser is similarly covered by affirmative covenants.

Covenants are normally absolute, and should be if a matter is within a party's sole control. However, the seller or its counsel may be fearful of a damage claim in the event that circumstances beyond its control keep it from fulfilling the promise. This fear is addressed by inserting in the covenants a reasonable-efforts qualification—the understanding that the seller will use its reasonable efforts to achieve the stated objective. Some covenants contain aspects of both absolute obligation and the reasonable-efforts qualification.

CONDITIONS OF CLOSING

Conditions of closing must be fulfilled by the obligated party or parties—or by a third party, the occurrence of an event, or the passage of time—in order to legally obligate the other party to close. Such conditions may be waived, in which case the waiving party can require the other party to close.

Closing conditions enjoy a greater symmetry than other areas of the acquisition agreement, although many of these conditions are designed solely for one party's benefit.

The first condition in every agreement is that the representations and warranties are true in all material respects at the closing, as if made at the closing, and that all of the covenants and agreements required to be performed at or prior to the closing have indeed been performed in all material respects. The condition is confirmed by each party's delivering to the other a certificate to this effect. Receipt by each party of an opinion of the other's counsel covering various matters is standard in all but the smallest acquisitions.

Other common symmetrical conditions include expiration of the waiting period under the Hart-Scott-Rodino Act, absence of litigation challenging or threatening the acquisition, stockholder approval, listing on a stock exchange of the shares to be issued, and securities registration statements becoming effective. The need for the obligations of both the purchaser and the seller to be conditioned upon stockholder approval, stock exchange listing, and registration statements becoming effective may not be entirely clear, but must be explored carefully.

In each instance, if the condition is not satisfied, not only does one party fail to receive a bargained-for benefit, but the other party incurs a legal detriment if it is forced to proceed. For instance, should the approval of the seller's stockholders not be obtained, the seller is violating corporate law if it proceeds with a closing. If the shares to be issued are not listed on an exchange, not only is the seller not getting the benefit of its bargain, but also the purchaser may be violating its listing agreement with the exchange should it proceed.

Other typical conditions include the following:

- Approval of regulatory authorities
- Receipt of third-party consents
- Receipt of favorable tax rulings
- Receipt of certain financial statements and, possibly, the achievement of a certain level of earnings or net worth
- Settlement of litigation

- Signing of employment or noncompete agreements by key employees
- Resignation of various officers and directors
- Satisfactory results of an investigation of environmental and other matters
- Any other occurrences deemed important to one party or the other

The interplay between the covenants and conditions should be considered. One might ask, "If an item is specified as a condition of closing, why include it as a covenant as well, or vice versa?"

Consider the need for the seller's stockholders to approve the acquisition. If receipt of such approval is made a condition of the purchaser's obligation to close, is the purchaser not adequately protected? But what if a seller gets cold feet in such a situation? Without a covenant, the seller has no obligation to call a stockholders' meeting or to attempt to get such approval. The converse, using a covenant but not a condition, does not work here inasmuch as the seller could not legally proceed without stockholder approval.

Yet consider a situation in which the seller must obtain a third party's consent to the acquisition. The purchaser may feel that the acquisition is so good that it is prepared to proceed without the consent. Including a covenant presumably will assure that the seller will make reasonable attempts to obtain the consent. Also including a condition may impose additional pressure on the seller to obtain the consent. Moreover, if only a covenant is included, the purchaser's only remedy may be monetary damages. But if a condition is included as well, the purchaser will be able to walk away from the transaction and, equally important, will have leverage to renegotiate the provision, the price, or the entire transaction.

If an acquisition involves a non-U.S. person, the conditions for closing would include compliance with the Exon-Florio Amendment relating to national security concerns. Under Exon-Florio, written notification of the proposed transaction must be sent to the Committee on Foreign Investment in the United States. The committee has 30 days to determine whether to conduct an investigation.

A final issue is the date of the closing itself. If all aspects of the acquisition were predictable, the parties could simply insert a date in the agreement and leave it at that. But any number of things may cause delays. Sometimes an agreement provides that the closing will occur a certain number of days after the last condition is met. Without also specifying an absolute date, however, this approach provides no time frame within which the acquisition is to occur.

A good approach is to set a target date and then provide that if a condition is not met, the party unable to meet the condition may postpone the closing until it is met, but in no event may postpone it until later than a specified date. If the specified date arrives and the closing is not held, either party may elect to terminate the agreement.

INDEMNIFICATION

To this point, the discussion has focused only on aspects of the agreement leading up to closing. After closing, a number of occurrences could cause damage or expense to the purchaser. The acquisition agreement usually contains provisions that entitle the purchaser to be indemnified by the seller or its stockholders against such damage and expenses.

Indemnification provisions are especially crucial in an acquisition agreement. Because of the potentially high costs of certain contingent liabilities such as taxes, environmental matters, product liability, litigation, and employee benefits, indemnification is used to protect the purchaser. With respect to such contingent liabilities, indemnification should cover inaccurate or incomplete representations and warranties, as well as liability to third parties. In the case of environmental liability, the indemnity should also cover liability for natural resource damage and cleanup costs, when such damage and/or costs result from activities prior to the closing (even if the cleanup is not required until well after the closing.)

Indemnification provisions are unusual in an agreement for the acquisition of publicly owned companies, except where there are one or a few major stockholders from whom it may be sought. This discussion therefore relates to the acquisition of a privately held company.

Items Covered

Indemnification provisions normally address damages incurred by the purchaser resulting from either (1) a breach of a covenant or a misrepresentation by the seller that is discovered after closing or (2) an allocation of responsibilities between the parties in the acquisition agreement.

The indemnity provisions typically begin by stipulating that the representations and warranties survive the closing and any investigation by the purchaser, and that the disclosure schedule and any other documents or written statements furnished by the seller to the purchaser are deemed to be representations. Then the items covered are set forth. Losses or expenses incurred as a result of a misrepresentation or breach of a covenant or agreement are invariably included. The typical harm likely to occur is that the purchaser may not receive an asset or that the value of an asset may be less than represented, or that the purchaser may incur liabilities to a third party that were not disclosed or are in amounts greater than disclosed.

The impact of the knowledge and materiality qualifications on the representations and warranties becomes much clearer in the context of indemnification. With a knowledge qualification, the purchaser must show not only that the factual representation was not correct, but also that the seller knew or should have known that it was not correct. If there is a materiality qualification, the purchaser must also establish that the inaccuracy or misrepresentation was material. As each of these qualifications is introduced, the purchaser's burden becomes increasingly difficult.

Another category of items is often covered by an indemnity. The most common are items disclosed in the representations or disclosure schedule that remain the seller's obligation. These involve an allocation of responsibilities. One often covered is pending litigation, for which the outcome may be uncertain or the amount of ultimate damages difficult to predict. Rather than factor the outcome into the purchase price, it may be easier simply to make it the seller's responsibility. The parties rarely attempt to refine the concept of damages, leaving it to be resolved at the time a claim arises.

It is also common to cover matters arising from the transaction itself, such as transfer taxes, bulk-sales liability, and similar items.

Finally, in some instances the purchaser will want protection beyond guarantees of the fair presentation of a balance sheet or the ability of a seller to warrant. Taxes are the most frequent subject of this type of indemnity, particularly if the purchaser is aware that the seller has been very aggressive with its tax returns. In this instance, it is common for the purchaser to insist on tax indemnity covering any and all taxes assessed to the extent that they exceed the reserve allocated on the seller's balance sheet.

Common Points of Negotiation

Indemnification provisions are usually the subject of heavy negotiations, and the seller and its attorney can be expected to challenge the scope of the indemnity.

The seller may seek a "basket provision," a clause that provides the purchaser indemnification of damages only if they exceed a certain amount. Although most indemnification provisions contain a basket, rarely does the purchaser offer it in the first instance. There is no fixed rule as to the amount, which varies depending on the size of the deal. The agreement normally provides that the seller has no liability to the purchaser for any claim until the aggregate of all claims exceeds the basket, and then the seller is liable only for the excess. There are any number of variations.

A second avenue of relief that may be pursued by the seller is a cutoff date beyond which the purchaser cannot assert claims. Most purchasers will agree in principle with the seller's desire for this kind of certainty and peace of mind. However, tax claims are normally left open until the expiration of the statute of limitations, and contingent liabilities such as litigation must be kept open until finally adjudicated. The cutoff date should be based on the concept of a reasonable period of time within which the purchaser, through reasonable diligence, should have discovered the misrepresentations and breaches, and within which any third party will have made its demands. Three years seems to be the outside limit for a general cutoff, with earlier cutoffs often being tied to completion of the first audit of the business by the purchaser's accountants.

Finally, the seller will likely seek an upper limit on liability. Although many experts have suggested that this limitation is normally inappropriate, it nonetheless is quite common. If the transaction is clean, the purchaser probably risks little in putting a limit on the seller's total liability. Although this argument can be turned against the seller, as the seller's actual exposure to liability is slight in a clean deal, if the principal owner is to continue working for the purchaser and is a critical part of the acquisition, his or her peace of mind may more than offset the additional risk the purchaser incurs through accepting an upper limit.

Two other arguments are often put forward by the seller. First, an indemnity should be reduced by the amount of any hidden assets of the seller that turn up or by the amount by which liabilities prove to be less than anticipated. This is rarely agreed to by the purchaser. A more troublesome argument is that the indemnity should be applied net of its tax effect. This frequently is agreed to by the purchaser, but the complications of attempting to apply it are great.

Second, the seller's counsel can be expected to insist that the seller have control of third-party proceedings if it is to be responsible for them. This would appear to be a fair and reasonable position until one considers certain situations in which the purchaser would have good reason to want control even though the seller is responsible. Internal Revenue Service claims that could affect future practices are a good example. Obtaining control may be desirable enough to the purchaser to warrant its giving up a portion of the indemnity.

Provisions to Facilitate Claims Settlement

Indemnification may result in an empty victory if the purchaser is unable to collect from the seller, and suing the seller may not be the most desirable solution. To protect itself, the purchaser may provide for a deferred payment or a nonnegotiable note against which it can offset the amount of any claim of indemnity. By allowing the purchaser to offset amounts it owes the seller under the note, by amounts it feels are due it under the indemnity, the note gives the purchaser direct access to the seller. The cautious purchaser—and its attorney—will write this into both the note and the indemnification provision.

To protect the seller and again to level the playing field, the seller's attorney will then insist that if the amount or the validity of the purchaser's indemnification claim is disputed by the seller, the purchaser must turn the note over to a third party pending resolution of the dispute amounts due under the note. Once the dispute has been resolved or adjudicated, the third party will turn over this sum to the party determined to be entitled to it.

However, parties often contemplate arbitration as a means to resolve disputes rather than resorting in the first instance to litigation. If arbitration is the chosen course, issues such as governing law, liability for punitive damages, awarding of attorneys' fees, the number of arbitrators to be involved, and the ability of one party to unilaterally request arbitration are addressed in this provision.

If the parties do not wish to arbitrate, the acquisition agreement may contain provisions relating to litigation procedures, such as choice of law, selection of forum, submission of jurisdiction, waiver of jury, payment of legal fees by the losing party, and so on.

The best and probably the fairest solution is to place a portion of the purchase price in an escrow account with a third party, which tends to equalize the bargaining positions of the purchaser and seller. Not having the funds, the seller is forced to bargain with the purchaser. Because the purchaser is denied the use of the escrow fund pending resolution, it too is forced to bargain.

The principal issues concerning an escrow are its size and duration. No formula exists, and without specific indemnity items to which dollar amounts can be fixed, most escrows range in size between 10 and 20 percent of the purchase price.

Invariably, the seller will attempt to limit the purchaser's recourse to the escrow. If the purchaser is willing to consider this condition, it obviously should argue for a larger escrow.

The duration of the escrow is also strictly a matter of negotiation. It never exceeds the indemnification period and is often shorter, on the theory that its principal function is to protect against misrepresentations and claims arising soon after the closing.

Typically, the escrow provides that if no claims are pending at the scheduled termination, all funds in escrow will be distributed to the seller; but if claims are pending, the amount in dispute will remain in escrow until resolution. If the amount and duration are difficult to resolve, one compromise may be to allow portions of the escrow to be released at various stages along the way.

The escrow agent should be independent of the purchasing and selling parties. A bank is normally the first and best choice. Usually fees are split or paid by the purchaser. It is common for the escrow funds to be invested or deposited in an interest-bearing account.

Although often very complicated in their mechanics, escrows are fairly simple in substance. The purchaser gives written notice of a claim to the escrow agent and the seller, along with details. If the seller does not object within a specified period of time, the escrow agent pays to the purchaser the amount of the claim. If the seller objects within the specified period of time, the escrow agent continues to hold the funds until resolution.

CHAPTER 10

ACQUIRING A PUBLIC COMPANY

Because of the publicity and extensive disclosures associated with acquiring a public company, such an acquisition often has an aura of glamour. But the lack of privacy brings with it both significant advantages and disadvantages. If they are properly understood and managed, neither the advantages nor the disadvantages are sufficient to control such a transaction. The issues involved generally are not very complex, but if mishandled may result in damage to an acquirer and may increase costs as well.

ADVANTAGES AND DISADVANTAGES

There are a number of advantages to acquiring a public company, including the fact that it has an established value. In addition, because of the regulatory framework set up to protect shareholders, most purchasers with the means can buy a part or all of the equity of a public company—so long as there are shareholders willing to sell their stock.

Researching a particular public company is easier than researching a private company, because of the multitude of required public disclosures that enable a prospective acquirer to gain easy access to a wealth of information. The various reports filed with the Securities and Exchange Commission (SEC) disclose information concerning suppliers, competitors, customers, property holdings, financial results, and other areas of interest. In addition to SEC disclosures, there are numerous independent reviews of a public company's performance and prospects. These reports provide useful, up-to-date coverage of events regarding a company and often reveal information not readily discernible from data released by the company itself.

A further advantage in acquiring a public company is the flexibility a bidder has in the mode of acquisition. Because a public company has a sufficient number of shareholders to create a public market for its stock, an acquirer can offer registered securities with liquidity as part of the purchase price. The advantage of offering noncash consideration to shareholders is that if such securities are publicly traded, they are significantly easier to value and may be more readily accepted by the selling shareholder.

Along with the advantages of acquiring a public company are a number of drawbacks. The most significant is that acquiring a public company may cost more in both time and money than would be necessary in acquiring a privately held company—principally because of the additional legal assistance needed and the time required to fulfill regulatory obligations.

The regulatory structure developed to protect shareholders sets up significant constraints in the acquisition of a public company. To complete such an acquisition, an acquirer has two basic choices:

- Merge, subject to shareholder approval, or
- Acquire controlling interest through a tender offer.

Of these two possibilities, a tender offer represents the fastest way to gain control of a company. However, a tender offer must be left open for a minimum of 20 business days and generally takes longer to complete than a merger. It is rare for either a friendly or a hostile tender offer to receive enough shares in the time the initial offer is open. It is also not unusual for other complications, such as litigation, to force an extension. And the tender process is expensive.

In the case of a merger, regulations require that a preliminary proxy statement be filed with the SEC at least 10 days prior to distribution to the target's shareholders. Under most circumstances the SEC will review the statement and request certain changes before it can go to shareholders. This can take anywhere from 30 to 45 days. It generally takes a minimum of 20 days after proxy materials are sent before a shareholder vote can take place.

Besides the problems of timing and cost, there are also issues of disclosure. An offer will become a matter of public record if it is accepted by the target or if the acquirer or target discloses it. Because of the increased awareness of their fiduciary responsibility by directors of public companies, such offers generally are publicly disclosed.

Disclosure of a bid often attracts other bidders, presenting the possibility that the initial offer might put the company "in play." If that occurs, the subsequent public auction increases the cost of the acquisition and frequently results in the original acquirer losing the acquisition to a "white knight" or other buyer. (A white knight is a friendly investor that acquires a part or all of the company to prevent an acquisition by an unwanted acquirer.) Thus, a "bargain purchase" of a public company is unlikely.

When an acquirer buys a private company, it must take into account corporate laws and federal antitrust considerations, but it is subject to none of the disclosure requirements or fiduciary responsibilities attached to dealing with a diverse group of public shareholders. Moreover, a private company need not entertain bidders until it is prepared to sell, whereas a public company, unless it has a control shareholder, is open to almost any bidder. It is this eminent approachability that sets acquisitions of public companies apart. The issue in dealing with a private company is first and foremost whether the owners will sell. The issues involved with a public company are significantly more complex.

ISSUES TO CONSIDER

The issues begin with the basic question of whether the target as currently valued is attractive and, if so, whether to buy shares prior to making an offer. In a public environment an acquirer can buy shares in the market and, to the extent that these shares are priced lower than an acquirer is willing to pay for the entire company, the acquirer should logically buy all the shares it can at the lowest price. However, an acquirer is limited in the amount of shares of the target that it can purchase (up to 5 percent) without having to disclose the purchase, as well as its intentions. Disclosure tends to drive up the price of the shares.

The advantage to buying shares prior to making an offer is obvious. To the extent that shares are purchased at low prices, the total cost of a transaction will be lower. If the acquirer is outbid in the process, the profit made on the lower-priced shares will defray the cost of attempting the acquisition. But the primary disadvantage is that the act of buying shares is often considered to be hostile by the target's management and directors.

One of the most important strategic decisions a potential acquirer must make is how critical it is to gain the support of the target's management. Because of disclosure requirements, even management-backed acquirers must be prepared to meet unsolicited bids.

Acquiring a public company takes place in a dynamic environment. Not only are the legal considerations complex, but the applicable laws and regulations change frequently. In addition, the diversity of financing methods currently available makes the potential universe of both acquisitions and acquirers extremely large. Because of the dynamic conditions in public markets, independent advisors can provide valuable advice regarding the current state of the market and regulatory considerations. Two other common roles that can be performed only by certain financial professionals are:

• Being dealer/manager of a tender offer, and
• Writing a fairness opinion as to the value of an offer.

To execute a tender offer requires the necessary legal filings; it also requires that a registered broker/dealer manage the offer. Because one generally needs a broker/dealer who operates in all fifty states, the major securities houses are generally used. In addition, both the buyer and the seller may wish to have an independent advisor draft a fairness opinion. This opinion is obtained so that the company's shareholders can feel confident that a knowledgeable third party agrees with management and the board of directors that the transaction is fair to the shareholders from a financial point of view. If a fairness opinion is requested, the shareholders may want a major securities firm or other professional valuation firm to issue it. It is important to have the credibility required to ensure shareholders of independent objectivity.

METHODS OF ACQUIRING CONTROL OF A PUBLIC COMPANY

A public company can generally be acquired in five ways:

1. Merger

2. Tender offer or exchange offer

3. Tender offer followed by a merger

4. Acquisition of a control position in the debt securities of a troubled company

5. Proxy contest

The first four methods involve acquiring control of a company by purchasing all or substantially all of its shares (or debt securities in a reorganizing company where the creditors will own the new equity). The fifth method implies acquiring control by aligning the company's other shareholders against management. The fifth is implicitly hostile whereas the other four may be friendly or hostile.

Whether an acquisition is hostile or friendly does not change the regulatory guidelines for acquiring a company. The SEC believes in the "level playing field" doctrine. One disadvantage of a hostile offer is that if management wishes to fight the bid, the acquirer may be forced to offer to buy shares without having an opportunity to conduct a due diligence examination before pricing the offer.

Figure 10-1 shows the frequency with which each type of acquisition has been used in recent years.

Note: The following comments deal with healthy companies; troubled companies are discussed subsequently.

FIGURE 10-1   Summary of types of public acquisitions* made 1/1/93–12/1/93

(Source: Securities Data Corporation)

Securities Offered	Merger	Tender Offer	Tender Offer Followed by Merger	Total
Cash	42%	4%	2%	49%
Cash and other considerations	24%	0%	0%	25%
Other considerations**	26%	0%	0%	26%
Total	93%	5%	2%	100%

*Based on transactions disclosing terms

**"Other considerations" includes, for example, contingency payouts, stock, and debt.

Merger

A merger following a shareholder vote is the most common means of acquiring control of a public company. Only with a shareholder vote (or implicit shareholder approval through the tendering of shares) can management sell a public company. From the acquirer's point of view, a merger agreement subject to a shareholder vote is probably the least complex and cheapest method of acquisition. This is true for several reasons. First, it gives the target's shareholders the best view of the transaction. Second, it allows the acquirer more time to conduct due diligence. Third, the expense of drafting a merger proxy statement and mailing it to shareholders is usually less than that of drafting an offer to purchase, tendering for shares, and drafting a "back-end" merger statement to acquire the non-tendered shares.

Moreover, in industries where regulatory approval is required, a merger is almost always used because gaining approval from the appropriate government agency generally takes longer than achieving shareholder approval, making the expense of a tender offer unnecessary. The savings and loan industry is a good example of one in which such regulatory delays occur.

The disadvantage of a merger is that it can take significantly longer than a tender offer. This may not be important if the acquirer already owns or controls enough shares to assure a favorable vote or if approval from agencies other than the SEC is necessary. However, if there is a real threat that another bidder may surface, the time required to file, receive approval, and mail a proxy statement may present a risk.

The benefits an acquirer gains by electing a merger followed by a shareholder vote are potentially offset by the acquirer's risk of losing the target company to others because of the length of time required to complete the transaction. Assessing the trade-off is necessary to making a critical strategic decision.

Following is the timetable for a merger.

	Cash	*Stock*
Preliminary	Begin due diligence investigation	Same as for cash
	Make open market or negotiated purchases	
	Negotiate lock-up agreements with key stockholders	
	Arrange financing	
	Prepare registration statement and proxy materials	
Day 1	Contact target	Same as for cash
Day 2	Begin further due diligence investigation	Same as for cash
	Begin further negotiations with target*	
Day 7	Execute merger agreement	Same as for cash, plus:
	Execute lock-up agreements with target and/or stockholders	Begin blue sky survey
	Issue press release	
	Engage proxy solicitors	
Day 12	Target files proxy materials with SEC	Same as for cash, plus: Bidder files proxy materials with SEC

*May take more time than allotted

Continued

	Cash	*Stock*
Day 12 (Cont'd)	File Hart-Scott-Rodino notice with FTC	File registration statement with SEC
		Mail blue sky applications, exemptions, and notices
		File listing application with appropriate stock exchange
Day 17	File Schedule 13D with SEC (if lock-up agreements cover 5 percent of shares)	Same as for cash
	File Form 3 with SEC (if lock-up agreements cover 10 percent of shares)	
Day 42	Hart-Scott-Rodino waiting period expires (unless second request)	Target and bidder proxy materials cleared by SEC**
		Registration statement declared effective by SEC**
		Receive all blue sky clearances
		Receive authorization of listing on stock exchange
Day 54	Target proxy materials cleared by SEC**	Target and bidder mail proxy materials
		Final prospectus mailed with proxy materials
Day 55	Target mails proxy materials	
Day 75	Target stockholder meeting to approve merger	Target and bidder stockholder meetings to approve transaction
Day 76	File short-form certificate of merger with secretary of state	Same as for cash
	Issue press release	
Day 78	Begin to pay for shares	Same as for cash
Postmerger	File Form 8-K for bidder with SEC	Same as for cash
	Delist target stock	
	Deregister target with SEC	
	Postmerger filings and approvals	

**May take more or less time, depending on SEC review

Tender Offer

A tender offer tends to have the most drama in the merger and acquisition business. The basic risk for a public company is that within the confines of the law, any person or company may go directly to a company's shareholders and offer to buy their shares.

Tender offers give shareholders a means to "vote" without a formal proxy. If enough shareholders are willing to sell—or tender—their shares at a certain price, a formal shareholder vote is not necessary. Avoiding a shareholder vote is important in an all-cash transaction or in a transaction in which the cash component is large enough to acquire a controlling interest. If an acquirer has been able to execute a merger agreement, it is important for it to do everything in its power to limit the potential risk of losing to another bidder.

A tender offer supported by the target is the fastest means of acquiring control of a company. This technique is more expensive than a merger, but the added expense generally is not significant in relation to the total cost of an acquisition and the risk of losing the bid.

Because a tender offer does not require a formal proxy, an unsolicited offer may be made to shareholders without the approval of the target's board. If management refuses to entertain a bid, a tender offer—taking the bid directly to the shareholders—can force management's attention and response.

Once a tender offer begins, the board of directors' ability to prevent or delay the acquisition is severely limited. If the bid is genuine, the board must find some alternative means of getting shareholders comparable value. If the board cannot find an alternative transaction and the hostile takeover prevails, the hostile bidder may eventually be able to negotiate the final bid with the target's management and board. Without a tender offer, a negotiated transaction would be much more difficult.

When an unsolicited acquirer has reached an agreement, it is unusual to request a shareholder vote. Waiting for a shareholder vote risks attracting another bidder and leaving control of the company in the old shareholder/management's control for a much longer time.

Following is the timetable for a cash tender offer.

	Friendly	*Hostile*
Preliminary	Begin due diligence investigation	Same as for friendly
	Make open-market or negotiated purchases	
	Negotiate lock-up agreements with key stockholders	
	Arrange financing	
	Prepare offer documents	
Day 1	Contact target	Same as for friendly
Day 2	Begin further due diligence investigation	Commence offer
	Begin negotiations with target	File Schedule 140-1 with SEC (copy to relevant stock exchanges and target)
		Request stockholder list from target*
		File Hart-Scott-Rodino notice with FTC
		Publish summary ad
Day 7	Execute merger agreement	Target or bidder (at target's election) mails offer documents to target's stockholders
	Execute lock-up agreements with target and/or stockholders	
	Issue press release	
Day 12	Commence offer	
	Mail offer documents to target stockholders	
	File Schedule 140-1/130 with SEC (copy to appropriate stock exchange and target)	
	File Hart-Scott-Rodino notice	
	Publish summary ad	
	Issue press release	

*Although the target is required by law to give the bidder its stockholder list, litigation may be necessary to obtain the list, causing delays in mailing offer documents.

Continued

	Friendly	*Hostile*
Day 17	File Form 3 with SEC (if lock-up agreements cover 10 percent of shares)	Hart-Scott-Rodino waiting period expires (unless second request)
Day 27	Hart-Scott-Rodino waiting period expires (unless second request)	
Day 28		Offer expires (unless extended)**
		Accept tendered shares for payment
		Issue press release
		File 140-1 amendment with SEC
Day 29		Begin to pay for tendered shares
Day 31		File short-form merger certificate with secretary of state
		Issue press release
Day 38	Offer expires (unless extended)	
	Accept tendered shares for payment	
	Issue press release	
	File 140-1 amendment with SEC	
Day 39	Begin to pay for tendered shares	
Day 41	File short-form merger certificate with secretary of state (if 90 percent of shares tendered)	
	Issue press release	
Postmerger	Mail Notice of Merger to remaining target stockholders	Same as for friendly
	Pay for remaining shares	
	File Form 8-K for bidder	
	Delist target stock	
	Deregister target with SEC	
	Postmerger filings and approvals	

**The litigation that is an inherent part of hostile bids may extend the offer. In addition, each new price will extend the offer for 10 days.

Exchange Offer

An exchange offer works much like a tender offer, except that the acquirer offers securities to the selling shareholders rather than cash. Like a tender offer, an exchange offer can be taken directly to a company's shareholders. However, unlike a cash tender offer, the securities offered in an exchange offer must be registered with the SEC.

The time required to register securities for an exchange offer negates the time savings available through a tender offer. The time required for an exchange offer may, in fact, exceed the time required to complete a merger via a shareholder vote. Because the same result can be accomplished in the same amount of time and less expensively through a direct shareholder vote, exchange offers are rarely used.

Following is the timetable for an exchange offer (common or convertible stock).

	Friendly	*Hostile*
Preliminary	Begin due diligence investigation	Same as for friendly
	Make open-market or negotiated purchases	
	Negotiate lock-up agreements with key stockholders	
	Arrange financing	
	Prepare offer documents	
	Prepare registration and proxy materials	
Day 1	Contact target	Same as for friendly
Day 2	Begin further due diligence investigation	Commence offer
	Begin negotiations with target	File Schedule 140-1 with SEC (copy to NYSE and target)
		Request stockholder list from target*

*Although the target is required by law to give the bidder its stockholder list, litigation may be necessary to obtain the list, causing delays in mailing offer documents.

Continued

	Friendly	*Hostile*
Day 2 *(Cont'd)*		File Hart-Scott-Rodino notice with FTC
		Publish summary ad
		Issue press release
		Engage proxy solicitors
Day 7	Execute merger agreement	Target or bidder (at target's election) mails offer documents to target's stockholders
	Execute lock-up agreements with target and/or stockholders	
	Issue press release	
	Engage proxy solicitors	Begin blue sky survey
Day 12	Commence offer	File proxy materials with SEC
	Mail offer documents to target stockholders	
	File Schedule 140-1/130 with SEC (copy to appropriate stock exchange and target)	File registration statement with SEC
		File listing application with appropriate stock exchange
	File Hart-Scott-Rodino notice with FTC	
	Publish summary ad	Mail blue sky applications, exemptions, and notices
	Issue press release	
	Begin blue sky survey	
Day 17	Hart-Scott-Rodino waiting period expires (unless second request)	Same schedule as Day 12 through Postmerger for friendly
Day 28	Offer expires (unless extended)	
	Extend offer	
	Issue press release	
	File Schedule 140-1 amendment with SEC	
Day 42	Proxy materials declared effective by SEC**	
	Registration statement declared effective by SEC**	
	Receive all blue sky clearances	
	Receive authorization of exchange listing	

**May take more or less time, depending on SEC review.

Continued

	Friendly	*Hostile*
Day 43	Mail proxy materials to bidder's stockholders	
	Mail final prospectus to target's stockholders	
Day 53	Bidder stockholder meeting to approve transaction	
Day 54	Terminate offer	
	Accept tendered shares for payment	
	Issue press release	
	File 140-1 amendment with SEC	
Day 55	Begin to pay for tendered shares	
Day 57	File short-form certificate of merger with secretary of state (if 90 percent of shares tendered)***	
Postmerger	Mail Notice of Merger to remaining target stockholders	
	Pay for remaining shares	
	File Form 8-K for bidder with SEC	
	Delist target stock	
	Deregister target with SEC	
	Complete postmerger filings and approvals	

***A long-form merger will take at least four weeks to complete, depending on SEC review of proxy material.

Tender Offer Followed by a Merger

The fact that an exchange offer is an unattractive means to acquire a company on a hostile basis does not mean that an offer has to be all cash. The prevailing thought is that the cash component of an offer needs to be large enough to acquire control. The shares that are not purchased for cash can be acquired through an exchange of securities through a shareholder vote that the acquirer controls. In other words, the acquisition can be accomplished through a cash tender offer for at least a majority (the percentage will vary based on state laws) of the shares, followed by a merger by shareholder vote.

Typically, this structure is used either when the acquirer wants to use securities as part of the purchase consideration or when an insufficient number of shareholders tender their shares to complete the transaction through a tender offer.

There is a very real possibility that not enough shares will be tendered to complete a merger. This may be due not to insufficient value, but to a lack of shareholder awareness. If enough shares are tendered, the acquirer may control the company but will be required to go to a shareholder vote to complete the acquisition.

This two-step structure enables the acquirer to use cash to acquire control and securities to complete the acquisition. As an example, assume that an acquirer has agreed to purchase a target company and pay shareholders cash for 51 percent of the shares plus stock in the acquiring company for the balance. This transaction could be handled in two ways.

On one hand, the target could conduct a shareholder vote, and if the transaction is approved, the target shareholders would exchange their shares for the cash and equity package being offered. On the other hand, the acquirer could make a tender offer for 51 percent of the target shareholders' share and then call for a shareholder vote in which the remaining target shareholders would exchange their shares for the acquirer's shares.

Again, the advantage of the latter technique is timing. If the acquirer believes there is significant risk of a competing bid, this is a valid reason for structuring the acquisition as a two-step tender offer followed by a merger.

The last principal use of this structure is the hostile bid in which the acquirer wants to use securities as acquisition currency. It is possible to take an offer that includes securities directly to the shareholders. The typical approach is a cash bid or tender offer by the acquirer for a sufficient number of shares to gain control, followed by a merger vote in which securities are exchanged. The percentage of shares of the target necessary to gain control and ensure a "back-end" merger will vary, based on the target's bylaws and the applicable state's laws. Essentially, including a cash component large enough to control a company is typically the only way an unsolicited offer can display enough substance to be considered a valid and competitive bid.

Acquiring Debt Securities of a Troubled Company

Buying a controlling position in the debt of a financially troubled publicly held company, with the intention of converting that debt to equity as a condition of the debt restructuring, is a seldom used though effective means of gaining control of a company. The recent use of this strategy has accompanied the wave of financial restructurings following the leveraged buyout boom of the late 1980s in both out-of-court and formal bankruptcy proceedings.

Both operationally troubled companies and those simply overburdened by debt as the result of an ill-conceived capital structure or overpriced acquisition are suitable for acquisition through this strategy. However, the lengthy negotiations involving the restructuring of a company's debt and the resources necessary to complete an operational restructuring make acquisitions of operationally troubled companies via the debt-for-equity route unattractive to most buyers.

The major players using this strategy are so-called vulture funds. These funds, as the name implies, specialize in buying the debt of distressed companies at a steep discount to their face amount. Some vulture funds invest with the intention of deriving long-term gain from the appreciation in the value of the restructured entity, whereas others focus more on the short term, intending to profit from increases in the price of the debt securities.

Buying distressed-debt securities with the intention of converting to equity is a strategy most effectively used when it is apparent that any restructuring will result in the substantial elimination of the existing equity holders' interest. It entails thorough research of the various classes of debt and the classes of debt's respective rights and priorities to ensure that the debt being purchased will enable the acquirer to strategically control the restructuring.

For companies in bankruptcy, generally at least one-third of the outstanding claims of a senior debt class must be owned to effectively control the restructuring. This amount is significant in that it allows the owners of such debt securities to block a restructuring plan that they oppose. This is due to the rules of the bankruptcy court, which require that at least two-thirds of the dollar amount and more than 50 percent of each creditor class voting must vote affirmatively to accept a plan of reorganization.

Acquiring such a sizable position in a company's debt securities may be accomplished either through open market purchases or through the use of a public tender offer. A tender offer establishes a fixed price for which a certain dollar amount of securities will be purchased. In this way, an investor can be assured of acquiring a position strong enough to substantially determine the outcome of the restructuring.

Proxy Contest

The proxy contest is a way to take control of a company without owning a majority of its voting stock. In its simplest form, a proxy contest occurs when a group of "dissident" shareholders (typically a noncontrolling group) attempts to elect a slate of directors who are not currently on the target's board of directors and are not supported by management.

The nomination and election process is carefully regulated by the SEC. The dissident shareholders must register their slate with the SEC through a proxy statement and solicit proxies from other shareholders. At the same time, management solicits proxies for its own slate of directors.

Dissidents try to gain control of a board for several reasons.

The proxy contest may be a prelude to a change-of-control transaction. The contest in this case is used to remove an entrenched board. Given the current view of directors' liability, few directors will ignore a bona fide bid, but they can take the position that the hostile bid is "inadequate," supported by a concurring fairness opinion from an investment banker.

The proxy contest is still used in transactions in which the management is entrenched and dissident shareholders want to effect a change in management to improve the value of their shares. Given the timing and expense of proxy contests, the potential increase in value for the dissident shareholders has to be significant to merit such action.

An area in which proxy contests of this sort were very prevalent was the savings and loan industry in the early 1980s. At that time many buyers were limited by regulations to owning less than 10 percent of a thrift institution. However, because these same thrifts were selling for a fraction of their book value, a common perception was that significant improvements could be achieved through a change of management.

In another area, proxy contests have become more common in response to corporate "poison pill" bylaws or state statutes designed to inhibit unfriendly offers. By gaining control of a target's board, an acquirer can repeal such bylaws or comply with the applicable statutes to make the offer "friendly."

Recently, encouraged in part by contests involving savings and loans where management was not prepared for the challenge, dissidents have been winning more frequently. However, the majority of proxy contests are still won by incumbents who have all the corporate tools at their disposal.

CHAPTER 11

SECURITIES LAWS AND OTHER REGULATIONS

Legal considerations significantly affect the timing and structure of an acquisition of a publicly held corporation. Indeed, they help to determine whether a proposed acquisition is viable at all. For a management that is considering whether to pursue a specific transaction, it is mandatory to completely understand the fundamental legal concepts that come into play in an acquisition.

Every acquisition is unique in terms of the legal issues involved, primarily because of differences in jurisdiction of incorporation, whether the companies are publicly traded, the nature of the target's business, and the structure and financing of the transaction. In the early stages of the process experienced counsel should become familiar with both the acquirer and the target in order to identify applicable legal issues in a timely manner.

Most frequently, the acquirer will need to consider state corporation laws, which govern the mechanics of significant corporate transactions, and the Securities Exchange Act of 1934 (the Exchange Act), which regulates trading in the securities of public companies, tender offers, and proxy solicitations. The Securities Act of 1933 (the Securities Act) and state securities laws may also be important, especially if the consideration for the company being

159

acquired includes securities or if it will be financed by issuing securities. With a clear understanding of the legal framework, the acquirer and its advisors can determine the most efficient structure for the transaction.

The following discussion is necessarily limited in depth and scope. Among the topics eliminated because of space constraints are the timing and substance of public announcements, the legality of various strategies used by acquirers and targets in acquisitions— including poison pills, lock-ups, "no-shopping" agreements, greenmail, dual-stock plans, defensive restructurings, self-tender offers, and "shark repellants."

STOCK PURCHASES

A significant or controlling interest in a public company can be obtained through a tender offer, negotiated block purchases, or an open-market purchase program. These techniques provide the only unilateral means for acquiring a public company without the participation or consent of the target's board of directors. The speed with which stock purchases can be accomplished is a great tactical advantage, even in friendly transactions.

Tender Offers

A tender offer can be described as a special form of stock-purchase program characterized by a concerted effort to purchase a significant amount of stock from the public at a fixed price over a short period of time. Prior to adoption of the Williams Act in 1968, tender offers went largely unregulated. The Williams Act amended the Exchange Act to impose significant procedural requirements on all tender offers and other accumulations of stock.

Disclosure Requirements.   At the time a tender offer commences, the purchaser must file with the SEC and deliver to the target a Schedule 14D-1. The 14D-1 must identify the purchaser, its source of funds for the offer, and the purpose of the transaction. It must also discuss any negotiations with the target, as well as certain financial information relating to the target and the purchaser, if material.

Most important, the purchaser must disclose "such additional material information, if any, as may be necessary to make the required statements, in light of the circumstances under which they are made, not materially misleading," according to the SEC. This requirement serves as the basis for including material nonpublic information concerning the target in the offering materials. For instance, if in the course of negotiations the target furnishes earnings forecasts or describes a pending new business development, the purchaser may publicly disclose such information because it is, or may be deemed to be, material. Releasing such information would defuse any allegations that the offer was made based on inside information.

The target is required to respond to the tender offer. It must recommend acceptance or rejection of the offer, or state that it remains neutral or that it is unable to take a position with respect to the offer. This response must be provided to stockholders within 10 business days from the date the tender offer commences. In addition, prior to making a public response, the target must file a Schedule 14D-9 with the SEC, disclosing the reasons for its recommendation as well as information about the target similar to that required by Schedule 14D-1 for the offeror.

Procedural Requirements. Tender offers are subject to complex and highly technical rules, the effects of which must be taken into account in structuring such an offer.

A tender offer commences at the time the offer is first published, sent, or given to stockholders. The target must facilitate the transmission of the offer. At its election the target must either mail the offering material to its stockholders or furnish to the offeror a list of its stockholders. If the offeror publicly announces the tender offer, within five business days it must file its 14D-1 and mail the offer.

A tender offer must be open to all holders of a class of securities for which the offer is made, and must remain open for at least 20 business days. If the offer is amended to increase or decrease the percentage of stock sought or the consideration offered, the offer must remain open for at least 10 days after the amendment. Where the number of shares tendered is greater than the number of shares sought, the shares must be purchased on a pro rata basis from all tendering stockholders.

Tendering stockholders may withdraw their tendered shares at any time while the offer is open. As a result, the purchaser may not purchase shares until the expiration of the offer. Because a higher competing bid could be made while the offer is pending, withdrawal rights provide a significant benefit to stockholders and a risk to the offeror.

Unconventional Tender Offers

If an acquirer determines that open-market purchases are strategically and economically superior to a tender offer, it must structure its buying program to avoid the tender offer rules. This task is complicated because the Exchange Act does not define "tender offer." The SEC considers the following factors when determining whether a stock purchase program constitutes a tender offer:

- Active and widespread solicitation
- Solicitation for a substantial percentage of stock
- A premium over the prevailing market price
- Terms that are not negotiable
- An offer that is contingent on a fixed number of shares or that is subject to a fixed maximum
- An offer that is open for a limited time
- Pressure on offerees
- Publicity

Several courts have adopted this eight-point test and have gone so far as to find a tender offer even when fewer than all of the factors are present. Therefore, if a purchaser wishes to engage in an open-market purchase program, it must structure its program to avoid as many of these eight points as possible.

Schedule 13D: 5 Percent Ownership

Frequently, an acquirer will accumulate a significant amount of the target's stock before commencing a tender offer or proposing a merger. Within 10 days after acquiring "beneficial ownership" of 5 percent of any class of equity security, an acquirer must publicly disclose such purchases by filing a Schedule 13D with the SEC and by delivering it to the target. Beneficial ownership includes the direct or indirect right to vote or to dispose of shares and the right to acquire shares, by option or otherwise, within 60 days. All shares beneficially owned by a group acting in concert must be aggregated in calculating beneficial ownership.

The purpose of a 13D is to inform the investing public of the existence of a significant block of stock that could form the basis for an acquisition or other market-sensitive transaction.

The 13D must identify the acquirer, the amount of securities owned, its sources of funds for the purchase, and any contracts with respect to the target's securities. Most important, the acquirer must describe the purpose of its investment, including any plans or proposals that may result in a change in control or other significant transaction. The 13D must be amended "promptly" upon any material change.

The 13D filing often signals the commencement of hostilities—or negotiations. Other potential acquirers and market professionals, such as arbitrageurs, frequently react to a 13D filing by putting the target "in play." Disclosure in the 13D is often the focus of litigation between the acquirer and an unwilling target. If the 13D filing is not forthcoming as to the purchaser's intention to seek control of the target, the target may seek to enjoin the acquisition.

Trading on Inside Information

A purchaser of publicly traded securities must be aware of the antifraud and insider trading prohibitions in the Exchange Act, primarily Rules 10b-5 and 14e-3 and Section 16(b).

The broad scope of Rule 10b-5 prohibits any scheme or device to defraud, any material misstatement or omission, or any act or practice or course of business that would operate as a fraud or deceit in connection with the purchase or sale of securities.

The SEC has used Rule 10b-5 and its tender offer counterpart, Rule 14e-3, to allege illegal trading on the basis of tips and other nonpublic information. The limits of Rules 10b-5 and 14e-3 in the acquisition context are neither obvious nor simple. The changing state of the law requires constant monitoring to determine whether it would apply to any specific transaction.

Section 16 of the Exchange Act regulates "short-swing" trading by certain "insiders" by permitting an issuer to recover any profit obtained by directors, officers, or 10-percent shareholders from the purchase and sale of securities within a six-month period. To monitor such short-swing trading, the SEC requires the filing of a Form 3 to report ownership of 10 percent of a public company's shares and a Form 4 or Form 5 to report changes in ownership.

The rule against short-swing profits in Section 16(b) is absolute and applies even if inside information is not used or available. Notwithstanding the draconian intent of Section 16(b), courts have been flexible in applying it to so-called unorthodox transactions.

For example, if the owner of 10 percent of the stock (who is not otherwise subject to 16(b)—that is, not an officer or director) of the company being acquired purchases an additional 5 percent and is then outbid for the company by a "white knight" or other offeror, the 15-percent stockholder incurs 16(b) liability—losing any profits made on the sale of the shares in excess of 10 percent—if it voluntarily sells those shares in a tender offer. The purchaser has a better chance of avoiding this liability if the shares are sold involuntarily, as in a merger.

State Takeover Laws

Many state laws purport to govern or limit acquisitions of corporations based in the state or those having substantial operations or stockholders in that state. These statutes take many forms and, in some cases, impose substantial burdens on the acquirer (usually applying only if the acquirer owns a threshold percentage of the target's stock). Many of these statutes have been declared unconstitutional, but in 1986 the U.S. Supreme Court upheld such a state law for the first time.

Since the 1986 Supreme Court decision, more than 35 states have adopted new takeover laws designed to withstand constitutional scrutiny. These statutes have been enacted by Delaware, Michigan, New York, Pennsylvania, and other states. They generally limit the ability of a large shareholder to vote its shares in a corporation and/ or to engage in a business combination with a corporation, unless the acquisition of shares or the business combination was approved prior to the acquisition of a threshold amount of shares. The definition of "large shareholder" varies from state to state, but generally applies to holders of 10 to 20 percent of the outstanding shares of a company.

Because of these possible adverse effects, an acquirer must survey all potentially applicable state takeover laws prior to commencing an acquisition and must develop a strategy for compliance or challenge.

MERGERS

Despite the advantages of stock purchases, it is virtually impossible to gain 100 percent ownership of a public company by stock purchases alone. The beauty of a merger is that the acquirer can obtain 100 percent ownership without 100 percent voluntary participation by stockholders. Nearly all acquisitions of public companies, therefore, involve a merger—either alone or as a second step following stock purchases.

State law governs the rights of stockholders and the obligations of corporations in a merger. Although the laws vary from state to state, a merger usually requires approval by the boards of directors and stockholders of both parties to the merger. The acquirer can often avoid having to obtain the approval of its stockholders by causing a subsidiary to merge with the target. Even then, the ultimate parent company may need to obtain the approval of its stockholders, depending on the jurisdiction and the financing structure of the acquisition.

The percentage of stockholders of the target who must vote to approve a merger is determined by state law and the company's charter. Most states also provide for a "short-form" merger, which requires no vote of the stockholders or directors of the target if the acquirer owns 90 percent of the outstanding stock.

Because mergers generally require approval of the board of directors of the target, even a successful tender offeror cannot complete a merger without the cooperation of management. In some cases, the owner of a majority of the target's stock may call a meeting or act without a meeting to vote its shares for the purpose of changing management. (Proxy contests are beyond the scope of this chapter, but the utility and risks of proxy contests as an acquisition tool should not be discounted.) In some cases, use of defensive tactics by the target leaves litigation as the only recourse.

Whenever it is necessary to solicit stockholder approval for a merger, the SEC requires the preparation of a detailed proxy statement. This statement includes a description of the transaction and of the parties, a description of stockholder rights, financial information, and other relevant data.

A proxy statement must be filed with the SEC at least 10 days prior to mailing, although in practice the SEC review process takes substantially longer. Depending on the complexity of the transaction and the SEC's work load, proxy material can take from four to six weeks to "clear." Allowing an additional three to five weeks to solicit proxies is usually recommended.

Even if proxies are not required, because the acquirer owns sufficient shares to approve the merger without a vote of other stockholders, an "information statement" must be prepared, cleared by the SEC, and mailed to stockholders at least 20 days before the merger is approved. The information statement must include data substantially equivalent to a proxy statement.

The surviving corporation in a merger will succeed to the rights and obligations of the merging companies. All stockholders are bound by the merger, provided that dissenting stockholders may have the right to receive cash equal to a court's appraised value of their shares. The availability of appraisal rights differs from state to state, and the procedural requirements for claiming those rights often deter stockholders from exercising them.

Certain mergers with affiliates of the target that "freeze out" the minority stockholders, such as situations in which a company goes from publicly traded to privately held status, are subject to an additional layer of regulations under the Exchange Act. In such "going private" transactions, including many leveraged buyouts, Rule 13e-3 requires additional SEC filings and public dissemination of disclosures concerning the fairness of the transaction, actual and potential conflicts of interest, and alternatives considered to achieve the same goals.

ASSET PURCHASES

Asset purchases have the advantage of permitting the parties to pick and choose the assets to be purchased and the liabilities to be assumed. Many assets, however, are not freely transferable.

Unlike a merger, where only stock is transferred and not a company's assets and liabilities, an asset sale is likely to require the consent of third parties with whom the target has contractual relationships. In addition, the target's debt is more likely to be accelerated and the acquirer more likely to be required to seek governmental licenses and permits relating to the business being purchased. This process inevitably creates delays and uncertainty and frequently results in substantial additional expenses.

Stockholder approval is required for a sale of all or substantially all of a corporation's assets. The solicitation of proxies for approving the sale is subject to the SEC proxy requirements described earlier. The transfer of assets may also require compliance with the "bulk sales" laws of the states in which the target conducts business.

FINANCING THE ACQUISITION

Although some purchasers are blessed with sufficient working capital or unsecured lines of credit to make an acquisition, many require financing. Acquisition financing presents a number of unique legal issues.

Issuing New Securities: The Need to Register

Whenever a company offers to sell securities to the public, it must register the offering under the Securities Act. The registration process, like the process of clearing a proxy statement, is time-consuming.

Some offerings are exempt from registration. The most important exemption for acquisition purposes is the so-called private placement. Although the initial offering is exempt, the securities may not be resold unless they are registered or an exemption from registration is available. Because successive private placements could be recharacterized as public offerings, issuers take precautions to minimize the risk of their appearing to make a public offering. These precautions may take the form of contractual restrictions on transfer and imprinting the stock certificates with a similar restriction.

The SEC and the courts have looked primarily to three criteria to determine whether an offering is a private placement:

• The number of offerees and their relationship to the issuer
• The number of units offered and the size of the offering
• The manner of the offering

Any offering within the SEC's "safe harbor" guidelines in Regulation D qualifies as a valid private placement. Regulation D provides that offerings to wealthy and sophisticated investors are generally permitted without registration. Regulation D contains many detailed requirements, but failure to fall within its safe harbor does not necessarily invalidate a private placement.

A corporation may exchange its own securities for the target's stock. The exchange may take place as part of a tender offer (as an exchange offer), in a merger, or as consideration in an asset purchase (which typically would be followed by a liquidating distribution to that target's stockholders). Each transaction is subject to the respective legal requirements described earlier for tender offers, mergers, and asset purchases, in addition to registration under the Securities Act.

Blue Sky Laws

States have regulated securities offerings since 1911, when Kansas adopted a law to protect unsophisticated investors from speculative schemes that had no more basis than "so many feet of blue sky." State "blue sky" laws, like the Securities Act, require the registration of securities prior to sale in the relevant state, unless an exemption is available.

Many blue sky laws also impose substantive requirements to ensure that an offering is fair. An issuer must consider the securities laws of every state in which the securities are to be offered.

Borrowing: The Margin Rules

The margin rules adopted by the Federal Reserve Board ("the Fed") currently prohibit secured lending unless the market value of "margin stock" securing the loan exceeds 50 percent of the loan. From time to time the Fed may amend this percentage. Margin stock includes all listed stocks and many stocks that are traded over the counter. Although the margin rules seldom apply to mergers, they are often an issue in highly leveraged tender offers and stock purchase programs.

The margin rules apply to loans that are secured by margin stock directly or indirectly. If the loan agreement prohibits the purchaser from selling the margin stock, the loan may be deemed to be indirectly secured by the stock.

The Fed has expanded its definition of indirect security in its "junk bond interpretation." If a highly leveraged "shell" corporation purchases margin securities with the proceeds of a financing, such financing may be deemed to be indirectly secured by those securities.

MISCELLANEOUS ISSUES

Every acquisition is affected by a myriad of laws. For example, New Jersey's Environmental Cleanup Responsibility Act (ECRA) may materially increase the cost of acquiring a target with manufacturing facilities in New Jersey. ECRA requires that when there is a change in corporate control, whether by stock purchase, asset purchase, or merger, the target's hazardous wastes must be cleaned up. This requirement is in addition to environmental discharge and Superfund requirements established by New Jersey or federal law. Accordingly, cleanup may be required even if the target is in compliance with its discharge permits. Connecticut adopted a similar law in 1986, and other states may follow.

The rules of the New York and American Stock Exchanges affect acquisitions of listed targets, particularly as to matters of corporate governance (such as stockholder approval) and the issuance of securities.

Employee benefits present numerous legal issues in acquisitions. Federal and state securities laws must be considered in the cancellation of stock options or in the substitution of the acquirer's stock for target stock in option plans.

The Employee Retirement Income Security Act of 1974 (ERISA) governs the disposition of pension funds and employee stock ownership plans. With the phenomenal growth of pension funds beginning in the 1970s and with the favorable treatment afforded employee benefit plans by the tax code, pension funds and employee stock ownership plans have become a potential source of acquisition financing—subject to state and federal limitations on those plans.

Other laws may apply, depending on the nature of the business being acquired. For example, the acquisition of banks and other financial institutions, insurance companies, public utilities, airlines and other transportation companies, and communications-related firms may require prior approval of the federal or state agency that regulates the industry. Prior approval may also be required for a transfer of licenses or with respect to foreign operations.

This list of regulated industries and required consents is merely exemplary. A determination of all applicable laws and regulations that will have an impact on a transaction begins with counsel's preacquisition review and generally continues through the closing.

CHAPTER 12

ANTITRUST CONSIDERATIONS

An important consideration in any contemplated acquisition is the potential constraint posed by federal antitrust laws. The principal antitrust law governing acquisitions is Section 7 of the Clayton Act. This statute prohibits acquisitions "where in any line of commerce ... in any section of the country, the effects of such acquisitions may be substantially to lessen competition or to tend to create a monopoly." The Clayton Act applies to acquisitions in all industries—except for those in regulated industries such as railroads and television stations, where mergers must be approved by federal agencies, including the Interstate Commerce Commission and the Federal Communications Commission, applying specifically tailored statutes.

Because the statute draws no clear line between lawful acquisitions and those that are potentially anticompetitive, hence unlawful, much is left to the discretion of federal agencies and the courts. Responsibility for enforcing federal merger laws is shared by the Department of Justice (DOJ) and the Federal Trade Commission (FTC). Representatives of the two agencies meet periodically to determine which agency will investigate specific acquisitions. Although one cannot predict with certainty which agency will proceed in a particular case, over the years the FTC and the DOJ each have established expertise in different industries.

In April 1992, the FTC and the DOJ jointly issued Horizontal Merger Guidelines. These guidelines outline the analytical framework that the agencies will apply in investigating proposed transactions where the merging companies are competing with each other at the time of the proposed merger.

Portions of DOJ merger guidelines issued in 1984 provide a framework for analyzing the legality of mergers between potential competitors or between suppliers and customers (often referred to as "vertical" mergers). Few if any such mergers have been challenged in recent years.

Horizontal merger enforcement policies have shifted dramatically over the past several years. In the 1960s the government successfully attacked acquisitions between parties with relatively low market shares. Perhaps the most cited example of this is *United States v. Von's Grocery Co.*, in which a merger between two Los Angeles–based supermarket chains, which together accounted for only 7.5 percent of sales in that city, was ruled unlawful by the Supreme Court. In retrospect, it is clear that the courts gave little consideration to how a merger of two parties with such small market shares could possibly affect price or output or otherwise reduce the level of industry competition.

Today there is a fairly broad consensus that this level of merger enforcement was both excessive and counterproductive. Thoughtful antitrust experts favor more careful economic analysis to determine whether a merger is likely to have anticompetitive consequences. As the DOJ has stated: "Most mergers do not threaten competition. . . . Many are, in fact, pro-competitive and benefit consumers."

A statute enacted in 1976—the Hart-Scott-Rodino Act—requires parties contemplating a significant acquisition to provide advance notification and extensive internal financial and economic data so that the antitrust enforcement agencies may undertake the careful analysis required under the DOJ guidelines prior to consummation of the acquisition.

When a merger between horizontal competitors is contemplated, careful planning and management of the antitrust defense of the acquisition is essential. It seems wise in such cases to involve counsel and a competent economic expert at an early stage. Before too much time and effort is put into planning an acquisition, these advisers should be asked to appraise the likelihood of a successful governmental or private challenge. If serious problems seem likely, attention should be devoted at an early stage to the possibility that a sale to a third party of part of the assets to be acquired might lessen the anticompetitive concerns.

ACQUISITION BETWEEN COMPETITORS: THE 1992 HORIZONTAL DOJ MERGER GUIDELINES

The best road map to current antitrust enforcement policies is the joint FTC/DOJ Horizontal Merger Guidelines issued in 1992. DOJ first promulgated merger guidelines in 1968, with a major revision in 1982 and additional revisions in 1984. The main purpose of the 1992 Horizontal Merger Guidelines is to identify and challenge only those mergers that are likely to make it easier for a business to exercise "market power"—defined as the ability to "maintain prices above the levels that would prevail if the market were competitive."

Market Definition

Central to identifying such competitively harmful mergers is the definition of the market—the geographic area and the product or bundle of similar products—potentially affected by the acquisition.

The importance of product and geographic market definition to merger analysis cannot be overstated. For example, in the highly publicized efforts by Coca-Cola and Pepsi-Cola to acquire Dr. Pepper and 7-Up, respectively, counsel for the companies seeking to make the acquisitions argued for an "all beverage" market, which would pit soft drinks against other cold drinks such as iced tea, fruit drinks, and juice. In such a broadly defined market, the shares of carbonated soft-drink manufacturers would appear to be relatively small and their ability to restrain competition correspondingly limited. But the FTC and Royal Crown, which would have been the only major carbonated soft-drink manufacturer other than Coke or Pepsi had the acquisition been approved, disagreed with the broad definition of the market. They argued that the carbonated soft-drink market was a discrete competitive arena and that the two proposed acquisitions would raise the level of concentration in that market to a level where vigorous competition might cease. The FTC prevailed in court in *FTC v. The Coca-Cola Co.*

Often, it is not easy to define the product market in which the acquisition should be judged. The 1992 Horizontal Merger Guidelines seek to resolve such questions by attempting to predict what would happen in the event of a "small but significant and nontransitory" postacquisition rise in price. In most cases, the government uses a hypothetical increase of 5 percent for this purpose.

If good substitutes exist to which consumers could readily switch in response to such a price increase, then the definition of the product market must be expanded to include those substitutes. For example, if juice and iced tea are substitutes for carbonated soft drinks, and if significant numbers of consumers would readily switch to them if the price of carbonated soft drinks were to rise, then an "all beverages" market definition might be appropriate.

As one former DOJ official observed, "One way to think about what is involved in defining a relevant market is to ask the question: whose membership would be necessary to make a cartel work in this market?"

Under the 1992 Horizontal Merger Guidelines, one begins with a provisional market definition consisting of the goods or services provided by both merging companies. Next, if readily available substitutes exist, the product market definition is expanded to include them. The analytical process continues to the point where prices could hypothetically be raised profitably without loss of customers to suppliers of still other substitute goods.

Similarly, the geographic market is determined by projecting what buyers would do in response to a "small but significant and nontransitory" increase in price by sellers in the area or areas where the merging companies are located. If companies located elsewhere could easily provide the relevant product to the merging companies' customers, a postacquisition attempt to raise prices would not prove profitable, and the tentatively identified, provisional geographic market definition would be too narrow and would need to be expanded to include the more distant sellers.

Permissible Postmerger Concentration Levels

Merger analysts today engage in intense debate about what constitutes "too few" companies to ensure vigorous competition. All of the experts agree that the fewer companies there are in a market, the easier it is for them to collude or to engage in parallel pricing policies. However, they disagree as to the precise point at which further increases in concentration should be precluded.

Robert Pitofsky, a respected commentator on antitrust issues who is viewed as a moderate on the subject, has suggested that allowing mergers that result in control of up to about 20 percent of the market—as long as four or five strong competitors remain—is probably acceptable to a majority of antitrust scholars (*New York Times*, July 27, 1986). Other experts, who are generally associated with the Chicago school of economics, have suggested that mergers that result in control of up to 40 percent, or even 50 percent, of the market are acceptable—if two or three vigorous competitors remain.

The 1992 Horizontal Merger Guidelines address this question by adopting a refined measure of market concentration and by characterizing specified levels of industry concentration as either "unconcentrated," "moderately concentrated," or "highly concentrated." The guidelines employ the Herfindahl-Hirschman Index (HHI) as a measure of market concentration.

The HHI for a market is computed in two steps. First, the number of HHI points contributed by each market participant is calculated by squaring the participant's market share. For example, a firm with a 20 percent market share would contribute 400 HHI points to the HHI of that market; a firm with a 30 percent share would contribute 900 points. This index gives greater weight to the market share of the larger companies, which the DOJ believes corresponds to their relative importance in any postacquisition effort to collusively raise prices.

The second step in the HHI calculation is to sum the HHI points of all market participants. For example, a market in which each of ten companies has 10 percent of the business has an HHI of 1,000 (each of ten companies contributes 100 points), and a market in which each of five companies has a 20 percent share of the market has an HHI of 2,000 (each of five companies contributes 400 points).

Under the 1992 Horizontal Merger Guidelines, where the market is "unconcentrated"—has a postmerger HHI below 1,000—the DOJ will not challenge the acquisition. That is because with so many companies remaining and with none of them being dominant, it would be difficult to coordinate pricing above competitive levels.

Where the market is "moderately concentrated"—has a postmerger HHI between 1,000 and 1,800—the DOJ is unlikely to challenge mergers that produce an increase in the HHI of less than 100 points. The increase in the HHI occasioned by a proposed merger is calculated by multiplying the merging companies' market shares and doubling the product. For example, a merger between a company with a 5 percent market share and one with a 10 percent market share would increase the HHI by 100 points (5 × 10 × 2). A merger that leaves market concentration in the moderately concentrated range, but which increases concentration by more than 100 points, "potentially raise[s] significant competitive concerns," depending on other economic factors pertaining to that industry which affect the likelihood of successful postmerger collusion.

Finally, in a market that is "highly concentrated"—has a postmerger HHI above 1,800—mergers that increase the HHI by more than 50 points, "potentially raise significant competitive concerns," depending on other industry factors. In the "highly concentrated" region, mergers that increase concentration by more than 100 points are presumed likely to create or enhance market power. This presumption can be rebutted, however, by showing that industry economic factors make anticompetitive effects unlikely.

ASSESSMENT OF POTENTIAL ADVERSE COMPETITIVE EFFECTS UNDER 1992 HORIZONTAL MERGER GUIDELINES

The 1992 Horizontal Merger Guidelines describe in considerable detail the potential adverse competitive effects of mergers that are of concern to the enforcement agencies. Those effects are divided into two forms: "coordinated effects" and "unilateral effects."

Coordinated Effects

For many years it has been accepted that mergers may decrease competition by making it easier for the firms remaining in a market to coordinate their pricing or to engage in other behavior that could harm consumers. For coordinated action to be profitable, firms in a given industry must be able to reach a tacit or explicit understanding on competitive conduct, to detect cheating, and to punish those market participants that deviate from that understanding. The 1992 Horizontal Merger Guidelines outline general market conditions that would be conducive to such coordination, detection, and punishment.

For example, it is generally easier for firms to coordinate their policies if the products at issue are fungible or homogeneous rather than differentiated. When firms in a market have different cost structures, coordination is more difficult. Similarly, in markets where there is ready access to transactional prices, it is easy to detect any deviation from the tacit or expressly stated pricing coordination.

One factor weighing heavily against the likelihood of coordinated effects is the presence in the market of "maverick" firms that have an economic incentive to deviate from any coordinated norms. In markets where there are several small fringe firms with significant excess capacity or capacity that could be diverted from other uses, coordinated effects may be very unlikely. On the other hand, the 1992 Horizontal Merger Guidelines indicate that acquisition of a maverick firm will be viewed as making collusion more likely.

Unilateral Effects

The entirely new concept of unilateral effects was introduced in the 1992 Horizontal Merger Guidelines. It reflects a more refined use of the economics of industrial organizations to predict ways that firms can increase their profits after a merger through unilateral action that may harm consumers. Unilateral effects typically found in markets for differentiated products are distinguished from unilateral effects that may be found in markets for fungible products.

1. Differentiated Products. Not all differentiated products in the same product market necessarily compete with one another to the same degree. For example, some cars may be closer substitutes for one another than other cars. If the products of the merging firms are the closest substitute for one another, it may be possible for the merged firm to raise prices on one or both products without losing so many sales as to be unprofitable. The reason is that consumers of one product will merely switch to the merged firm's other product. A variation of this analysis can be applied to mergers in markets where location is important and where, by virtue of location, some firms are closer competitors than others.

Where there is some evidence that the merging parties are each other's closest substitutes, where a numerical HHI threshold of concern is crossed, and where the merging parties have a combined share of 35 percent of the market, the antitrust agencies will *presume* that anticompetitive unilateral effects are likely to occur. However, if other firms in the market could readily reposition their products to provide an equally close substitute, it should be possible to rebut this presumption.

2. Fungible Products.   The potential unilateral effect of concern here is that subsequent to a horizontal merger involving a market with relatively fungible products, a large merged firm will find it profitable to raise prices and reduce output. The theory is that the merger provides the merged firm with a larger base of sales for the resulting price rise. It also eliminates a competitor to which customers otherwise could have diverted their purchases. However, unless the merged firm has a market share of 35 percent or more, and unless there is some reason that customers could not turn to the remaining suppliers to offset the results of the unilateral suppression of output, this concern should not be sufficient to precipitate a government challenge.

Ease of Entry

The 1982 DOJ Merger Guidelines stated, "If entry into a market is so easy that existing competitors could not succeed in raising prices for any significant period of time, the department is unlikely to challenge mergers in that market." In the 10 years between adoption of those guidelines and the 1992 revision, there was considerable attention and litigation devoted to the question of when "ease of entry" contentions should be accepted by the government as a basis for not challenging an otherwise potentially anticompetitive acquisition.

The 1992 Horizontal Merger Guidelines attempt to clarify the antitrust agencies' thinking on entry. They require that entry be "timely, likely, and sufficient" to defeat any anticompetitive effect that may result from the merger. Entry is deemed "timely" if the new entrant can move from "initial planning to significant market impact" in two years. Entry is deemed "likely" if new participants could participate profitably in the market at premerger prices after committing whatever "significant sunk costs" are necessary to enter. Finally, entry is deemed "sufficient" if the new entrant or entrants are likely to be able to provide a product that will be perceived by customers as an acceptable substitute for the products of the merged firm, and to produce it in sufficient volume so as to return prices to the premerger level.

Evaluation of each component of this three-part entry test is likely to be a complex, factually intensive, economically oriented undertaking. A variety of factors should be considered in assessing ease of entry. These include the following:

- Recent instances of entry and exit, including any examples of vertical integration by customers choosing to make rather than to buy
- Cost advantages of existing competitors, including advantages afforded by technology, distribution systems, or natural resources acquired at a lower price than presently available
- The existence of patents that would block entry or make it more expensive
- Environmental or other governmental regulatory barriers
- Economies of scale: savings associated with relatively high levels of production that make entry on a small scale difficult

In many cases, careful economic analysis of entry barriers may make a substantial difference in the attitude of enforcement authorities toward a particular acquisition. Indeed, even where post-acquisition concentration levels are in the "moderately concentrated" or "highly concentrated" ranges and where an increase in the levels occasioned by the acquisition is substantial, a strong case documenting that new entry is easy has been known to lead to the conclusion that an acquisition is not unlawful.

Efficiencies

When deciding whether to block a merger, antitrust agencies consider whether the merger will create a more efficient, low-cost operation than is possible if the companies remain separate. The rationale is that such gains in efficiency increase competitiveness and result in lower prices to consumers.

The enforcement authorities take into account potential efficiencies such as economics of scale, better integration and utilization of production facilities, and lower transportation and distribution costs. Reductions in duplicate selling costs or administrative and overhead expenses are also considered.

It remains unclear how sympathetic government enforcement agencies will be to efficiency defenses. The 1992 Horizontal Merger Guidelines state that the merging parties have the burden of demonstrating that a merger which would otherwise be challenged should be permitted to go forward because of significant efficiencies that cannot be achieved by less anticompetitive alternatives.

STATE ATTORNEYS GENERAL ACTIONS AND PRIVATE SUITS TO BLOCK MERGERS

Although this chapter emphasizes the 1992 Horizontal Merger Guidelines and the possibility of challenge by the FTC or the DOJ, the possibility of an action by a state attorney general or by a private-party lawsuit against the merger should not be overlooked.

In the 1990 case *California v. American Stores Co.*, the Supreme Court held that state attorneys general have standing to seek to enjoin mergers under federal, as well as state, antitrust laws. Several such challenges have been mounted in recent years. Moreover, the National Association of Attorneys General has adopted its own merger guidelines which, in many respects, suggest that mergers that would be cleared by federal officials might be challenged by one or more state attorneys general.

Private-party litigation might be instituted by competitors, customers, suppliers, or, in the case of a hostile takeover, the target company.

In *Cargill v. Monfort of Colorado*, the Supreme Court considered the extent to which a competitor has the right to challenge a contemplated acquisition. The Court ruled that a competitor does not have standing to file a suit, except in the relatively rare situation in which the challenged merger would create such a high level of concentration that the merged entity would likely have sufficient market power to drive smaller competitors from the market by below-cost, predatory pricing; the ultimate result of which would be higher prices for consumers after the competition has been driven from the field.

The mere fact that a merger will create a more efficient entity that will compete vigorously and take sales from the complaining competitor does not give that competitor the right to sue. That kind of injury, the Court pointed out, flows from the very conduct—vigorous competition—that the antitrust laws are designed to protect. In sum, the Court restricted but did not eliminate the ability of companies to block acquisitions. In any event, the ability of customers or suppliers of the merging parties, or of unwilling targets, to challenge an acquisition on antitrust grounds is unaffected by the *Monfort* case.

The likelihood of a potential challenge by a state attorney general or by a company or other private party must be considered at the acquisition-planning stage. The reason for this is that the federal courts are not bound by the 1992 Horizontal Merger Guidelines, and many of them have not fully accepted the more lenient attitude reflected in the guidelines. Some courts continue to apply the more expansive antimerger precedents established in the 1960s and to block acquisitions that the government has decided not to challenge. Thus, where state or private challenge is anticipated, the likelihood of successfully completing a horizontal merger is harder to predict.

PREMERGER NOTIFICATION

The Hart-Scott-Rodino Antitrust Improvements Act of 1976 introduced the concept of premerger notification. A basic understanding of the Act is necessary for those involved in planning for a merger, particularly when the timing of the consummation transaction has significant business consequences.

Basically, Hart-Scott-Rodino provides that parties of a specified minimum size must report and provide information to the FTC and the DOJ concerning their intention to acquire voting securities or assets having a specified minimum dollar value. After filing this report, the parties must wait a prescribed period of time before consummating the transaction.

The purpose of this premerger notification mechanism is to allow the antitrust enforcement agencies sufficient information and time—prior to completing an acquisition—to consider whether to seek a preliminary injunction to prevent the closing of the deal pending a full trial concerning the anticompetitive potential of the transaction.

If both the purchaser and the seller meet one of several "size of person" thresholds outlined in Hart-Scott-Rodino and the implementing regulations issued by the FTC, and if the assets or voting securities to be acquired are valuable enough to meet applicable "size of transaction" criteria, the parties must complete and file a standard reporting form. At present the implementing regulations exempt from filing requirements those transactions that involve the purchase of assets valued at $15 million or less and those that involve the acquisition of a controlling interest in the voting securities of a company with annual net sales or net assets of less than $25 million.

The initial report provides enforcement authorities with various kinds of information, principally revenue data by Standard Industrial Code (SIC) category. These data provide them with a general sense of the product markets, if any, in which both parties participate.

CEOs and other management officials planning an acquisition should be aware that most documents prepared by or for officers or directors of a company to assist in their analysis of the acquisition must be submitted as part of the initial filing. These documents often provide insights into the parties' motives for entering into the transaction and can be suggestive of likely areas of competitive concern, if any exist.

After both companies have filed these initial documents, they must wait 30 days before they can close the proposed acquisition. In the case of cash tender offers, the initial waiting period expires 15 days after the acquiring company files the notification form.

When the enforcement agencies perceive no antitrust problem, the companies are formally notified—usually at the end of the 30-day period—that the waiting period has expired and that they are free to close. Where delay could cause adverse business consequences and where no antitrust problems exist, requests for early termination of the waiting period are usually granted.

In cases where the initial filings raise potential antitrust concerns that the FTC or the DOJ wants to pursue, the agency involved serves the companies with a request for additional information. This "second request," as it is called, must be issued before the expiration of the initial waiting period, and it has the effect of prolonging the period of time before the companies can consummate the transaction. The second waiting period does not end until 20 days after both companies have substantially complied with the government's second request. In a cash tender offer, the second waiting period expires 10 days after compliance with the second request.

The second request can be quite formidable. In larger merger cases, it is not unusual for the request itself to exceed 25 single-spaced typewritten pages and for the responsive documents to be tens of thousands of pages long. Typically, the request for additional information seeks a wide range of information designed to facilitate an economic analysis of a merger's anticompetitive potential.

For example, extensive company data concerning shipment patterns and transportation costs might be called for to help delineate the geographic market. Companies are often asked to provide historical sales and capacity data for all goods or services deemed to be within the product market. They are asked for their own data on this subject, as well as for whatever information they have regarding the sales and capacity of their competitors. Such information enables the government agency to calculate market shares and the extent to which the proposed acquisition will affect market concentration. Customer files typically are sought to gain insight into the level of competitive intensity in the industry. Companies are also asked to provide detailed information about the costs of building new facilities or substantially expanding existing ones; these particulars are used to shed light on the extent to which new entry into the market would be likely in the event of a postacquisition price increase.

It should be noted that the government has taken the position that a request for additional information need not be limited to existing documents. Requests for data to be compiled and for essay-length answers to questions concerning range of economic issues are quite common. Moreover, the antitrust agencies have also taken the position that detailed cross-indexes to all documents and data must be submitted in order to facilitate expeditious review before the second Hart-Scott-Rodino waiting period expires.

In most instances, government authorities do not insist on literal compliance with the second request. Where particular requests are unduly burdensome, there is an opportunity to negotiate with agency staffs to determine a sensible shortcut to providing the essential information. However, in the end, an agency has considerable leverage when it insists that documents be produced. Few parties wish to engage in litigation to determine whether the request is unauthorized or unreasonable, inasmuch as they are usually precluded from closing the transaction while such litigation is pending.

SUMMARY

When a merger between horizontal competitors is contemplated, it is essential that the antitrust defense of the acquisition be carefully planned and managed. At an early stage in the process, it would be wise to involve counsel and a competent economic expert. Before too much time and effort is expended in planning an acquisition, these advisors should be asked to appraise the likelihood of a successful governmental or private party challenge. If serious problems seem likely to arise, attention should be devoted at an early stage to the possibility of lessening anticompetitive concerns by selling to a third party part of the assets to be acquired. Careful management of the Hart-Scott-Rodino notification and document-production process is also essential if needless delay and disruption of the business is to be prevented.

PART IV

Accounting and Tax Considerations

INTRODUCTION

Most nonfinancial executives tend to avoid reading all treatises on the subject of accounting. When it comes to acquisitions, however, senior management needs to have at least a basic understanding of the implications of the accounting treatment that will accompany different transaction structures. Both the negotiations and the way an acquisition is portrayed to shareholders may depend on the accounting method chosen by, or imposed upon, the parties at the time of the transaction.

The tax implications of alternative transaction structures must also be understood by the acquiring company's senior management. In keeping with the complexity of U.S. tax law, the impact on financial reporting and tax planning of any two alternative structures may not be the same.

The financial staff of the acquiring company, working with qualified accounting and tax advisers, will undoubtedly identify the issues. But the CEO frequently becomes the final arbiter, choosing the trade-offs between conflicting accounting and tax considerations. A transaction frequently can be structured to achieve a tax treatment providing an economic benefit at the expense of future reported earnings, for example. Such a decision clearly rests with the CEO, who must live with the consequences.

Obviously, the tax implications and, to a lesser extent, financial reporting differences frequently become bargaining points. In the later stages of the negotiations, senior management may have to make the final call on these issues.

Finally, one acceptable method of accounting for a transaction may seem to represent the intent and result of the acquisition more appropriately than another, equally acceptable method. Does the acquirer want to restate historical earnings? How much goodwill is the acquirer willing to carry on its balance sheet and amortize against future earnings? These are policy-level decisions.

The first chapter in this section, Chapter 13, presents the two acceptable methods of accounting that may be adopted to reflect an acquisition: pooling of interests and purchase of assets. Richard P. Miller explains the rules that govern the adoption of each method and discusses the implications of each.

Gerard B. Pompan, the author of Chapter 14, identifies the tax issues that pertain to an acquisition. The chapter also presents the seller's tax considerations, describes how those frequently are in opposition to the buyer's tax objectives, and outlines how buyer and seller can work toward their mutual tax benefit in structuring a transaction.

CHAPTER 13

ACCOUNTING PRINCIPLES

Accounting Principles Board Opinion No. 16 (APB No. 16) is the principal authoritative source of generally accepted accounting principles (GAAP) governing procedures for a merger or acquisition (technically a business combination). APB No. 16, Accounting for Business Combinations, was issued in 1970 by the Accounting Principles Board of the American Institute of Certified Public Accountants. APB No. 16 establishes two mutually exclusive accounting methods for dealing with business combinations:

- The pooling of interests method
- The purchase accounting method

The first step is to evaluate the proposed structure of the acquisition and determine whether the pooling or the purchase method is the appropriate form. Once the form of accounting is selected, the acquirer usually must prepare projected financial statements on a combined basis to evaluate the proposed transaction or to obtain required financing. Because these two accounting methods result in significantly different postacquisition financial statements, the acquirer's financial reporting objectives may dictate a change in the proposed structure of the transaction.

Determining whether a proposed transaction qualifies as a pooling of interests requires a significant degree of professional judgment. Many transactions that appear on the surface to be exchanges of common stock, and that would therefore be accounted for as poolings, do not meet the pooling criteria; such transactions must be dealt with by the purchase method.

The pooling of interests method may offer certain advantages to a public company for acquisitions involving payment of a large premium. Because the pooling method does not adjust the historical carrying value of assets and liabilities acquired, there are no charges against future earnings for additional depreciation or goodwill amortization. Of course, the acquirer must take into account the dilutive effect on earnings per share that may result from issuing additional shares.

THE POOLING OF INTERESTS METHOD OF ACCOUNTING

When an acquisition involves issuing common stock by an acquirer for substantially all of the shares of another company, it generally necessitates using the pooling of interests method—if the transaction meets certain criteria. Conceptually, a pooling results in a combination of shareholders' interests, so that each group shares proportionately in the risks and rewards of ownership in the new entity. Under the accounting rules for a pooling, the accounts of the two companies are simply combined and carried forward at their previously recorded amounts. In addition, the results of operations of each company for the periods prior to the combination are restated and presented on a combined basis.

The pooling criteria set forth in APB No. 16 fall into three general categories:

• The combining of companies

• The combining of interests

• The absence of planned transactions

There are a number of specific criteria for each category. Unless a business combination meets all of the criteria, it must be accounted for as a purchase.

Combining of Companies

The necessary conditions for combining of companies are as follows:

1. Each of the combining companies is autonomous and has not been a subsidiary or division of another corporation within two years before the plan of combination was initiated (generally announced to shareholders).

2. Each combining company is independent of all other combining companies. For purposes of meeting this test, intercorporate investments of less than 10 percent are allowed.

The intent of these two conditions is to require that a pooling involve the combination of two independent shareholder groups. If one of the companies is or has been a subsidiary of a third company, the transaction could be viewed as a spin-off by the parent; thus the venture would not qualify as a pooling.

Combining of Interests

The criteria regarding combining of interests are intended to reinforce the concept that the separate stockholder groups of the combining companies share mutually in the risks and rights of ownership in the combined entity. Accordingly, transactions that alter the relative voting rights of the stockholder groups or involve a distribution of assets or debt for common stock do not achieve this goal.

The specific combining of interests criteria are as follows:

1. The transaction is effected in a single transaction or is completed in accordance with a specific plan within one year from the date the plan was initiated. (Delays owing to governmental authority or litigation do not affect this requirement.)

2. The transaction involves issuing only common stock with rights identical to those of the majority outstanding voting common stock, in exchange for substantially all (at least 90 percent) of the voting common stock interest of another company.

Cash or other consideration may be issued to acquire fractional shares or holdings of dissident shareholders. However, the exchange offer cannot include a pro rata distribution of cash and stock to all shareholders, even if such distribution meets the 10 percent test. In addition, any cash offered to acquire a portion of shareholders' stock holdings is considered, for the purpose of this test, to be an offer for all of the holdings.

3. None of the combining companies changes the equity interests of the voting common stock in contemplation of the combination (within two years before the plan of combination is initiated). "Normal" distributions based on earnings or prior history are allowed. Such distributions can consider the normal dividend pattern of either the acquirer or of the potential acquisition. Accordingly, a private company that is being acquired in a pooling can pay a dividend based on what the shareholders would have received had the combination been effective earlier.

4. Each of the combining companies reacquires treasury stock for purposes other than the combination, and only a "normal" number of such shares are reacquired.

Conditions 3 and 4 are intended to prevent large distributions to some shareholders; such distributions in substance would be cash purchases of the shares, and would thus be contradictory to the theory of pooling. In addition, significant reacquisitions after a transaction that otherwise qualifies as a pooling may invalidate the applicability of the method.

5. The ratio of the interest of an individual common stockholder to the interests of other common stockholders remains exactly the same.

6. The stockholders retain the voting rights they are entitled to. Conditions 5 and 6 are intended to require the continuation of ongoing shareholder relationships, again stressing the "sharing" of risks concept.

7. The combination is resolved at the date the plan is consummated.

This precludes the acquirer from agreeing to distribute stock as additional consideration contingent on future results—such as in the form of an earn-out agreement—and still qualify the transaction as a pooling. It does not preclude the acquirer from revising the number of shares exchanged based on a contingency existing at the acquisition date if settled at an amount different from the amount recorded.

Absence of Planned Transactions

Three additional conditions relating to future transactions must be met in order to qualify an acquisition for the pooling treatment:

1. The combined company does not agree to reacquire all or part of the common stock issued. To do so would be, for all intents and purposes, a cash purchase from the former shareholders and would violate the pooling concept.

2. The combined corporation does not enter into financial arrangements on behalf of stockholders. These arrangements, including the guarantee of a loan secured by stock issued in the combination, are prohibited, because they would, in effect, negate the exchange of equity securities.

3. The combined corporation does not plan to dispose of a significant portion of the assets of the combining companies within two years after the combination, other than dispositions typical during the usual course of business.

THE PURCHASE METHOD OF ACCOUNTING

Many business combinations involve payment of cash or other consideration in addition to or in place of issuing common stock. Therefore such combinations do not meet the pooling of interests criteria. Generally, any transaction in which more than 10 percent of the purchase price is paid in cash, notes, or other nonstock form must be accounted for as a purchase.

The accounting for an acquisition using the purchase method is more complex than one using the pooling method in that it goes beyond a mere combination of corporate accounts. Rather, it establishes a new basis of accounting for the acquired company beginning on the date of acquisition. From that date forward, the companies are merged for financial reporting purposes.

The purchase price is generally determined based on the cash and fair market value of other assets (including stock) issued and liabilities assumed, plus direct acquisition costs incurred. This is allocated to the assets and liabilities of the acquired company, based on a revaluation at fair market value of all assets and liabilities acquired. It includes any acquired assets and liabilities that may not have been previously reflected on the acquired company's historical balance sheet.

Any excess of the purchase price over the net fair market value of the assets and liabilities acquired is recorded as goodwill, an intangible asset. Goodwill should be amortized to income, generally using the straight-line method, over the future period during which it is expected to be beneficial. However, under no circumstances can that period exceed 40 years. Many factors must be considered when determining the appropriate amortization period of goodwill—including market conditions, product demand and obsolescence, and legal or contractual provisions. For tax purposes the amortization period for deducting goodwill and similar intangibles is 15 years by statute, regardless of its otherwise determined economic life. Accordingly, it is very likely that book and tax amortization will differ.

Any part of the purchase price that is contingent on the outcome of future events, such as earnings, should not be recorded until the amount of the additional consideration can be determined.

In many cases, the process of determining fair market value is a subjective one, requiring the use of numerous estimates and assumptions. Considerable professional judgment must be exercised throughout the process of allocating purchase price, inasmuch as it will have a significant impact on the future reported earnings and, possibly, the acquirer's tax liabilities.

Careful analysis may be required in some situations to determine the accounting acquirer, as it may be different from the legal acquirer. A company that distributes cash or assets or that incurs liabilities to acquire another company is clearly the acquirer. However, in a purchase transaction effected principally by the exchange of stock, the identity of the acquirer is not always evident. The SEC has issued a Staff Accounting Bulletin (SAB Topic 2A) giving guidance as to its views on the topic.

CASE STUDY: CGA AND ALLEN SERVICES CORPORATION

The following case study illustrates the effect of financial-statement differences between the pooling and purchase methods of accounting. CGA Computer Associates purchased Allen Services Corporation. The transaction was originally accounted for as a pooling, but the Securities and Exchange Commission disagreed with the use of this accounting treatment. In the settlement, CGA was required to prepare financial statements in accordance with both the pooling and purchase methods. For this reason, the case provides an excellent example of some of the differences between the two methods.

On February 27, 1981, CGA acquired from the sole stockholders of Allen, computer software program packages that had been marketed by Allen. CGA issued approximately 1.4 million common shares to the Allen shareholders in exchange for the net assets and business acquired. Shortly thereafter it filed a registration statement covering approximately 1 million common shares, principally those owned by the former Allen shareholders.

CGA accounted for the acquisition of Allen as a pooling, based on the fact that the transaction involved issuing common stock. The SEC disagreed with this accounting treatment, however, and instituted proceedings under Section 8(d) of the Securities Act of 1933.

The SEC alleged that CGA's treatment as a pooling rather than as a purchase was inconsistent with GAAP. It argued that this was due to the fact that CGA and the selling shareholders entered into a financial arrangement that provided the following: that within two years the shareholders would sell at least 50 percent of their stock through a registration statement filed by CGA, and that in the event they did not sell the stock, CGA was to make them a loan that would be secured by their stock.

CGA and the SEC reached a settlement on this issue in January 1982, in which CGA agreed to report its financial statements by both a pooling interests and purchase method of accounting in "equal prominence"—meaning that neither method was designated as supplemental. This dual presentation will continue for as long as the financial statements differ materially as a result of using the different methods.

The primary differences between the two methods of accounting are the recording of certain assets, the amortization of those assets, the tax effects of such amortization, and the time period relative to the inclusion of the result of Allen in CGA's consolidated income statements. Specifically, the differences are these:

1. The purchase method valued the transaction at $19.5 million, based on an independent appraisal of the value of stock issued. This amount was allocated principally to the value of software acquired ($11.8 million) and goodwill ($6.5 million).

2. Software packages and goodwill were amortized over five years under the purchase method. Amortization of the software was deductible for tax purposes, resulting in a reduced tax bill. However, under the pooling method, the software tax savings had to be accounted for as an increase in capital.

3. In the year the transaction occurred, the results of Allen's operations were included in the purchase accounting financial statements for only two months from the date of acquisition. For the pooling of interests income statement, they were included for a full year.

It is interesting to note the differences between results produced by the two methods, at the acquisition date and thereafter. Specifically, these differences are as follows:

1. Net income under the purchase method ($815,000) was less than under the pooling method ($2,175,000) because of the effect of the amortization of the software packages and goodwill, and related tax effects, and because Allen's results were included for only two months. After the amortization period, however, reported net income was the same under both methods.

2. At the end of the five-year amortization period, the balance sheet was the same under both accounting methods, except that two components of stockholders' equity, retained earnings and capital in excess of par value, differed in offsetting amounts. Retained earnings under the pooling method were $19,349,000 greater than under the purchase method. This is simply the difference between the amounts in the capital in excess of par value accounts under the two methods. It results from recording the value of the stock issued in the transaction in the capital in excess of par value account under the purchase method, amortizing such amounts in subsequent income statements and incorporating Allen's income prior to the transaction into the combined retained earnings.

Cash flow was the same under the two methods of accounting.

The following information extracted from the CGA Annual Report for the year ended April 30, 1981, highlights the differences between the pooling of interests and purchase accounting methods. The difference codes in the right-hand column are explained in notes below the table.

	Pooling of Interests Method ($ thousands)	Purchase Method ($ thousands)	Difference
Condensed Income Statement			
Revenues	20,358	15,510	A
Income interest, net	640	536	
	20,998	16,046	
Direct costs	10,091	8,587	A
Selling, general, and administrative	6,668	4,893	A
Amort. of software	–	392	B
Amort. of goodwill	–	219	B
	16,759	14,091	
Income before taxes	4,239	1,955	
Income tax provision	2,064	1,140	C
Net income	2,175	815	
Condensed balance sheet			
Current assets	11,034	11,034	
Fixed assets, gross	701	603	
Accumulated depreciation	(232)	(134)	
Fixed assets, net	469	469	

Continued

Software packages, net of accum. amort.	–	11,387	D
Goodwill, net of accum. amort.	–	6,343	E
Other	75	75	
	11,587	29,299	
Current liabilities	2,711	2,711	
Stockholders' equity common stock	326	326	
Capital in excess of par value	4,024	23,373	F
Retained earnings	4,517	2,889	G
	8,867	26,588	
	11,578	29,299	

A. This difference is due to the inclusion of the results of Allen's operations for a full year along with the results of CGA's operations for a full year under the pooling method, rather than from the date of the acquisition under the purchase method.

B. This difference results from the amortization, over a five-year period, of software packages (appraised at $11,770,000) and goodwill ($6,562,000) for two months during the year ended April 30, 1981, under the purchase method.

C. This difference in the income tax provision results primarily from two offsetting components: (1) Under the purchase method, income before taxes is substantially less than under the pooling method because the results of Allen's operations for only a two-month period are included. There are also additional charges to expense for amortization of software packages and goodwill, thus resulting in a lower tax provision. (2) The tax provision under the purchase method also includes taxes related to the amortization of goodwill that is not deductible for income tax reporting purposes.

D. This difference results from allocation of acquisition costs to software packages acquired, based on an independent appraisal of fair market value, under the purchase method.

E. This difference results from acquisition costs not allocable to identifiable tangible and intangible assets (goodwill), under the purchase method.

F. These differences result from the issuance of CGA common stock with an appraisal of $19,500,000 to acquire Allen under the purchase method.

G. This difference results from different net income achieved under the purchase and pooling methods. It also reflects the incorporation of Allen's income for years prior to the transaction into the combined financial statements, distributions to former Allen stockholders, and the related tax effect of such distributions.

NOTE: The above example demonstrates the difference in accounting treatment between the purchase and pooling methods. It is not intended to reflect current tax treatment for an acquisition, since several significant tax law changes have taken place subsequent to the date of the transaction.

CHAPTER 14

FEDERAL INCOME TAX CONSIDERATIONS

For an acquirer, the value of an acquisition may be significantly affected by the structure of the deal. For the seller too, the structure chosen may have a major tax impact and will help determine the amount the seller nets. Achieving the most beneficial tax structure requires recognizing that a zero-sum game exists, one that involves the buyer, the seller (including shareholders if the acquired company is incorporated), and the government. If the parties minimize the current value of their combined tax payments, they will increase the size of the pie over which they are negotiating. This chapter addresses some of the key tax considerations for both the buyer and the seller.

As noted in the prior chapter's example of the ASC/CGA combination, the difference in the accounting treatment of an acquisition—as a pooling or as a purchase—may have no current or cumulative effect on the resulting business. Differences in tax treatment, however, have an impact both on reported earnings and on cash flow. Clearly these differences go beyond financial statement reporting: the amount and timing of taxes paid has direct value implications for the shareholders of both the acquirer and seller.

BUYING ASSETS OR STOCK

One of the key issues facing a purchaser of a company is whether to acquire the company's stock or its assets. From an economic standpoint these transactions may be similar if not identical, but significantly different tax results may occur from the purchase of assets, stock, or a combination of both.

A purchaser often acquires assets in order to acquire only selected items, to avoid incurring responsibility for liabilities that are undisclosed on the balance sheet, to avoid having to continue with a perceived unfavorable accounting method, or to get a stepped-up asset basis (to turn the current fair market value of assets into its tax cost).

A seller, on the other hand, often wishes to sell stock instead of assets in order to get rid of contingent liabilities, to avoid the need to value components of a purchased business, or to avoid the tax that may arise from prior depreciation or LIFO (last-in-first-out method of accounting for inventory) reserves.

A tax-free reorganization (as discussed on pages 207–208) will help the seller's cash flow at the time of the initial transaction, because the recognition of the seller's gain is deferred and it is not required to pay any taxes at the time of the sale. However, this type of transaction may cost the purchaser more over time. This would be the case if at a later date the acquired company is deprived of the benefit of decreased income tax payments that would have resulted from additional depreciation and amortization deductions from a taxable asset acquisition or stock purchase with a basis step-up election.

For acquisitions before 1987, the conflict between the purchaser's desire to buy assets and the seller's desire to sell stock could be resolved by having the acquired company sell its assets and liquidate. Under the "General Utilities" doctrine, which was eliminated by the Tax Reform Act of 1986, a corporation being liquidated could sell its assets and distribute the cash proceeds without recognizing gain or loss on those sales; the only tax on the liquidating corporation would be the "recapture" or repayment of the value of some past tax benefits (such as depreciation).

Accordingly, the acquirer would reflect its acquisition cost in the depreciable basis of the assets without the selling corporation having to recognize full taxable gain. The shareholders of the selling corporation would, of course, have to recognize taxable gain; they

would have done so anyway if they had sold their stock rather than
having their corporation sell assets in liquidation.

As a result of the Tax Reform Act's elimination of "General
Utilities," a liquidating corporation must recognize full taxable gain
or loss on the sale of its assets. In addition, this treatment of the
liquidating corporation cannot be avoided by having the corporation
distribute the assets to its shareholders in liquidation; the liquidating
corporation will be treated as if it had sold its assets to its shareholders at fair market value.

Such treatment of the acquired corporation does not mean that
an asset sale should always be avoided. The acquired company may
have tax attributes, such as past tax losses, which can be carried
forward to offset the taxable gain that will be triggered by the asset
sale. If the use of those tax losses would be subject to restrictions
should the stock of the corporation be sold (as discussed on pages
210–211 under *Assess Sec. 382*), it may make more sense to have
the acquired company sell assets, so that restrictions can be avoided.
The benefit to the purchaser would be that losses would take the
form of a higher depreciable basis in the assets.

Most corporate acquisitions involve tax considerations for four
taxpayers or groups of taxpayers:

• The purchaser
• The purchaser's shareholders
• The seller (or target)
• The seller's shareholders

Most acquisitions fall within one of four basic formats:

• Taxable purchases
  — stock
  — asset
• "Nontaxable" or tax-deferred acquisitions
  — stock
  — asset

These four forms of acquisitions have different tax consequences
for the four taxpayers/groups, as summarized in Figure 14-1.

FIGURE 14-1 The four basic acquisition formats

| | Type of Transaction | | | |
| | Transfer of stock | | Transfer of assets | |
Parties to the transaction	*Nontaxable*	*Taxable*	*Nontaxable*	*Taxable*
Shareholder of target	Selling shareholders of target company have no taxable gain or loss. The basis of the stock of the purchasing company received by the selling shareholders is the same as that of their target company stock.	Selling shareholders will recognize gain or loss.	Selling shareholders have no taxable gain or loss. The basis of the stock of the purchasing company received by the selling shareholders is the same as that of the target company stock.	Shareholders of target company will have gain or loss if target company liquidates.
Purchasing company	Purchasing company recognizes no gain or loss. The basis of the target company stock received by purchasing company carries over from the target stockholders.	Purchasing company generally recognizes no gain or loss. The basis of the target company stock received by purchasing company will be what was paid.	Purchasing company has no gain or loss. The basis of target company assets acquired by purchasing company is the same as if owned by target. Tax attributes of target, including net operating losses, are transferred to purchasing company. Net operating losses may be limited.	Purchasing company has no gain or loss. Assets acquired at fair market value by purchasing company. Tax attributes of target do not carry over.

200

Target company	Target company is unaffected, except that net operating loss carryovers may be limited.	Target company is unaffected, unless Sec. 338 applies. Net operating losses may be limited.	Target company goes out of existence. No gain or loss is recognized.	Target company will recognize a gain or loss on the sale of its assets. Tax attributes of target company are unaffected unless target company liquidates, in which case they disappear.
Shareholders of purchasing company	Shareholders of purchasing company are unaffected. However, dilution of their control of purchasing company will result.	Generally, there is no dilution of control to shareholders of purchasing company.	Shareholders of purchasing company are unaffected. However, dilution of their control of purchasing company may result.	Generally, there is no dilution of control to shareholders of purchasing company.

TAXABLE TRANSACTIONS (STOCK OR ASSET PURCHASES)

Taxable purchases of another company are similar to transactions accounted for as purchases under generally accepted accounting principles (GAAP), as discussed in Chapter 13.

From a tax perspective, the sale of many assets at the same time is similar to the sale of a single asset. Only the magnitude of the transaction and the need to allocate the purchase price among the assets differ. In addition, non–income tax considerations related to transfer of title and transfer taxes enter into a bulk sale.

Whenever assets are purchased in a taxable transaction, their tax cost (the basis) is the amount paid (cash plus any assumed liabilities). When something other than cash is paid, the basis is the fair market value of the assets transferred. A sale of assets by a corporation is taxable to that corporation. The same result occurs regardless of whether the sale is made by the corporation in contemplation of liquidation.

Seller's Shareholders in a Taxable Acquisition

In any acquisition the purchases must be mindful of the seller's tax status. Because a taxable acquisition will likely result in a tax liability for the seller, its shareholders will frequently want a higher price in a taxable transaction. Thus, tax cost will affect the acceptable purchase price.

For example, assume a sale of a going business is being negotiated. The purchaser wants a minimum cost. The selling stockholders own stock in a corporation that, in turn, owns land. (For purposes of this example, the selling corporation is assumed to own just one asset.)

The fair market value of the land is $200, and its original cost was $20. Assuming that $200 is agreed upon as the purchase price, the sale of corporate stock would clearly be preferable, as is illustrated in the following comparison:

	Stock Sale	Asset Sale
1. Gross proceeds	$200	$200
2. Corporate basis in land	—	20

	Stock Sale	*Asset Sale*
3. Corporate-level gain	—	180
4. Corporate tax @ 34 percent	—	63
5. Proceeds to shareholder (item 1 − item 4)	200	117
6. Shareholder basis in stock	20	20
7. Shareholder-level gain	180	97
8. Shareholder tax @ 33 percent individual rate	60	38
9. Net proceeds to shareholders (item 5 − item 8)	$140	$ 79

For the seller's shareholder to net the same amount of cash ($129) from the land sale as from a stock sale, the price for the land would have to be $293.

	Asset Sale
1. Gross proceeds	$297
2. Corporate basis in land	20
3. Corporate-level gain	277
4. Corporate tax @ 35 percent	97
5. Proceeds to shareholder (item 1 − item 4)	200
6. Shareholder basis in stock	20
7. Shareholder-level gain	180
8. Shareholder tax @ 39.6 percent the maximum individual rate	71
9. Net proceeds to shareholder (item 5 − item 8)	$129

In effect, the asset sale would transfer the cost of all tax burdens relating to the sale from the seller to the purchaser. The purchaser, in that case, would have a higher basis for the acquired assets, representing the amount paid. However, the benefit would at best result in future cash savings owing to a lower capital gain at the time of resale, whereas the cost would be more cash paid now. Accordingly, it is difficult to predict the circumstances under which the parties would willingly agree to a sale of assets instead of stock— unless, as noted above, the selling corporation had tax attributes such as tax loss carryovers that could offset the corporate-level gain, and such tax attributes would otherwise become limited if the stock of the selling company were sold.

An acquisition of the stock of a selling company for cash or other property also results in a taxable gain or loss to the seller's shareholders. The purchaser's basis in the acquired stock equals the amount paid. However, the purchaser gets no other advantage until the stock is sold, because no depreciation is allowed on stock cost.

When the Acquired Company Is a Subsidiary

When the acquired company is a subsidiary, its parent has a choice of selling the stock of the subsidiary or having the subsidiary sell its assets. Either structure would involve the recognition of gain or loss. Thus, the parent might be tempted to base the decision on whether it has a higher tax basis in the subsidiary's stock or the subsidiary has a higher tax basis in its assets. However, this ignores the tax impact on the purchaser. A sale of stock might minimize the seller's tax but prevent the purchaser from reflecting its acquisition costs in the depreciable basis of the acquired company's assets.

For example, assume that the subsidiary being acquired has assets with a tax basis of $100, a fair market value of $1,000, and no liabilities, and that the parent has a tax basis in its subsidiary's stock of $200. If the subsidiary sells its assets, it will derive a taxable gain of $900, whereas a sale of the subsidiary's stock would limit the taxable gain to $800.

However, the asset sale would give the purchaser a depreciable basis in the subsidiary's assets of $1,000. In contrast, the stock sale would leave the new owner of the subsidiary with an undepreciable basis of $1,000 in the subsidiary's stock, whereas the subsidiary's depreciable basis in the assets remains at $100. As long as the present value of the tax savings from depreciating the additional $900 of acquisition cost exceeds the "seller's" extra tax cost on the additional $100 of taxable gain ($900 on the assets versus $800 on the stock), the transaction should be cast as an asset sale. The parties can then negotiate a formula for dividing their combined tax savings from this structuring and reflect the results in the acquisition price.

When the Acquired Company Is an "S Corporation"

A special election in the Internal Revenue Code permits an unaffiliated corporation owned by 35 or fewer individuals to be treated as a conduit. That is, no corporate-level tax is imposed, and the shareholders take into account on a current basis their share of the corporation's taxable income or loss. Generally, such an "S Corporation" can sell its assets to the acquirer and liquidate without incurring a double tax—a corporate-level tax and another shareholder-level tax.

Section 338 Treatment

Under Section 338 of the Internal Revenue Code, a purchaser of stock may elect to treat the corporate assets acquired by stock purchase as if they were acquired directly. Where the acquired company is a subsidiary, a special election under Sec. 338(h) (10) permits the parent to sell the stock of its subsidiary while treating the transaction as if its subsidiary had sold its assets instead. These elections generally achieve the same tax effect as a taxable asset transfer without undesirable side effects such as recording of deeds and exposure to state and local transfer taxes.

For the purchaser to elect Sec. 338 treatment with respect to an acquisition, many requirements must be met. Some of them are as follows:

- Acquisition of control (80 percent of the vote and value of outstanding shares)
- Maximum 12-month acquisition period
- Acquisition by purchase
- Purchaser must be a corporation

It should be noted that a Sec. 338 election generally places the additional tax cost liability on the purchaser, while the Sec. 338(h) (10) election results in the additional tax liability remaining with the seller.

A Sec. 338 election must be made within eight and a half months after the end of the month in which the acquisition occurs. In addition, the target's tax attributes, including net operating loss carryovers, capital loss carryovers, credit carryovers, and earnings and profits, as well as its accounting methods, disappear following a Sec. 338 election, because such a transaction is treated as an asset sale.

Allocation of Purchase Price as Tax Basis

A major factor in the purchase of a business is the price the purchaser is allowed to allocate for future tax purposes to each of the assets acquired. This allocation consideration applies either to a taxable asset purchase or to a purchase of stock followed by a Sec. 338 election. The 1986 Tax Reform Act placed strict limits on how such a purchase price can be allocated.

The specific mechanism for allocating the tax cost of a purchase is as follows: basis is allocated first to cash and cash items, then to marketable securities and like items, then to the various other assets acquired. If the total purchase price paid exceeds the total fair market value of the identified assets acquired, the excess is goodwill. Goodwill is amortizable, by statute, over a 15 year period.

Goodwill, "going concern" value, and assets of a similar nature, now referred to as Section 197 intangibles, are amortizable for tax purposes over a prescribed 15 year amortization period on a staight line basis. An allocation of purchase price to assets such as inventory, which is expensed as sold, allows the purchaser a deduction for tax purposes. Therefore, in valuing the seller's assets, a purchaser will want to first identify assets which will be disposed of quickly, e.g., inventory and depreciable assets with short lives, and then intangibles and goodwill/going concern value, in order to maximize recovery of the acquisition cost through depreciation or amortization.

Included in the definition of Section 197 intangibles, subject to 15 year amortization, are covenants not to compete, regardless of their contractual terms. This treatment applies to noncompete agreements either in asset or stock acquisitions. To sustain a noncompete agreement with the IRS, it must be separately bargained for and have "economic significance."

Many similarities exist between the methodologies used to value an acquired company's assets for tax purposes and for GAAP purposes. For example, the purchase price allocable to the assets is generally determined in the same manner for tax purposes as for GAAP. In both cases, it is the sum of cash and fair market value of any other assets paid plus liabilities assumed.

The rules differ in accounting for contingent liabilities. To maintain the accounting records of the company, GAAP requires recording contingent liabilities based on both the probability of occurrence and the reasonable estimation of amount. However, tax rules do not permit contingent liability recognition until such liabilities are "fixed and determinable" with reasonable accuracy.

Generally, GAAP definitions would result in the recognition of some liabilities that are not liabilities for tax purposes. On the other hand, the liability assumed by the purchaser for outstanding long-term debt may be greater under tax rules, which do not permit discounting such debt at current market rates, whereas such discounting is required for GAAP.

Valuation difficulties may arise when assets are acquired for stock and/or noncash assets. In these cases, the value of the assets acquired is the value paid. If stock given as consideration is traded on a recognized market, then the exchange quotes for the valuation date are generally the best evidence of fair market value. However, there are cases where market quotations are unavailable or where they may be considered an unreliable indication of value because of specific market conditions or stock characteristics. For example, if the stock is closely held, various factors are weighted for valuation purposes. These factors include the company's earning capacity, the industry's economic outlook, and the market price of similar stocks; they are similar to the guidelines for valuing closely held stock for estate tax and gift tax purposes.

NONTAXABLE TRANSACTIONS (STOCK OR ASSET PURCHASES)

As in the pooling of interest method of accounting, an acquisition can be treated as a nontaxable transaction (technically a tax-free reorganization) only if a variety of conditions are met. But although pooling of interest accounting will result where conditions set by the American Institute of Certified Public Accountants and the Securities and Exchange Commission are met, tax-free treatment requires that conditions set by the Internal Revenue Code, income tax regulations, the Internal Revenue Service, and the courts be met.

In a tax-free acquisition, financial gain that would otherwise be realized in the transaction from the exchange of stock or assets is generally deferred. The historical basis of assets carries over. In addition, the purchaser acquires the acquired company's tax history. Tax-free control of a target may be acquired by acquisition of either assets or stock.

In addition to the technical requirements of the Internal Revenue Code, a variety of conditions set by the courts must additionally be met before an acquisition can receive tax-free reorganization treatment, including the following:

- Continuity of business enterprise
- Continuity of shareholder interest
- Business purpose to the reorganization

Continuity of Business Enterprise

The requirement for continuity of business enterprise stipulates that the buyer either continue the acquired company's historical business or use a significant portion of the acquired company's historical business assets in a business. If the acquired company has more than one line of business, the first alternative is satisfied if the acquiring corporation continues a significant line of business of the acquired company. Where the acquired company is a holding company, the application of these rules will depend on an analysis not only of the acquired company but also of its subsidiaries.

Continuity of Shareholder Interest

All tax-free reorganizations require at least some of the acquired company's shareholders to receive an equity interest in the acquiring corporation or its parent. The rule is most liberal in a statutory merger, or "A" reorganization. Any kind of stock may be used—common or preferred, voting or nonvoting—and as long as 50 percent of the acquired company's stock is exchanged for stock in the merged corporation, the continuity of shareholder interest requirement is satisfied. This is true regardless of whether all shareholders receive stock and other consideration on a pro rata basis. (However, any shareholder receiving nonequity consideration will have to recognize any taxable gain to the extent of cash and/or value of nonequity consideration.)

In other types of reorganizations, such as acquisitions of target stock or target assets, by contrast, much more stringent requirements are imposed. In a stock acquisition, only voting stock may be used, and 80 percent control of the target must be achieved. In an asset acquisition, on the other hand, voting stock must be used except under very limited conditions. In addition, 90 percent of the fair market value of the net assets and 70 percent of the fair market value of the gross assets must be acquired.

Business Purpose of the Reorganization

To receive tax-free treatment, a proposed reorganization must have a business (or nontax) purpose separate from its shareholders'. This requirement originated in the courts, but now is reflected in the income tax regulations. Common business purposes include cost savings, economies of scale, and expansion into new markets.

SURVIVAL OF TAX ATTRIBUTES

Over its life, a corporation will accumulate various items of tax history, which are referred to as tax attributes. These attributes fall into several categories:

- Accounting methods and similar items
- Accumulated earnings and profits
- Carryovers of certain tax losses and benefits

Most of these items are transferred in tax-free acquisitions but are eliminated in a taxable sale of assets or in a stock acquisition with a Sec. 338 election. Many of the items also survive a taxable acquisition of the acquired company's stock where no Sec. 338 election is made to treat the transaction as an asset acquisition. Even where tax attributes survive a transfer, the law limits the extent to which a purchaser may use carryovers of certain tax losses and credits.

One commonly prized attribute is the net operating loss (NOL). An NOL arises when permitted deductions exceed gross income subject to tax. In other words, the excess amount is allowed as a deduction in computing taxable income in the three years prior to the loss year and for fifteen years following the loss year.

The steps used to determine the extent to which a net operating loss deduction survives a tax-free reorganization or a taxable acquisition of stock without a Sec. 338 election are as follows:

1. *Assess the NOL:* Determine whether income and deductions originally reported in the loss years were correct.

2. *Assess the business purpose:* Determine whether the principal purpose of the acquisition is a business (nontax) purpose.

3. *Assess consolidated return rules:* If the acquired company will survive the acquisition and be included in a consolidated return with the purchaser, the acquired company's loss carryover will be permitted only to offset future taxable income of the acquired company. Sometimes this limitation can be avoided by liquidating the acquired company into the acquirer.

4. *Assess Sec. 382:* When direct and indirect ownership of a corporation changes by more than 50 percent within a three-year period—as would be true in most stock acquisition transactions—the annual amount of the acquired company's net operating loss carryovers that may be deducted will be limited to a "reasonable" return on the investment in the acquired company. "Reasonable" is defined as the long-term tax-exempt interest rate, which is currently about 5.5 percent.

The investment in the acquired company is net of acquisition debt, whether or not the debt is pushed down to the acquired company. For example, if the company is acquired for $10,000 using $9,000 of acquisition debt, only $55 of the acquired company's net operating loss carryover (5.5 percent of the difference between $10,000 and $9,000) may be deducted annually. However, this annual limitation can be increased to accommodate gains resulting from a Sec. 338 election with respect to the acquisition. And for the first five years it may be increased to accommodate certain gains that were accrued economically but not realized at the time of the acquisition.

5. *Assess Sec. 384:* When either the acquired company or the acquiring corporation has net operating loss carryovers, the carryovers of the loss corporation generally cannot be used to offset the gains of the other corporations—to the extent that they were accrued but not realized at the time of the acquisition.

DISPOSITION OF UNWANTED ASSETS

When stock of the acquired company is acquired and no Sec. 338 election is made to treat the stock acquisition as a purchase of assets, the acquired company's tax basis in its assets will not reflect the purchaser's acquisition cost. If the acquisition price represents a premium over the acquired company's basis for tax purposes, the acquired company most probably would have to recognize taxable gain on the sale of any of its assets that the purchaser does not want it to retain.

Prior to recent tax legislation, the acquiring corporation could form several subsidiaries that would "mirror" the groups of assets in which the acquirer was not interested and the group to be retained. The acquired company would then be liquidated into the mirror subsidiaries, with one receiving the assets to be retained and each of the others receiving a group of assets that would be sold as a separate package. In this way, the acquisition cost of the stock of each mirror subsidiary would equal the fair market value of the net assets it contained, despite the fact that the subsidiary itself would have the acquired company's old tax basis in its assets. The stock of each mirror subsidiary could then be sold immediately in a transaction that would produce little or no taxable gain, even though the mirror subsidiary might have had substantial taxable gain if it had sold its assets instead.

Recent legislation has blocked the use of this technique, as well as several variations on the theme. However, it may be possible to achieve the same tax result with other techniques. It may also be possible for the acquirer and parties interested in the unwanted assets to achieve essentially the same economic result as a breakup of the target without actually breaking it up and incurring adverse tax consequences.

MULTINATIONAL ACQUISITIONS

When the acquired company is a multinational corporation, many complications arise in regard to taxes. The most pressing problems usually stem from the acquisition debt. If a portion of the acquisition debt is not passed on to the foreign subsidiaries of the acquired company, the interest expense may exceed the worldwide U.S. taxable income of the target (and, if the acquirer is a corporation that will file a consolidated return with the acquired company, consolidated U.S. taxable income). To the extent that interest expense does not exceed preinterest taxable income, the interest expense will be allocated in part to foreign-source U.S. taxable income.

To the extent that such foreign-source taxable income has already borne foreign income taxes that exceed the U.S. tax on such income, the U.S. tax on that income will already have been offset by the foreign tax credits. In that event, no U.S. tax savings may be available for the interest expense allocated to that income. Even the portion of the interest expense allocated to U.S.-source taxable income may exceed such income; in this case, there may be no U.S. tax benefit for the excess amount.

These problems can be solved or minimized by pushing acquisition debt down to the foreign subsidiaries of the acquired company. This can be achieved in several ways, depending on the countries in which the acquired company's foreign subsidiaries operate.

In addition, for income tax purposes, an acquirer should not overlook the opportunity to reflect its acquisition cost in the tax basis of the assets of the foreign subsidiaries of the acquired company. And the most tax-efficient way of repatriating excess cash from the acquired company's foreign subsidiaries should be reviewed.

CONCLUSION

There are many ways in which the combined tax burdens of the acquirer, the seller, and the seller's shareholders can be minimized and deferred. The transaction should be structured in such a way as to optimize the combined tax burden. The goal, after all, is to negotiate over as large a corporate pie as possible.

PART V

Integration After the Acquisition

INTRODUCTION

The authors in this section all maintain that the time to plan for postacquisition integration of the people who come with a purchased company is before the transaction closes. Each chapter identifies different types of "people" issues and offers ideas for dealing with them.

In Chapter 15, Philip D. Robers points out that no matter what so-called experts may say, there is no formula for postmerger integration. That is because no two acquisitions are alike and no two acquirers are alike. But if there is any axiom for engineering a successful acquisition, it is this: the acquisition must make sense for the acquirer from the beginning.

Larry E. Senn describes different management styles and corporate cultures in Chapter 16 of this section. Although mergers and acquisitions must be based primarily on strategic, financial, and other objective criteria, ignoring a potential clash of cultures can lead to financial failure.

Many issues must be addressed in studying how the employee benefit plans of two merging corporations should be integrated. John E. Vaught and Tom Shea discuss the alternatives of merging into one plan or following other options in Chapter 17 of this section. Each alternative has different implications for the companies and for their respective employees.

CHAPTER 15

POSTMERGER INTEGRATION

If an acquisition came with an owner's manual—complete with a section on how to start it and operate it, a maintenance schedule, a guide to repairs, and perhaps even a warranty—all a CEO would have to do would be to follow the guidelines, keep to the timetables, and fill in the blanks. The idea sounds farfetched, yet some theoreticians act as if postmerger integration were just that cut-and-dried. They prescribe what in essence are formulas or recipes for corporations to follow after they buy a company.

Some try to help a company decide when to introduce its financial systems. Some advise on how to replace the acquired company's inventory methods with those of the acquirer. Others discuss the importance of combining computer operations. Still others advise on how to impose a sales force onto another company's marketing network. As a bonus, some even tell how to run periodic checks to make sure that everything negotiated in the deal turns out as planned.

If anything, this is a formula for failure—and failure is something that has plagued far too many U.S. corporate acquisitions.

There is no formula for postmerger integration. The reason is simple: no two acquisitions are alike and no two acquirers are alike.

If there is any axiom for engineering a successful acquisition, it is this: the acquisition must make sense for the acquirer from the beginning. A close second is that there must be a carefully prepared plan for integrating the acquisition.

WHAT MOTIVATED THE ACQUISITION?

Before a company can successfully integrate an acquisition, its leadership must stop and reflect on why it wanted to buy the company in the first place. Here are some of the usual motives for acquisitions and the problems that they may present after the deal is done:

- *Pure diversification:* Companies with cash or credit to spare realize that the marketplace is beginning to eclipse them, so they buy a company in another industry to reverse their core industry's expected decline.

  These transactions are fairly rare. Almost any company that has been reasonably well run has been diversifying over time. If a company has been asleep, it is probably too late to save it through diversification. And if a target company is worth buying, it is clearly going for a premium. The acquirer needs not only money but patience, because it will have to wait a long time to get its money back. But if a company can afford the price of admission, and if it does not interfere too much in the company it buys, such an acquisition can succeed.

- *Improved market position:* Improving market position through acquisition may be tricky to pull off, particularly if the impetus for the acquisition originated with a small unit within the acquiring company. The unit may have convinced the CEO that it could boost its market share from, say, 3 percent to 30 percent if Company X were purchased. That is a dubious motive for an acquisition; if the division's management is that good, it should have more than a 3 percent market share to begin with.

  Here is what often happens. Many CEOs of acquiring companies do not want to see their managers report to executives of the acquired company, even if it has the larger market share. In these cases, one of the acquirer's managers is put in charge of the combined company, even though he or she may lack the experience to run a company of that size. Key executives of the acquired company object to this practice and resign. In the end, the little fish may have eaten the whale, but no one truly qualified remains to run the new company.

- *Turnaround situations:* A company goes "bottom fishing," deciding to pick up another company that has a good market position but is in trouble, which is why it is cheap. The potential acquirer's top team thinks: "We're smart folks; we will manage this better."

  Maybe so. But often cheap companies are in real trouble and need a great deal of managing. And if the acquirer is running lean, it probably cannot afford to cut loose some of its key people to play doctor.

  What sometimes happens in turnaround cases is that the acquirer fires everyone who got the acquired company in trouble, then quickly hires replacements. Often these people are unknown or untested, or worse still, as bad as the people who got the company into trouble in the first place.

- *Acquiring technology:* Acquisitions motivated by a desire to acquire technology can work out fairly well—*if* a company succeeds in making its corporate culture mesh with the other company's culture. But that is a huge *if.*

WHAT SHOULD BE INTEGRATED?

A company in any industry depends on a series of interrelated business processes to provide products and/or services to its internal and external customers (See Figure 15-1). Business processes are composed of activities that transform raw material and data input into value-added products and/or services for customers. These processes use an organization's resources to provide results. A list of typical processes in a manufacturing company is shown in Figure 15-2, and in an insurance company in Figure 15-3. Similar lists could be developed for other industries.

Companies in virtually every industry are adopting a "process point of view" rather than the traditional vertical one. Management teams complete focused improvement projects to achieve major

FIGURE 15-1   Viewing a company from a process perspective

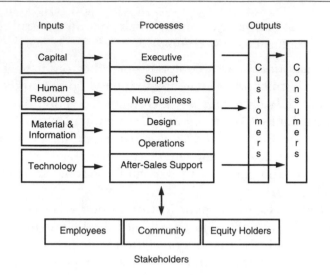

FIGURE 15-2   Typical manufacturing industry processes

Executive
- Financial planning
- Strategic planning
- Monitoring and control

Support
- Financial management
- HR
- Legal
- MIS
- Facilities

Gaining New Business
- Identification customer requirement
- Proposal/bid/quote generation
- Configure/customize
- Order

Produce/Service Design
- Idea/concept generation
- Development
- Test
- Commercialization

Operations
- Order
- Scheduling
- Manufacture/process
- Deliver/install
- Cash collection

After-Sales Support
- Customer complaint/need definition
- Solutions design
- Service dispatch
- Conduct service
- Resolution

FIGURE 15-3   Typical insurance industry processes

Executive
- Financial planning
- Strategic planning
- Monitoring and control

Support
- Financial management
- HR
- Legal
- MIS
- Facilities

Gaining New Business
- Marketing
- Underwriting
- Policy issues
- Renewals

Produce/Service Development
- Product pricing
- Product development

Property & Casualty
- Settlement
- Litigation mangement

Life
- Loans/surrenders
- Benefits

Health
- Network management
- Provider relations
- Utilization management
- Claims processing

Member Services
- Policy administration
- Billing
- Customer inquiries
- Generating customer reports

reductions in cost and in process cycle times, as well as to improve the quality of the product or service produced.*

One of the most useful things that management can do in an acquisition situation is to conduct a "current state assessment" of the business processes of *both* the acquired and the acquiring company. That is, it should prepare a "map" of the processes, assess how well they are performing from the perspectives of time, resources, and quality and determine how compatible the corresponding processes are. Ideally, this should be done prior to the acquisition.

A current-state assessment provides a solid foundation for asking the following key questions:

- What are the costs, benefits, risks, and barriers to integrating individual business processes of the two companies?

---

*For more information, see Harrington, H. J., *Business Process Improvement: The Breakthrough Strategy for Total Quality, Productivity and Competitiveness,"* McGraw-Hill, 1991. Also see Davenport, T. H., *Process Innovation: Reengineering Work Through Information Technology,* Harvard Business School Press, 1992.

- Which processes should be integrated and when?

- For those processes to be integrated, how should the combined process be structured (i.e., adopt the process from one of the companies, a hybrid of both, or a totally new reengineered process)?

Most successful managers realize that asking the right questions is often the toughest part of management. Asking questions from the perspective of process rather than organization adds clarity to the postmerger integration procedure. Ironically, one of the prime causes of "nonmerger mergers" is that management has not considered in advance how to integrate processes.

DEVELOPING AN INTEGRATION PLAN

Although there is no formula for postmerger integration, management must develop a plan to guide the integration. Indeed, the operating environment may become hectic after a merger, and, without an agreed-upon plan, a company runs the serious risk of not achieving the merger's objectives.

What issues and areas should be addressed in the plan? Process integration is one of the most basic. In fact, the performance of any company rests squarely on three closely interrelated factors—its processes, people, and technology. A successful integration strategy must address all three (see Figure 15-4). Fortunately, adopting a "process point of view" can clarify many of the issues pertaining to people and technology.

Figure 15-5 indicates some of the issues that are likely to be considered in guiding the integration plan, depending on what motivated the acquisition.

Many acquirers do not go through a planning process of this type. They simply do not give postmerger integration much thought. It is the conquest that thrills; once they bag their prey they lose interest. Surely, the senior management of most large corporations get heavily involved in the decision to acquire companies. Far too many, however, turn over the "do work"—the details of integrating the acquisition—to someone else.

FIGURE 15-4   Focus on integrated impact

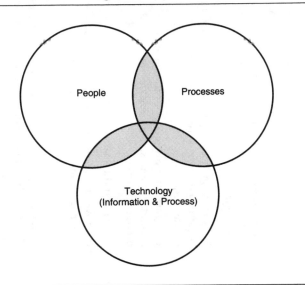

Unless an exceptional management team is in place, which has the requisite experience in integration, that may be irresponsible. After all, it takes a tremendous amount of time and effort to acquire a company. Unless one company bails another company out of trouble, it usually takes a year. In many ways, an acquisition is like having a baby. After going through the necessary effort and labor, it hardly makes sense to walk away and abandon it to someone else's care.

KEEPING THE STAFF AT BAY

The early days—lasting from a couple of months to as long as a year—are the most critical in integrating and acquisition. Acquiring the company was important enough to occupy the CEO's time from beginning to end. It then stands to reason that the CEO must stay involved for a reasonable length of time after the deal is closed if it is going to succeed. It is equally important to keep the acquirer's staff out of the target's operations for as long as possible. One of the gravest sins in assimilating an acquisition is to allow staff mem-

FIGURE 15-5 Key issues to consider in developing an integration plan

Motivation for merger	Short-term issues	Longer-term issues
Pure diversification	• Retain key personnel needed to operate the acquired business. • Maintain customer focus to avoid losing market share.	• Integrate key business processes in "support areas" (e.g., customer service, logistics, MIS, etc). • Establish strong "balanced scorecard" performance measurements to effectively manage the acquisition.
Improved market position	• Integrate marketing and selling programs and related business processes. • Maintain customer focus to avoid losing leverage in marketplace being sought.	• Fully leverage high-impact personnel from the acquired company across the combined operations. • Integrate business processes to eliminate redundancy and standardize operations and products/services.
Turnaround situation	• Focus on immediate cost reduction opportunities. • Concentrate on training programs related to business fundamentals. • Initiate a quality assurance function.	• Strengthen the management team. • Improve and reengineer business processes of the acquired company, integrating as desired.
Acquired technology	• Retain key personnel needed to protect the technology acquired. • Maximize leverage obtained from acquired technology through application to existing operations.	• Search for opportunities to broaden the horizons of the combined company through application of the acquired technology. • Assure that appropriate investments are made to keep the combined company on the technology "power curve."

bers to move in and force changes before they are necessary. That only creates ill will and drives up costs.

When buying a company, a CEO must rely on his or her support staff for fact-finding. Experts must evaluate the target and look for things that could hurt the acquiring company later. Once the acquisition has been accomplished, however, senior management must take over and make the value judgments about what should be fixed and when.

The typical acquisition often becomes an attractive nuisance. It is a new toy and everyone wants to play with it—especially individuals in staff positions, because they can ususaly find some free time. But well-meaning staff can damage an acquisition faster than almost anything else. Most low-level managers are function-oriented. They seek excellence in their specialized areas of interest. And when they strive for excellence in their functional areas, more often than not they rapidly drive up costs.

They may visit the acquired company and pester the staff there with countless petty requests for information. They arrive with a stack of policy manuals 10 feet high and say: "Thou shalt, and within 90 days." Or worse, they may tell the acquired company's employees that top management wants things done a certain way. "What do you mean, you don't have a personnel manager? Here's our organizational chart. See those blocks. Fill them in. And get a computer like our computer."

The CEO needs to make it clear to staff not to invoke his or her name in the interest of change. Moreover, the CEO must be careful about what he or she says to the new company in those early days. Too often, what comes out of a CEO's mouth is interpreted as mandate.

When a nice, profitable company is overburdened with new rules and regulations, it sags. One morning the acquiring company's CEO may wake up and find that the acquired company is not making money anymore because some of his or her staff are trying to reorganize and staff it as though it were an enterprise 10 times its size.

INTRODUCING CORPORATE CULTURE

Some observers have reported that they are amused to read that one thorny issue in assimilating new companies is introducing overhead allocations or transfer pricing to the new unit. That should be a nonissue, but too often it is not.

Engineer-entrepreneur companies go into culture shock the first time they are told, "You're going to be selling your product to another division. Your gross margin will no longer be 50 percent, but cost plus 20 percent. Now don't worry; it won't mean anything after the books are consolidated."

And trying to explain that the company routinely charges all of its businesses a certain percentage of assets employed for corporate services usually upsets entrepreneurs. In situations such as these, it is best to institute changes gradually. The acquired company should not be charged for the first year. Then the company's standard transaction costs should slowly be introduced. The new company should be given time to assimilate and understand the so-called charges. Although they are simply memo journal entries, they may well be unknown to anyone who is not familiar with a large corporation's structure.

PERSONNEL PROBLEMS

A sticking point in many acquisitions becomes evident when personnel compensation in the acquired company is out of line with the acquirer's policies. Frequently, the top three or four people in a small company are paid extremely well. Before the deal is closed, it must be made clear that the acquirer does not pay $300,000 a year to someone running a $25 million business.

If it is important for the top managers to stay on for a while, the acquirer might have to agree to an inflated salary for a specified number of years. This becomes part of the written deal and can help ease personnel problems later on. If other employees of the company ask what the new manager is being paid, they should be told the truth, and that the payments will be made for three years (or for any other specified length of time) so that the new manager—formerly the owner—will stay on during a transition period.

Personnel problems are not limited to small, entrepreneurial companies. Although public companies or corporate spin-offs are usually the easiest to assimilate because of the closer similarity of their corporate cultures, such problems may still occur. The key people in an acquired company might not want to be acquired and may feel rejected.

WINNERS AND LOSERS

The CEO's job is to prevent the rise of such feelings as "us versus them," "winners versus losers," "first-class versus second-class citizens." This is crucial in stopping the loss of good senior people. The best way to prevent the development of a winners-losers mentality is to be alert for any sign of it, and to eliminate it as quickly as possible.

But a company may invite such problems if senior managers redirect their attention after the acquisition is completed. The acquired company's employees are certain to feel doubly rejected if, after seeing the acquirer's CEO frequently during the negotiating period, they hardly ever see that person when the acquisition has been completed.

Although it is rare, one occasionally hears about a reverse situation in which the acquired company is glorified and the acquirer starts to feel like a loser. In such cases, sometimes the new company is given responsibilities it cannot handle. Sometimes its employees are given special perks or its methods are forced down the throats of old employees. Long-time employees may find this unbearable, and they rebel. In the end, a power struggle ensues that erodes morale and productivity.

WHY PEOPLE LEAVE

After almost every acquisition, people leave. Some get fed up after finding themselves at the low end of a winner-loser situation. Some, such as an engineer-entrepreneur made quite rich, would prefer to leave than to adapt to the corporate culture. And some, unfortunately, end up being purely redundant. They are reassigned or given incentives to leave. No one enjoys having to let staff go, but a CEO faced with this situation must be open and candid about it. If there is going to be any bad news, it should be made public quickly, rather than forcing those who will be affected to wait and fret.

A CEO courting a target company should tell that company's management about potential major changes before the deal is closed and money is exchanged.

THE WORST ENEMY

Change is the worst enemy in mergers and acquisitions because it erodes morale so badly. That is why it is important to delay change as long as possible in the acquisition of a company. And change costs money. If one or two operations are changed, it might not make much difference. But if an acquirer installs its own systems all at once, this can generate excessive costs.

Sometimes, of course, it is not possible to delay change. Clearly, the speed at which an acquisition is integrated varies according to two factors:

- *The condition of the company:* In a turnaround situation with a company that is in trouble, the acquirer must go in and do whatever is necessary, and do it quickly.
- *The price:* Sometimes the acquirer must get rid of unnecessary expenses—or staff—to justify the premium paid for the company.

In the absence of these two conditions, however, acquirers should go as slowly as possible, nurturing the company even if the technology is known and even if the acquirer could do everything the target is doing better and cheaper. Acquirers should ask whether the money saved is worth the damage that could be caused by switching the target's initiatives.

The goal of postmerger integration is a transformation, not a revolution. When changes must be made, the acquirer should follow established best practices in organizational change management. In fact, significant new approaches to change management are proving highly useful.

SYNERGY

In the world of mergers and acquisitions, one of the most over-worked—or most misunderstood—words is *synergy*. Reduced to its simplest equation, the idea of synergy is $1 + 1 = 3$. It means that the new combination is greater than the sum of its parts.

Yet that definition is too facile and may be deceptive. In a poorly conceived merger and its aftermath, a corporation might borrow heavily to buy a company, slam it together with its existing business, eliminate a lot of costs at the outset—and call that synergy.

Yet it is not. Over the short term, the reductions in overhead may look good. But the surviving corporation by then has exhausted its profit-producing and credit capabilities; it has nothing left to invest in the combined company. Over time, it is going to look pretty bad.

Synergy is an acquirer's capacity to use its significant strengths to improve the performance of an acquired company, or take one of the acquired company's strengths to counter a weakness of its own. Two strengths or two weaknesses combined do not make synergy. Synergy is much more than just eliminating some duplication at the outset. Synergy is taking a company that sells $50 million worth of its product a year in the United States, putting it through an acquirer's distribution system, and selling $100 million worth a year worldwide. Opportunities for synergy are most likely to be identified by studying the processes of both companies.

NO PANACEA

If recent history is a guide, a company that views acquisition as its core strategy or as a panacea will probably be disappointed in the end. One need only look at the conglomerates of the 1960s. Most deconglomerated in the 1970s and began "restructuring" in the 1980s. *Restructuring* is just a nice-sounding word for: "Let's write off all those mistakes we made in the last 10 or 20 years." With a little help from the tax code, companies that "restructure" can make their earnings look better and push up their stock price. Some companies talk about "rebenefiting the core." That means getting back to basics by disposing of bad acquisitions that do not help a company's primary industry.

Except in rare circumstances, a company's rule of thumb should be to acquire new companies only to supplement or complement its own basic industry. A second rule is: Stay involved in the postmerger integration.

CHAPTER **16**

CULTURE

Although it is clear that successful mergers and acquisitions must be based primarily on strategic, financial, and other objective criteria, ignoring a potential clash of cultures can lead to financial failure. Far too often, personnel and organizational issues are assigned a low priority during the preacquisition evaluation process. Other times they are an afterthought—only after the decision has been made that the acquisition is a good deal.

Many acquisitions that initially appear to be very promising from a number of viewpoints subsequently fail or require major surgery and extensive hand-holding as a result of neglect in evaluating critical personnel and organizational issues. One of the most celebrated examples is Exxon's ill-fated journey into business products through its acquisition of Vydec.

Exxon's large oil company culture conflicted with the sense of urgency and bias for action required for decision making in the more technological electronic business products market. As a former Vydec manager said, "They were oil men used to three- to five-year planning cycles. But we were frequently required to make a change because of something that had happened at two that afternoon."

There is increasing evidence that cultural incompatibility is the single largest cause of lack of projected performance, departure of key executives, and time-consuming conflicts in the consolidation of businesses.

UNDERSTANDING THE POWER OF THE INVISIBLE SIDE OF ORGANIZATIONS

Mergers and acquisitions currently constitute one of the primary strategies for growth of organizations. Successfully negotiated and then integrated, they can play a major role in the growth and success of organizations. Unfortunately, statistics indicate that up to one-third of all mergers fail within five years, and that as many as 80 percent never live up to full expectations. Many of these shortfalls are due to human factors, not to the quantitative analyses. As *Personnel Journal* noted (April 1992, p. 70), "Mergers and acquisitions have the potential to affect practically every aspect of an organization. Morale and productivity often suffer. Work processes and quality control may be thrown out the window. Group and inter-group relationships may be damaged."

It is interesting to note the parallel between the divorce rate in the United States (approximately 50 percent) and the fallout in mergers (virtually half). Because the human factor is so critical to success in both ventures, it is important to understand its role and to address it in each phase of the merger or acquisition process.

Over a period of time, organizations, like people, develop distinctive and unique personalities. In recent times, this personality of the organization has been referred to most often as "corporate culture." An individual's personality is made up of his or her beliefs, values, and behavioral traits. In like manner, a company's culture is made up of its value system, customs, and all of the unwritten rules that govern behavior within the organization.

Popular management books such as *In Search of Excellence* (Peters and Waterman), *Creating Excellence* (Hickman and Silva), and *Corporate Culture* (Kennedy and Deal) have highlighted the role of a healthy culture in the success of organizations and the implementation of their strategies. The term *culture clash* has been coined to describe a situation in which two company's philosophies, styles, values, and missions are in conflict. That may, in fact, be the most volatile factor when two companies decided to combine.

CHALLENGING COMBINATIONS
(DEADLY COMBINATIONS)

There are a number of constraining qualities in organizations which under normal circumstances may be a problem, but, predictably, are even more challenging when it comes to combining two entities that typify opposing styles. One set of typical contrasting qualities is shown in Figure 16-1.

A merger that experienced difficulty, which approximates Figure 16-1, is the Fluor Corporation's acquisition of St. Joe Minerals Corporation. Many of the problems in the acquisition of St. Joe by Fluor were due to differences in their organizational values. St. Joe was decentralized, lean on staff, frugal, informal, and run with a light hand. Fluor was highly centralized and had a large corporate staff, more reporting levels, and greater controls on decision making. In contrast to St. Joe's frugality, Fluor had planes and helicopters for its large central staff.

Although other business challenges certainly existed, it is interesting to note that none of the senior St. Joe managers who went to Fluor stayed on, and of the 22 senior officers in St. Joe at the time of acquisition, only a few remain today.

There are a large number of potential conflicting culture qualities; some of the classic features are outlined in Figure 16-2.

Cross-industry mergers and acquisitions often yield conflicting cultures. Mobil's management of Montgomery Ward is a challenging

FIGURE 16-1 Contrasting styles

Style A	Style B
Highly participative	Hierarchical
Nondirective	Directive
Informal	Formal
Decentralized	Centralized

FIGURE 16-2   Conflicting cultural qualities

Seniority-based compensation and promotion	vs.	Performance-based compensation and promotion
Conservative, risk averse	vs.	Innovative, risk taking
Cost and control driven	vs.	Service and quality driven
Long-range planning and deliberate decision making	vs.	Opportunistic, rapid decision making
Analytical, cautious	vs.	Intuitive, daring
Autocratic	vs.	Participative

enterprise because of the differences between a long-term exploration mind-set and a short-term retailing one. (What will be the level of oil reserves in the year 2000? versus today?)

When there is a fit in strategies and cultures, the probability of success is dramatically improved. Nabisco and Standard Brands represent a compatible marriage of complementary products and distribution systems. There was an orderly period during which two management groups were integrated. The two presidents did not talk only about undervalued assets and discounted cash flow. Instead, they discussed business philosophy, the similarity of their customers, and their plans for teamwork and mutual support.

HUMAN PROBLEMS TO BE AVOIDED IN ACQUISITIONS

Loss of Key People

When acquiring an organization, it is important to remember that "the natives have the maps." Even if a company ultimately wants to trim some dead wood, if this is not handled correctly, the wrong people will leave and the venture may be jeopardized. A number of studies document the high rate of exit from acquired firms. A survey in *Mergers and Acquisitions* magazine indicated that only 42 percent of managers remained with an acquired firm for as long as five years.

Uncertainty and insecurity are associated with almost all mergers or acquisitions. When a merger is announced, fears and anxieties are fueled by uncertainty about what the changes will bring. There is typically a feeling of personal vulnerability and loss of control. In beginning to explore their options, people often spend time updating their resumes.

It is essential to identify those people who are critical to the continued success of the acquired company and to put into motion a plan to ensure that these key people do not leave.

Loss of Organizational Effectiveness

The uncertainty associated with the change often leads employees to experience a loss of enthusiasm about their work and their organization. A decrease in morale and organizational pride is also common. Countless hours are spent in feeding the rumor mill, and large numbers of people adopt a "wait and see" attitude.

The sooner some semblance of certainty about the future can be communicated, the sooner people will settle down. Once a new vision for the organization is created and new future targets are set, people can refocus their energy in a forward direction.

INSECURITY IS THE ENEMY

Causes of Loss of People and Effectiveness

A spy was once caught in the Middle East. He was brought before the commandant who said to him, "You know, of course, that the penalty for spying is death by firing squad." The spy asked the commandant whether he had any choices in the matter or whether there was anything that he could say in his own behalf. The commandant replied, "Yes, you do have a choice. You can either be shot by the firing squad at dawn, or you can go through that door," he said, pointing to a large and ominous black door in the far corner of the room.

The spy asked what was behind the black door. The commandant answered, "That's for us to know. You decide: is it the black door, or the firing squad?" The spy requested time to come to a decision and was told that he had until dawn. One can only imagine what he thought as he paced in his small cell throughout the night. It is likely that most of his thoughts were focused on the question, "What could possibly be so horrible behind the black door that they would give me a choice?"

In the morning he was brought before the commandant and asked for his decision. "Shoot me," he said. "At least I know what that is." After the spy was shot a Red Cross observer who was present asked the commandant, "What was behind that black door?" The commandant replied, "Freedom."

During the acquisition process it is virtually impossible to overcommunicate. Anything that can be communicated should be communicated, because people find it easier to face the known than the unknown.

Harry Levinson, a psychologist and professor at Harvard, stresses the psychological consequences of the merger experience. He states that even when a merger offers new opportunities, it still tends to be perceived as a threat to one's equilibrium. Whether a merger is for the better or for the worse, it disrupts relationships, norms, work behavior, and support systems. If the psychological losses of employees are not addressed early in the process, they may lead to chronic problems in attitude and behavior.

One of the issues to address as early as possible is the new organizational structure. Failed mergers are characterized by a tendency to have unclear reporting relationships and frequent changes in the reporting structure. "The successful merger or acquisition of the 1990s may be less a result of financial manipulation and more dependent on what happens within the workforce after the papers are signed. Regardless of the specific type of deal, change in ownership is unsettling to many employees simply because it is change. The challenge is to persuade employees that the new ownership has business objectives they can understand and support. Three distinct elements need to be addressed: (1) emotion; (2) information; and (3) action" (*Executive Briefing* Feb. 1991).

WINNER VS. LOSERS—US VS. THEM

When companies are acquired or combined, their staffs almost immediately begin to focus on the differences between the companies.

It is typical in an acquisition for the staff of the acquiring company to see themselves as the winners and those of the acquired company as the losers. Typically, the controlling company wants to impose changes, and it sees the acquired company as highly resistant to change.

On the other hand, the most frequent complaint of companies that are being acquired is that the new owners "don't appreciate us." People immediately begin to keep score, tallying which side won or lost on each issue.

In such situations, it is critical for the acquirer to go out of its way to acknowledge as many positive aspects of the acquired firm as possible, and at the same time to create an environment in which there is a high level of openness to change.

It is, in fact, important to identify which cultural factors have historically made an organization great in order to avoid "throwing out the baby with the bath water." For example, if a company's historical success was based on its culture of service and quality, rapid and insensitive cost cutting could begin to destroy what made it great.

In like manner, the acquisition of a small, highly entrepreneurial firm by a larger, more formalized one poses cultural challenges. It is often important to provide direction and additional structure. However, this must be done without killing the entrepreneurial goose that lays the golden eggs.

One of the difficulties in meshing two organizations is that each group tends to see the world through its own biased cultural filter. This is often referred to as "familiarity blindness" or as a "cultural trance." For example, if everyone in a person's circle seems averse to risk, then it will seem to that person that the world is that way—and should be.

This phenomenon may be partially explained by the classic psychological example in the picture shown on the following page.

When a person looks at the picture, what does he or she see? Is it an old woman or a young woman? Upon first seeing it, the odds are that a person will see one or the other. The fact is that both are there but, typically, if the viewer has locked in one image, the other will be difficult to discern.

That is often the case when two organizations combine. They each look at the same events, the same decisions, the same situations—but colored by their culture and past experiences. And they legitimately do see things from two different points of view.

Learning mutual respect and being open to exploring different points of view are two of the keys to the human factor in any merger or acquisition.

VARIATIONS IN THE NATURE OF MERGERS AND ACQUISITIONS

The specific steps needed to deal with the human side of a merger or acquisition are greatly influenced by the basis for the merger, as well as by the cultures of the firms. For example, when an acquiring company in a merger is interested only in the physical and financial assets of a target company and expects to lay off most managers and employees, major efforts to manage culture are unnecessary. However, when a true marriage of two firms is the final goal, attention to the management of culture becomes critical, and detailed planning is required. The varying goals for merger outcomes in their three most common forms are discussed below.

Autonomy or Semiautonomy

In a hands-off scenario, the goal is to create mutual support and synergy without necessarily changing the nature of the organizations. It is unrealistic to assume that the acquiring company will not want some modifications. For example, it might want some shift in one or more qualities, such as innovation, bias for action, and a higher level of expectations. However, when the basis for the acquisition is autonomy or semiautonomy, it is important to respect the reasons for the differences in culture and to proceed slowly in any transformational activities.

The result of such a shift is shown in Figure 16-4.

Absorb and Assimilate

If the goal is to completely absorb and assimilate the acquired firm, then the primary need is to educate the acquired employees about the rules in their new organization. It should be remembered that they have been playing a different game under a different set of unwritten and written ground rules. Orientation to the new organization should include informing employees about the vision and

FIGURE 16-4   Merger outcome: autonomy or semi-autonomy

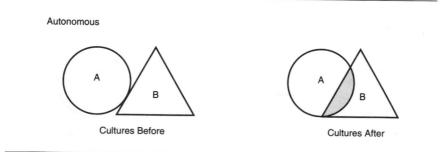

values of the organization as they were determined during the preacquisition process.

Cocreate a New Entity

When a true marriage of two firms takes place, there should be significant effort in the area of cultural integration.

In such cases, a joint integration team should decide on the new vision and mission for the combined organization. In addition, they should adopt a new set of shared values. Thus, neither of the old ways is determined to be right or wrong; instead, all staff members move toward a joint definition of the new culture. Merger outcomes are illustrated in Figures 16-5 and 16-6.

MANAGING THE HUMAN SIDE OF MERGERS AND ACQUISITIONS

A specific plan should be developed and implemented for merging cultures, as well as for merging operations and finances. This process can be broken down into the pre-acquisition phase, the due diligence and negotiation phase, and the postacquisition phase.

Pre-acquisition

The guiding principle during pre-acquisition or merger is "Know thyself." This may be implemented through an instrument known as a cultural profile. Both computerized and manual versions exist.

FIGURE 16-5   Merger outcome: absorption and assimilation

Absorb

Cultures Before

Cultures After

FIGURE 16-6 Merger outcome: cocreation of a new family

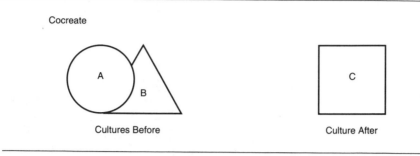

Cocreate

Cultures Before | Culture After

One sample of a straightforward manual that is easy to administer is shown in Figure 16-7.

Cultural Profile

A cross-section of the management team is asked to rate the organization on a series of cultural traits. In the example shown, the organization received high marks in terms of high standards and expectations, a healthy pace, and a sense of urgency.

Cultural barriers may be evidenced by too many excuses and blaming others (lack of personal accountability), too much focus on "my area" (lack of teamwork), lack of clarity about goals and direction, and finally, lack of a customer-centered focus.

There are also some organizational characteristics and support systems that differ from company to company. These characteristics and systems may be evaluated in a manner similar to that used for the corporate culture profile. In Figure 16-8, two companies (Company A and Company B), which in general represent the extremes in the list of characteristics, are profiled.

Organization Characteristics and Support Systems Scale

Once an organization has greater awareness of its own cultural strengths and weaknesses, as well as its organizational characteristics, it can use that information to begin to reshape a healthier culture to support acquisition and added internal success. Armed with that knowledge, it can begin to create a profile of appropriate

FIGURE 16-7 Cultural profile—strengths and weaknesses: board respondents' statistical summary

Always / Mostly / Occasionally / Sometimes Both / Occasionally / Mostly / Always	
7 6 5 4 3 2 1	

Left labels:
- Clear Alignment and Common Focus of Leadership at Top
- Clear Goals and Direction (Common Vision)
- Two-Way Frequent Open Communications
- High Trust/Openness Between People
- Teamwork/Mutual Support and Cooperation
- People Assume Accountability for Their Results
- Self-Starters/High Initiative
- High Performance Expectations
- People Feel Appreciated and Valued
- High Levels of Feedback on Job Performance
- High Performance Is Recognized and Rewarded
- Open to Change
- Encouraged to Innovate/Creativity Welcomed
- Healthy/Fast-Paced Environment
- Sense of Urgency/Bias for Action
- High Quality/Service Awareness and Focus
- High Cost Consciousness and Drive to Be Cost Competitive
- High Pride—Feel Like Winners

Right labels:
- Obvious Lack of Alignment at the Top
- Unclear Goals and Direction (Confusion)
- Top-Down Inadequate Communications
- Low Trust/Highly Political
- Narrow Focus/My Area Only/High Internal Competition
- Find Excuses/Blame Others/Feel Victimized
- Need Direction/Low Initiative
- Low or No Performance Expectations
- People Don't Feel Appreciated and Valued
- Infrequent or No Feedback on Job Performance
- High Performance Is Always "Expected" But Not Recognized
- Resistant to Change
- Do What Is Told/Don't Rock Boat/Poor Support for New Ideas
- High Stress/Burnout Pace
- Indecisive/Bureaucratic/Slow to Respond
- Quality and Customer Service Not a Priority
- Low Expense Consciousness—Don't Treat Money Like Their Own
- Don't Feel Like Winners

FIGURE 16-8   Cultural profile: Company A versus Company B

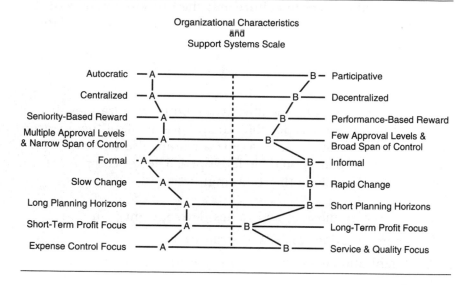

Organizational Characteristics
and
Support Systems Scale

Autocratic	Participative
Centralized	Decentralized
Seniority-Based Reward	Performance-Based Reward
Multiple Approval Levels & Narrow Span of Control	Few Approval Levels & Broad Span of Control
Formal	Informal
Slow Change	Rapid Change
Long Planning Horizons	Short Planning Horizons
Short-Term Profit Focus	Long-Term Profit Focus
Expense Control Focus	Service & Quality Focus

cultures for acquisition. These may be similar to its own culture or deliberately different, to support new strategic directions.

The Due Diligence Process

The analysis of mergers and acquisitions during due diligence understandably focuses on financial information. An internal resource specialist or outside consultant should also assist in the human aspects of the due diligence process. This includes the following tasks:

1. Develop a profile of the culture of the acquisition candidate, noting similarities and differences.

2. Determine similarities and differences in the internal reinforcement systems, including:
- compensation/benefit systems
- performance review systems
- performance criteria (written and unwritten)
- hiring and firing criteria and practices

3. Compare philosophies of the corporate leaders, especially if they are both staying on.

4. Openly discuss not only financial considerations, but the similarities and differences in culture and the proposed nature of the cultural integration, that is, autonomous organizations, assimilation, or creation of a new entity.

Postacquisition

An integration team with members from both organizations should be established as soon as possible. In addition to all of the financial and physical integration plans, a separate human resources and cultural integration plan should be developed. The key components of this plan should include the following:

1. New vision, mission, and values development plan
2. Communications plans and strategies
3. Organizational structure and reporting relationships
4. Personnel plan, including:
   • benefit packages
   • compensation packages
   • policy and procedure packages

POSTACQUISITION IMPLEMENTATION

Communications

Most people understand that mergers or acquisitions take place for business reasons. It is important at the outset to communicate the benefits of a merger. People may not like it, but if they see that it has a legitimate purpose and that the benefits are obvious, they are less resentful and more likely to accept the combination.

When one company is acquiring another, it is important for the new dominant firm's leaders to communicate in person as much as possible. It is easier to be resentful toward an unknown, invisible ogre than toward a real, rational, and concerned human being with whom one has had personal contact. Successful mergers happen only when high-level managers make themselves visible and accessible to all employees affected by the merger and when they promote the benefits at all levels.

Written communications and group meetings should be offered as frequently as possible and should communicate as much information as can be made available. This is a good way to minimize the impact of rumors and speculation, which can have a paralyzing effect on an organization.

Vision, Mission, and Shared Values

During a merger or acquisition, people need to be inspired to move toward new goals and visions. Without knowledge of a compelling purpose for the new organization, people tend to stay locked in the past and in speculation. In a true merger that is designed to create a new combined entity, the senior teams of each organization must work together to clarify the new organizational mission, shared values, and managerial game rules by which they are all going to play. The relationships between vision, strategies, and values are shown in Figure 16-9 along with one organization's stated set of shared values.

Typically, this process is best handled with assistance from outside facilitators. It is useful to create a common, shared, off-site experience for the new team to facilitate the consolidation process.

Organizational Structure

The greatest amount of speculation often surrounds the reporting relationships in organizational structures. The sooner these relationships are finalized and begin to function, the sooner uncertainty and speculation will end. Although they must be established quickly, it is important that reporting relationships are given enough thought so that short-term revisions are held to a minimum, as they merely reignite the fire of speculation and uncertainty.

Compensation and Benefits

When it comes to sensitive issues, at the top of the list is overall compensation. In the minds of individuals, the level of their compensation communicates a great deal regarding their relative worth, perceived value, and overall status within the company.

FIGURE 16-9   How vision, strategies, and values relate

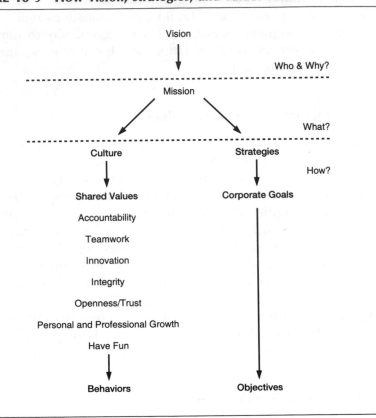

The more autonomous the combining companies are, the less urgency there is to match compensation packages. However, when companies are assimilated or truly merged, nothing will create more resistance and resentment than differentials in pay and benefits. Assuming that the salaries of the "better-paid" employees are in line with industry standards, a plan to move toward equalizing salary grades should be implemented over time.

THE EMOTIONAL CYCLE OF CHANGE

The integration process should be entered into realistically and with full knowledge of the potential obstacles that may be encountered. Most acquisitions considered to be successful follow a pattern that

FIGURE 16-10 The emotional cycle of change

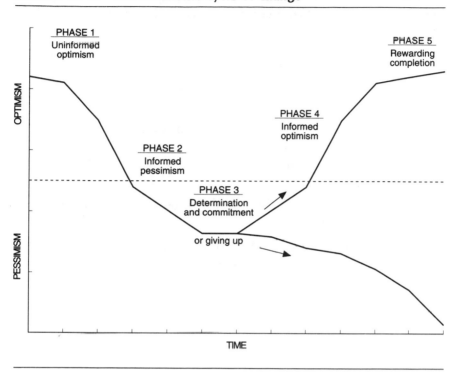

has been described as the "emotional cycle of change." Figure 16-10 illustrates this phenomenon.

Phase 1 is *uninformed optimism*, when people are excited about the new venture and have not yet faced its challenges and complications. Phase 2 is *informed pessimism*, when all of the issues, rumors, and disruptions are faced.

Phase 2 may take one of two courses. Without a systematic plan, pessimism may become reality and may also be long lasting. However, with a plan in place and with continued commitment, the tide will begin to turn. Then, the final phase will be success and *realistic optimism*, as the planned benefits begin to be realized.

BENEFITS OF A SYSTEMATIC INTEGRATION PROCESS

Using the ideas and tools described in this chapter can dramatically increase the probability of success in any organizational integration.

Following are some of the many benefits that may result from dealing systematically with the cultural aspects of mergers:

1. Staff members know how to operate effectively and more quickly in their new or newly revised organization.

2. There is a sense of community, because shared values link individuals to the organization and bind the staff together.

3. The process of creating a vision, mission, and shared values inspires excitement, inspiration, and commitment, with the entire staff working toward a new future goal as opposed to living in the past.

4. There are fewer defections in the organization, and the impact on morale is lessened.

5. There is improved productivity and profitability for the organization in a shorter period of time.

CHAPTER 17

EMPLOYEE COMPENSATION AND BENEFITS

Employee compensation and benefit plans are key components of any acquisition strategy. Their impact has become so great that they may actually dictate the structure of an acquisition. And in some instances, their unfunded or unreported liabilities have led to canceled transactions.

In recent years, the impact of employee compensation and benefit plans on acquisitions has increased significantly. This is due to a labyrinth of legislation governing their design, administration, funding, and accounting. The larger role of the Financial Accounting Standards Board (FASB), the effects of constant new legislation, and the influence of the courts all serve to restrict an employer's freedom of choice and its ability to control benefits and compensation costs. The incessant escalation in medical claim costs and the inherent risks associated with the investments that fund the pension liabilities combine with these factors to constitute one of management's most complicated, yet essential, issues when integrating two disparate companies joined as a result of an acquisition or merger.

Under ideal circumstances, it is desirable to begin the analysis of compensation and benefit issues in the acquisition process—possibly even before an acquisition candidate has been selected. More often than not, however, the choice of an acquisition/merger candidate is based on other criteria, and benefit and compensation issues are identified only during the due diligence process.

It is generally during the due diligence phase that benefits and compensation issues are first raised, and it is during this stage that potential courses of action should be contemplated. Disclosure of unreported or misreported liabilities and identification of dissimilar benefit and compensation programs should alert management as to potential costs (or savings) that various courses of action would have after the merger. Clearly, the results of this initial groundwork should be taken into account when designing the approach to integrating the companies.

DECIDING TO INTEGRATE PLANS

The decision on whether to integrate benefit and compensation plans of the acquired/merged companies depends on several factors:

- The purpose of the acquisition or merger
- The locations and/or businesses of the two entities
- Corporate philosophy and objectives
- Other influences (e.g., labor contracts, etc.)
- Cost considerations

Purpose of Acquisition/Merger

If the purpose of an acquisition/merger was to leverage the two companies' strengths, it could imply a complete integration of one company into the other and/or the creation of a new, single entity. This would lead to the conclusion that one set of benefit plans covering all employees would be desirable.

On the other hand, if the objective of the acquisition/merger was to gain control of an entity, spin off any unwanted subsidiaries, and then merge the remaining companies, it would probably make sense to maintain separate programs for a period of time.

Location and Business Considerations

If the acquired/merged companies are in totally separate locations and it is anticipated that such locations will remain totally separate, it could be argued that the benefit and compensation plans for each location should remain as they are for competitive reasons.

Even when the companies have the same location, if they represent totally separate lines of business it may make sense to maintain the plans separately so as not to change the competitive posture of the total compensation schemes for each entity.

Corporate Philosophy and Objectives

If the corporate philosophy is to let each company within the corporation have control of its bottom line, it may make sense to allow each individual company to maintain design control over its compensation and benefit plans.

On the other hand, if the acquired/merged companies are to be folded into one company and identification with, and loyalty to, that new organization is a major corporate objective, then having one plan reinforces that objective.

Outside Influences

The decision to integrate plans can be affected by other influences, such as existing labor agreements, potential labor organizing movements, composition of employee groups, and unique programs that cannot be easily modified or eliminated.

Existing labor agreements require reopening collective bargaining talks if benefits or compensation plans covering such employees are to be changed. This is generally an undesirable result and, for at least the covered employees, any changes should wait until the end of the existing bargaining agreement. If one of the companies is the target of a labor movement, any change in benefit or compensation programs that could be construed as a decrease in benefits could lend viability to the labor movement.

If one of the companies has an employee group that has noticeably different age and/or sex characteristics than the other group, implementation of a uniform benefit program could have significant adverse effects on certain benefit costs.

Cost Considerations

Maintaining only one employee benefit program is generally most efficient and should cut administration costs. Legally required changes are then required for only one plan, and communications with employees are simplified and more efficient. In addition, staffing needs can be minimized and, over time, the use of outside consultants such as actuaries and lawyers reduced.

Moreover, merging two entities into one plan can have the effect of increasing the predictability of claims and fostering movement into a self-administered claims environment for health insurance coverage, with its inherent administrative savings.

The Integration Process

Once it is decided to integrate the acquired/merged companies, careful consideration of the compensation and benefit issues is important. The timing of any compensation and benefit change is likely to be dictated by the circumstances surrounding the acquisition, as well as by the purchaser's objectives. Changes coincident with the acquisition may be achieved if the acquirer assumes legal and compliance obligations. Such changes are often made to reinforce a management objective, such as bringing everyone onto the same team from day one, or to reinforce control by emphasizing clearly who bought whom.

Delayed timing is better at meeting some objectives. The process of finding and negotiating the acquisition may not always permit adequate analyses by compensation and benefit planners. A delay in implementing changes could result in a more appropriate plan for the organization and could reinforce the message that employees need not fear rapid organizational change.

Delayed timing may also be appropriate if pending legislation is expected to affect the design of the compensation and benefit plan. If the outcome of pending legislation is unclear, it may be prudent to postpone making any changes until such time as they may be properly integrated and made to conform to the requirements of the new law. Pending legislation also has an impact on the establishment of the objectives for benefit plan treatment.

ANALYZING COMPENSATION AND BENEFIT PLAN VARIABLES

Each plan within the total compensation and benefit program of the acquired/merged company needs to be reviewed to determine its impact, not only individually, but also in terms of the outcome when it is combined with other plans. The effects of acquisition-related changes on each plan vary considerably in complexity. The effects of changes in salaries and wages are relatively straightforward, whereas changes in pensions have highly complex ramifications. The most seemingly insignificant details can have staggering financial impacts. For example, in an acquisition involving a multi-employer pension plan, the cost of withdrawing from that plan after an acquisition could amount to as much as $10,000 per employee.

A number of variables must be considered when integrating the compensation and benefit plans of the merged companies. Among these are the following:

Compensation:

• Salaries and wages

• Annual incentive and employee bonus awards

• Long-term incentive and stock awards

• Employment contracts

• Perquisites

Benefits:

• Retirement plans

• Health care plans

• Other welfare plans

• Labor agreements

Salaries and Wages

The key comparison is between the acquired company's salaries and wages and those of the acquirer, as well as of other employers in the acquisition's industry and geographical location. It is not always practical to review the salaries for each position. Instead, the acquirer may decide to compare pay scales for benchmark jobs at the acquired company with those of the purchaser and competitors; this approach usually provides a reliable indicator of relative cash-compensation ranking.

In addition to analyzing the level of salaries and wages, management should also note the number of employees of the merged group. Severance pay rising from reduction-in-force programs initiated after the integration may be a hidden cost. Alternatively, necessary staff additions may lower profit expectations.

Annual Incentive and Employee Bonus Awards

A review of the acquired company's executive incentive and employee profit-sharing or bonus programs (including recent payout history) will indicate whether they are consistent with the purchaser's philosophy in terms of participation, award size, performance measures, and formula for payment. To the extent that they are not in accord with the purchaser's philosophy or objectives, the purchaser needs to balance the potential for morale and turnover problems if a change is made against the need to conform to the purchaser's philosophy. In addition, any potential negative impact on productivity or financial results must be considered. If facility relocation or downsizing is planned, termination costs should be calculated, including "stay-on" bonuses to help retain key employees during transitional periods.

Long-Term Incentive and Stock Awards

It is usually more difficult to integrate long-term incentive awards into a purchaser's program. If, for example, the acquired company's stock is involved, how will the reward opportunities be continued if the acquired company's stock ceases to exist after the acquisition? If immediate vesting and payouts are triggered by so-called golden parachutes, this may materially impact acquisition costs and add to the complexities of structuring replacement programs. The transaction might also trigger adverse personal income tax treatment for U.S. or overseas executives, possibly requiring "tax offset" relief. In addition, the acquisition is likely to take place during one or more of the performance-measurement periods. The procedure for measuring performance and providing for pro rata payments needs to be resolved. Finally, it should be recognized that the long-term plan will become the key retention tool for executives, if properly structured.

Employment Contracts

Executive contracts should be reviewed, particularly if they take the form of golden parachutes, which provide compensation under certain conditions resulting from a change in control. If the contract makes it easy for an executive to claim a diminished position, and if the size of the payments under the contract are significant, the purchaser may be faced with hiring an entirely new management team. The situation can be exacerbated if the contracts remain in place after the acquisition. In that case, not only is the acquirer faced with losing the management team, but it must also pay the cost of the contracts—which can be as high as three years' total compensation per executive.

Perquisites

By any objective standard, perquisites are not as important an issue as most other compensation and benefit items. In the United States perks tend to account for about 3 to 5 percent of an executive's total compensation package. Yet removing perquisites can have an impact on morale disproportionate to their real economic value. Conversely, maintaining a rich perquisite package at the acquired company while the acquirer's executives have a more modest package can be equally disruptive.

Outside the United States, perquisites are typically much more significant and are provided to a large number of executives as a tax-effective way to deliver compensation value.

Retirement Plans

Determining the optimum treatment of retirement plans is likely to be the most complex of all compensation and benefit issues. The administration of qualified retirement plans is guided by many tax and labor laws, as well as by numerous accounting guidelines. Such plans typically involve the investment of funds in significant amounts, sometimes amounting to more than the net worth of the sponsoring employer.

There are two kinds of retirement plans: defined benefit and defined contribution. A defined benefit plan is one in which the ultimate amount to be received at retirement is defined by the plan formula; for example, 1 percent of final average pay multiplied by years of service, payable for life. The employer must contribute whatever it takes to fund such a benefit promise. Defined contribution plans fix the employer's contribution to the plan by means of a formula; for example, 10 percent of net income or fifty cents for every dollar contributed by the employee. The ultimate retirement benefit varies, depending on the amount contributed and the investment earnings on all contributions.

Defined Benefit Plans.   If the potential acquisition maintains a defined benefit plan, the purchaser needs to determine whether the plan or the portion of the plan to be received is partially funded, fully funded, or even overfunded. Are the assets of the plan less than, equal to, or in excess of the present value of accrued or projected retirement benefits? In most cases, an actuary using the latest actuarial report and asset statement can estimate whether the plan is an asset or a liability.

One of the most difficult challenges in evaluating the compensation and benefit plan of an acquired company is to determine the financial status of its defined benefit retirement plan. The issue is complicated because the retirement-benefit promise is not only expressed in terms of years of service, but also frequently based on salaries at some future date of retirement, death, disability, or termination. Thus, the benefits earned by employees up to the date of acquisition, in the absence of any plan changes, will continue to grow with future pay increases. If the plan is continued unchanged after the acquisition, the buyer funds the growth. It is important to recognize that the growth of benefits in such plans is leveraged; that is, increases in pay apply equally to all years of service, including those years prior to the acquisition/merger. This leveraging effect must be considered in any decision on whether to continue the plan unchanged or to modify or even terminate the plan.

If the plan is terminated, future pay changes will not affect the actual retirement benefits, but employees may expect to see some growth in benefits. The resulting situation is that the buyer needs to determine the adequacy of plan assets in relation to the liabilities of the plan, both on a termination basis (to assure that no additional money needs to be added if the plan is terminated), and on an ongoing basis (to reflect the impact of future pay changes). The buyer's anticipated action on terminating versus continuing the plan unchanged is likely to determine which measure of the plan's financial status deserves primary attention.

Defined benefit plans may be significantly underfunded or overfunded. Accordingly, funding status could have a major impact on the purchase price of the business. Therefore, the adequacy of the defined benefit plan's funding should be determined during the due diligence phase of the acquisition/merger.

It is also important to recognize that the plan's liabilities are determined by calculations made by the actuary, based on assumptions regarding future interest rates, mortality rates, turnover rates, disability rates, retirement ages, and marital status, as well as assumptions regarding future increases in pay and Social Security benefits. An analysis of the assumptions used, and even the methods chosen, to determine costs is necessary for proper evaluation of the "true" funding status of the plan.

Some other factors the purchaser needs to consider so that decisions can be made on adopting, modifying, merging, or terminating a defined benefit plan after an acquisition include the following:

- The plan must be in compliance with current legislation. If it is not, additional, unrecorded liabilities may exist. Furthermore, any recent changes in the plan are often submitted for approval to the appropriate government agencies. Evidence of approval—an IRS qualification letter, current plan documents, and recent annual report filings—must be reviewed. Finally, any pending legal actions against the plan must be disclosed.

- In determining whether a given plan is in compliance with the applicable nondiscrimination sections of the tax code, it is important to recognize that proof of nondiscrimination can be substantially affected by the acquisition itself. There are strict rules governing a controlled group of companies that can change the way the various tests are performed. It may make sense to terminate the plan prior to the acquisition to avoid such problems posed by the rules for controlled groups.

- The method of distribution of any excess assets should be identified if an overfunded plan is terminated. The plan must state whether the excess assets are for the benefit of the participants or whether they revert to the company. The plan may also have a "pension parachute" clause that in the event of a takeover requires any excess assets to be allocated to the plan's participants.

- The responsibility for continuing benefits for former employees must be addressed, and funds allocated accordingly.

- The nature of the plan's assets can change the "real" funded status of the plan. If the potential acquisition's stock is among the plan's assets, the disposition of shares and value may have to be determined. Unrealistic values for assets may be on the books; these include nonliquid insurance contracts, bonds carried at book value or real estate owned by the plan, with carrying values above current market value.

- Commitments to continue the plan made in employee communications may create unexpected liabilities that have not been valued as a part of the normal actuarial process. All current communications related to the plan should be reviewed.

- Many companies offer Supplemental Executive Retirement Plans (SERPs) for their senior executives. These plans often provide substantial additional pensions over and above the company's qualified defined benefit plan, and are increasingly "secured" through vehicles such as "Rabbi Trusts." In many cases such plans provide for an acceleration of vesting and/or earlier receipt of benefits if termination occurs after a change in control. Although companies are required to disclose the liabilities under such plans, these liabilities are usually calculated on an ongoing basis, that is, do not reflect trigger events such as a change in control. The increased liabilities for such a clause can be significant, particularly if a number of executives are involved.

In reviewing plans for companies outside the United States the same issues arise, although the specific approaches may be different. Funding requirements, for example, are very different from country to country. In Japan and Germany there may be no outside assets to cover benefit liabilities. In Belgium and the Netherlands insured, deferred annuity contracts may not be adequate—by U.S. standards—to meet accrued benefit liabilities. In Italy and some Latin American countries there may be no pension plans at all, but these countries do have statutory severance indemnities payable upon any termination, including retirement. Such liabilities could be significant, and not supported by outside assets. The prudent buyer should investigate carefully those acquisition situations in which unfunded liabilities could be relevant in the future.

Defined Contribution Plans. Savings, profit sharing—including 401(k) plans—and other defined contribution plans normally do not have the same potential liability problems as defined benefit pension plans. The benefit derived from a defined contribution plan is generally limited to the assets available at retirement or termination and, therefore, no unfunded benefits or significant excess funds will result. However, other issues do have to be reviewed during the integration process.

The plan's investments may require change, even if the buyer decides to retain the plan in its current form. For example, if the acquired company's stock is involved in the plan, the buyer should be aware that this stock may not exist in the future. In addition, some investments such as guaranteed investment contracts may not be transferable to a new buyer, particularly if the newly acquired operation was a division of a large company that had master contracts with the Guaranteed Investment Contract (GIC) insurer.

Other Considerations. Beyond considering factors related to the defined benefit plan and the defined contribution plan individually, the buyer needs to review the total benefits provided by the retirement program. Many companies maintain both types of plans, with the pension plan providing the basic benefit and the defined contribution plan serving as a supplement. The total amount of protected retirement income provided by the acquired company's plans may be inconsistent with the buyer's objectives. Moreover, the mix of defined benefit and defined contribution plans may be inconsistent with the buyer's ideal mix. It may also be that neither the buyer's nor the acquired company's plans meet the target retirement income level. In this case an acquisition may provide a unique opportunity to address the weaknesses in both the buyer's and the target's programs by instituting a new retirement program for the newly combined corporation that more closely meets the corporate objectives.

Health Care Plans

For employees whose company has been acquired, one of the most often affected areas of benefits is health care. Health care plans are highly visible, and employees react strongly to any tampering with the benefit levels. And at many companies medical plans represent the largest single employee-benefit cost. Therefore, the basis for the potential acquisition's provision of health care becomes critical to the acquisition decision.

A comparison of the acquired company's medical plan with the purchaser's objectives in such basic areas as cost sharing with employees (copayments, deductibles, and employee-paid contributions) and postretirement health coverage is appropriate. These are areas in which most companies have entrenched, well-defined philosophies, and in an acquisition these philosophies may clash. Where they do conflict, both the cultural and cost issues must be addressed and communicated.

Although some variations may be permitted, the major features must usually conform to a predetermined set of guidelines. In addition, postacquisition discrimination tests must be applied to ensure continued compliance with applicable legislation.

A major area of potential liability is health care for retirees. By now most companies that have plans covering retirees have recognized their liability on the books through application of FAS 106, the new GAAP accounting standard. The magnitude of such recognition in many cases is substantial and has a material effect on the affected companies' earnings.

There are, however, a number of companies who do not realize that they have an FAS 106 liability because they do not provide benefits after eligibility for Medicare. Often these companies provide for continued medical coverage after early retirement until individuals are eligible for Medicare. These liabilities must be recognized under FAS 106 and can be substantial, depending on the level of cost subsidy by the company. In integrating such a company into the purchaser's benefit programs, care must be taken not to inadvertently include such a benefit without adequate recognition of the FAS 106 liability. Even for those companies that recognize an FAS 106 liability for postretirement medical benefits, a careful analysis of the assumptions used for the determination of the liability is in order. For example, a buyer should be aware that a 1 percent increase in the projected medical inflation rate can result in increased liabilities of 15 percent or more.

Other Welfare Plans

Life insurance and disability plans are two other welfare benefits that require analysis to determine whether they match the buyer's objectives.

To a lesser extent, supplemental unemployment benefits, vacation and holiday pay, severance-pay plans, tuition reimbursement, and other more occasional benefits such as prepaid legal plans and child-care plans also require attention. Although the costs of these benefits are generally lower than the costs of retirement and medical plans, the benefits themselves may be equally important to employees who benefit from such programs.

Labor Agreements

Collectively bargained plans present a unique set of issues. Typically, the collective-bargaining agreement contains the obligation for a defined benefit plan and, in some cases, additional benefit promises. The additional promises may include full vesting or unreduced early retirement benefits in the event of a takeover or plant closing. Therefore, "successorship" of the plans may be determined by the buyer's successorship obligation to the union in general.

If the buyer purchases a company by acquiring stock, it assumes all of the acquisition's obligations, including any relevant collective-bargaining agreement. These obligations also include the provision of agreed-upon benefits and the assumption of the plan's assets.

Of particular importance is a company's participation in a multiemployer plan, sometimes called a Taft–Hartley plan. The potential liability for withdrawal from a multiemployer plan requires careful analysis prior to any decision that might lead to withdrawal at the time of or after the acquisition. When an employer ceases participation in such a plan, the requirement for additional contributions depends on whether the employer is assessed any withdrawal liability under the plan. Withdrawal liability provisions vary widely among plans. However, even under those plans with no withdrawal-liability provisions, the plan's board of trustees can change the benefit provision so that the liability for vested benefits exceeds the assets—which creates a withdrawal liability.

If the acquirer is purchasing assets, the multiemployer pension liabilities remain with the seller unless the acquirer voluntarily assumes them. Thus, the purchase of assets generally provides more freedom to negotiate appropriate treatment of defined benefit plans than does stock purchase.

A note of caution: Asset sales may trigger a withdrawal and result in a liability to the seller, unless specific conditions are satisfied.

COMMUNICATING ABOUT COMPENSATION AND BENEFIT ISSUES

Invariably, employees view a merger as something of a threat. A merger implies uncertainty, change, and a disruption of existing work patterns. Most people resist major organizational change, and executive and rank-and-file employees alike may become jittery and insecure. During the acquisition period, rumors and doubt infect employees' attitudes and may negatively affect company performance. It is a well-documented fact that many acquisitions functionally "fail" because some employees lose their career motivation or because some experienced managers feel compelled to leave the merged company.

As an acquisition approaches, the major concerns facing employees typically center on job security and career potential. The following are the most serious of these concerns:

- Will I still have a job here?
- Will I continue to serve in my present management role?
- How will the new owners view me and evaluate my performance?
- Will the current top management continue to influence and control my career?

And the $64,000 question:

- Will I be better or worse off?

Employees and managers often do not articulate these important concerns. Rather, such issues invariably emerge within the relative privacy of individual and small-group interviews, or are anonymously written as survey responses. Their concerns are not raised in open discussion with management because employees often feel that if they do admit to insecurity and doubt, management will perceive them as being negative or weak.

"Safer" questions about compensation and benefits tend to be raised as a way to mask larger, overriding personal concerns. It is therefore imperative that from the outset buyers assure employees that their benefit issues are receiving immediate attention and that they will not lose any benefits to which they are currently entitled. If it is determined that the companies will not integrate benefit and compensation plans in the short range, assurances should be given that existing benefit programs will continue pending any future integration of such plans.

PART VI

Cross-Border Transactions

INTRODUCTION

In recent years, United States companies have shown an increasing affinity for foreign, and particularly European acquisitions. In Chapter 18, Thomas J. Kichler cautions that when approaching an acquisition abroad, a U.S. investor must recognize the critical differences between foreign and domestic investments. Among the key areas which must be considered when dealing with foreign entities are corporate structure, regulations, taxation, and culture-based issues.

Two of the most important aspects of any acquisition are the determination of the value of the target company and the manner in which its acquisition is to be financed. Valuation and financing become even more significant issues when the proposed transaction involves a company based in a foreign country, where valuation conventions and the local financing environment may be vastly different from those found in the United States, presenting a plethora of risks and opportunities to the U.S. acquirer.

Elaborating on principles dealt with in a domestic context, in Chapter 19 Ian P. Wilson addresses the valuation and financing issues confronting an acquirer in a cross-border acquisition.

Cross-border transactions present an additional set of due diligence issues which do not occur when both parties are in the same country. When the companies are located in different countries, the political systems of both countries must be well researched and understood. In A. J. Matsuura's discourse (in Chapter 20) on due diligence in the cross-border context, he cautions that the acquirer and its advisers must have an intimate knowledge of the rules which govern the decisions before considering the essential business issues to be addressed.

A key issue in international tax planning is considering the multiple tax jurisdictions which become involved in a cross-border merger or acquisition. In Chapter 21, John S. Karls suggests that parties to a cross-border merger or acquisition retain the best international tax advisers available to ensure that their combined worldwide tax burden is minimized and deferred insofar as possible, and that opportunities for multiple tax benefits are seized.

In this book's final chapter, Eric R. Pelander points out that in the past five to ten years there has been an explosion in the number of joint ventures and other strategic alliances formed by U.S. companies. These alliances are becoming increasingly important to companies that are consolidating in order to remain competitive. CEOs recognize the utility of strategic alliances, which involve two or more companies that join together and pool risks, rewards, and resources to achieve specific but sometimes different strategic goals.

CHAPTER 18

THE ACQUISITION PROCESS

In recent years, U.S. companies have shown an increasing affinity for European acquisitions. According to *Acquisitions Monthly* (February 1993), U.S. acquisition activity in Europe increased 66 percent in 1992 from 1991, representing 222 acquisitions with reported prices of over $9 billion. And the trend shows no sign of abating.

The present growth in European acquisition activity by U.S. corporations can be attributed to several principal factors. First, the supply of acquisition candidates has been bolstered by the pool of aging proprietors of thousands of businesses—primarily in France and Germany—established after World War II. Many of these entrepreneurs have no obvious successors, and so choose to opt for a sale.

Second, the relaxing of investment and exchange controls by most European nations has acted as a catalyst to cross-border activity. Third, the formation of the European Community has encouraged many larger U.S. corporations to establish a market presence in one or more of the EC member countries. Fourth, global consolidation in several industries, notably electronics and telecommunications, food, transportation, and financial services, has led to a number of large strategic acquisitions by major U.S. corporations. And finally, fundamental changes in the political and economic structures of much of Eastern Europe have fueled acquisition activity in Germany and other access points to these emerging markets.

When approaching an acquisition abroad, a U.S. investor must recognize critical distinctions between foreign and domestic investments. To succeed, the U.S. buyer must adopt a transaction strategy that accommodates the needs of the seller as well.

The principal areas of difference, which are outlined below, include corporate structure and ownership, financial reporting, information availability and acquisition review, takeover regulations and consents, valuation conventions, taxation, and perhaps most significant, culture-based issues.

CORPORATE STRUCTURE AND OWNERSHIP

There are many different types of corporate entities throughout Europe. Notwithstanding the existence of numerous unlimited liability associations in France and Germany, the limited liability company is by far the most common form of European business entity. As in the United States, European countries differentiate between private and public limited liability companies. But unlike those in the United States, European firms do not define "public" as synonymous with "listed," and a significant number of public companies do not have stock exchange quotations. In most European countries, public and private corporations are differentiated on the basis of the number of employees and capital structures.

Two-tiered board structures, consisting of a supervisory board (appointed by the shareholders) and a management board (appointed by the supervisory board) are common in a number of countries including Germany, the Netherlands, and France. Under such organizational structures, employee representatives often play a significant role in the direction of a company.

In Germany, for instance, members of the management board of public and large private companies are appointed by the supervisory board for fixed terms. In addition, under the time-honored system of codetermination, half of the members of the supervisory board are appointed by employees. To avoid certain management and employee obligations, U.S. investors may seek to acquire only the assets of a target company. Under certain circumstances, however, the acquisition of most of a company's assets renders the buyer responsible for the work force.

Share ownership structures vary widely throughout Europe. The United Kingdom, like the United States, has broad public ownership and an active capital market. But for most of continental Europe's public markets, much of the ownership and control of large corporations is highly concentrated.

Stock Market Capitalizations (in billion $ U.S.) as of November 30, 1992
(Source: Morgan Stanley Capital International Perspective, Geneva)

United States	3,988.0
United Kingdom	876.9
Germany	331.5
France	327.5
Netherlands	128.7
Italy	126.7
Switzerland	184.2
Japan	2,335.3

Of Italy's top 200 listed companies, less than 5 percent have the majority of shares in public hands. In Germany, the nation's large banks control the votes for approximately 30 percent of listed shares. In Spain, three-quarters of all listed company voting rights are controlled by the country's major banks. French companies, through the separation of share ownership and control, are protected from the advances of unwanted bidders through a combination of cross-shareholdings and hard-core investors. The state government is the majority shareholder in many of the largest companies. Still, the vast majority of European companies are family-controlled concerns. As in the United States, transactions involving privately held companies must generally be friendly.

FINANCIAL REPORTING

Depending on their size, European companies are frequently required to file annual reports with state authorities. However, financial-reporting regulations vary significantly from country to country, and filed information may not be publicly available. EC nations are required to comply with the Fourth and Seventh Directives on Company Law, which standardize the formal presentation of company accounts but do not address accounting principles. Although all EC-quoted companies are required to file financial statements, the United States is the only country in which all companies are also required to have an annual audit.

Accounting treatments among EC countries are not consistent. In Germany and Italy, companies show a bias toward the strict application of rigid accounting rules. Thus, two companies with identical economic results could present financial results that vary widely, yet still comply with accepted accounting principles. In the United Kingdom as in the United States, emphasis is placed on reflecting a true and fair view of the commercial substance of a transaction. A commonly held view is that U.K. companies' profits are overstated, whereas German firms tend to understate their income. German long-form audit reports may also contain a great deal of information not found in U.S. companies' public filings.

Variations in accounting standards and reporting requirements have an impact on the acquisition process. Valuation analysis, based on financial information compiled with the use of different accounting policies, may require significant adjustments.

If the purchase price is adjusted for final balance sheet or income statement results, the buyer must ensure that accounting policies have been applied in a consistent manner. If a subsidiary is to be consolidated following an acquisition, it must be able to generate financial statements based on U.S. generally accepted accounting principles (GAAP).

INFORMATION AVAILABILITY AND ACQUISITION REVIEW

In addition to finding differences in financial-reporting standards, a U.S. acquirer embarking on an acquisition search will quickly discover that general business information available on acquisition targets varies significantly from country to country. For example, corporate data bases, a common source of company information in U.S. and U.K. acquisitions, are still in the process of being compiled in several European countries such as Italy and Spain.

Where a European company is being marketed actively, an information memorandum describing an acquisition candidate may not be available or may be less detailed than those customarily encountered in the United States. The increasing tendency for European companies to engage specialized professional advisers has led to the introduction of Anglo-American techniques in marketing a company. The general standards and comprehensiveness of information memorandums have been greatly improved.

Because of the inherent risks associated with buying a foreign company, the U.S. acquirer must be prepared to accept a costly and time-consuming acquisition review process. In some cases, typically where the target is a small or medium-sized family-owned concern, detailed records that would be required for the satisfactory investigation of a U.S. target simply do not exist. To avoid undue risk in such situations, the buyer may be able to compensate through purchase price by including a significant deferred-consideration element contingent upon future performance or by avoiding unknown liabilities through structuring the transaction as an asset purchase.

The due diligence process in cross-border acquisitions should begin long before a specific target has been identified. Entry into a new geographic market requires an evaluation of the market, logistical issues, and geopolitical risks. As the industry structure may be substantially different from that in the United States, a good understanding of the competitive market is critical.

REGULATIONS AND CONSENTS

In addition to local stock-exchange rules, the principal types of regulations an acquirer may encounter in the context of a European acquisition include national takeover rules, investment and exchange controls, and merger regulations.

National takeover rules, which are designed to ensure equal treatment for all shareholders, as well as to provide sufficient disclosure for an informed shareholder decision, vary widely from country to country. The United Kingdom, for example, has a rule book entitled *The City Code on Mergers and Takeovers* (the Takeover Code), which sets out in detailed, prescriptive form the obligations and procedures to be observed by parties to a transaction involving a U.K. public company (which need not be a listed company).

Although the Takeover Code lacks the force of statute, it is considered unwise to flaunt its rules, which are administered by a panel of distinguished city figures ("the Panel"). In contrast, Spain has little in the way of mechanisms for regulating and administering takeover bids. France has a regulatory mechanism bearing resemblance both to U.S. SEC rules and to the U.K. Takeover Code, and the Netherlands has a set of rules that aim to ensure fair treatment not only for shareholders, but also for employees.

Takeover rules apply principally to listed and to larger unlisted public companies and usually do not affect acquisitions of private companies. The EC, in an effort to harmonize such rules, issued in draft form the Takeover Directive (Thirteenth Directive on Company Law), based loosely on the U.K. Takeover Code.

Despite major reforms, investment controls still apply to some extent in most European countries. A non-EC acquirer of a French company, for example, must obtain prior authorization from the French Treasury Department in order to proceed. Acquisitions of more than 50 percent of a Spanish company by a foreign buyer, where the consideration exceeds about $25 million, must be cleared with the country's exchange-control authorities. Usually, a response to such clearance requests can be obtained within one month.

Merger regulations are designed to prevent the impairment of effective competition by acquisition or other means. Whereas most European countries have national merger controls, the European Commission, through the Merger Control Board (a European equivalent of the Hart-Scott-Rodino Antitrust Improvements Act of 1976), generally has jurisdiction over transactions involving very large corporations with a "community dimension." In middle-market transactions, where EC regulations usually do not apply (because the parties to the deal do not meet the size criteria), national merger rules may still be enforceable, potentially preventing the transaction from taking place. In the United Kingdom, Spain, France, and Germany it is possible to obtain advance clearance for proposed transactions. Other regulatory bodies may be required to approve transactions as well. For example, food, pharmaceutical, or banking companies may need to be granted approval for change in ownership by the national industry regulatory authorities.

VALUATION CONVENTIONS

In any successfully negotiated acquisition, it is important for an acquirer to understand the seller's perception of the value of the target company. This becomes even more important where the valuation conventions of the seller's country differ significantly from methods generally applied in the acquirer's country.

It is therefore advantageous for the buyer to make an effort to understand the seller's position. The U.S. buyer should conduct two valuations: the first using domestic techniques to determine how much the target is worth to the buyer (discounted cash flow and multiples); the second, to evaluate the seller's perception of the company's value.

Both discounted cash flow valuations and comparable company multiple analysis are predicated on the existence of liquid equity markets. Both techniques require the compilation of stock market information pertaining to companies operating in the same or a similar sector as the target company.

Frequently, a search for comparable listed companies in the target's country may produce only one or two candidates. A possible alternative approach is to derive a comparable company portfolio from the appropriate U.S. sector. However, this can produce misleading results because margins, growth rates, market structures, and competition often differ substantially.

Another potential problem with applying discounted cash flow is that this technique requires detailed cash flow projections for a period typically of five years. Medium-sized and smaller European companies usually do not prepare projections for periods beyond the next fiscal year; those that do may be reluctant to release such information until negotiations have reached an advanced stage. A possible approach, which avoids both the market-liquidity issues previously referred to and the need for detailed projections, is to apply representative transaction multiples, focusing on price-to-operating earnings and price-to-cash flow, where sufficient information is available. Although such analysis can provide a useful "first-cut" valuation, it will require cautious interpretation, particularly where the number of representative deals is limited.

TAXATION

As in most business activities, taxation is an important aspect of the acquisition process, one that can significantly affect the benefits to both the seller and the buyer. Adding cross-border dimensions to a transaction introduces new tax regimes to the equation—and attendant complications. Notwithstanding differences in national tax laws, the basic question is whether to purchase assets or shares and, therefore, how to structure and finance the acquisition.

The same basic considerations apply to this decision for a foreign acquisition as for a domestic acquisition. Generally, a seller may prefer to sell shares in order to minimize the charge to capital gains tax, among other reasons. In an asset sale, the company from which the assets are acquired will be liable for tax on any gain upon the disposition of the assets. A further tax charge will be levied on the seller upon distribution of the sale proceeds by the company in which it holds shares.

On the other hand, the most significant potential tax-related benefit to a corporation in acquiring shares is that the target's carried-forward tax losses may be available for offsetting against future taxable profits. However, in most European countries, a change in control linked to a cessation in trade will usually prevent the company from obtaining tax loss carryforward. In Belgium and France a material change in activities may be sufficient for a company to be denied loss relief.

Another tax-related benefit of the share-sale route is that transfer taxes are generally lower for this approach than for an asset sale (and are nil in some countries). In France, for example, transfer taxes can be 14 percent. There are other minor advantages—unrelated to taxes—to acquiring shares, including continuity of trading relationships and employment contracts and, possibly, the lack of need to establish a new company.

U.S. buyers generally prefer to acquire the assets of foreign companies for much the same reason that they commonly favor this approach at home. The principal advantage is the ability to "step up" the book values of depreciable assets in the allocation of the purchase price. This results in higher depreciation deductions than may be realized in a share purchase, where the seller's depreciated asset values are inherited by the buyer. Related to this process is the reduction of capital gains tax on a subsequent sale of the target company or its assets—as a result of a higher base cost—by reference to which any gain is calculated.

If the assets are bought by a local subsidiary of the U.S. corporation, it may be possible for the subsidiary to finance the acquisition by borrowing against the assets acquired. This may enable the local subsidiary to offset the borrowing costs against income generated by the assets, thereby reducing the income tax charge on the local operation. This is possible only in a share purchase, where local tax rules permit consolidated returns and where rules designed to prevent excessive leverage do not apply.

Furthermore, financial assistance rules applicable in most European countries prevent a target company from providing security on loans to its acquirer to finance the acquisition. An additional benefit of the asset purchase is that it allows the acquirer to determine what is acquired, obviating the need for excessive warranties and representations with respect to potential liabilities.

CULTURE-BASED DIFFERENCES AND OTHER ISSUES

At the risk of diminishing the importance of the previously discussed issues, the most fundamental areas of difference distinguishing an international acquisition from a domestic one lie in the cultural and human dimensions of the deal. Not only should the U.S. buyer recognize that Europe is not North America, but also that Switzerland is not Germany and that England is not France. Social structure, political environment, cultural background, and historical development all play a part in determining a country's identity.

These elements of national complexion differ for each European country. A U.S. buyer embarking on a European acquisition should research the relevant country (and in some cases, the region) thoroughly before approaching a target. Early and detailed analysis of the country will aid the identification of risks and potential problems and facilitate the avoidance of possible embarrassment or conflict.

Although many European business executives are fluent in English, their national language is typically the one they use to conduct business. The acquisition agreement, too, is likely to be governed by the laws of the country in which the target company is based and is frequently drafted in that country's language. It is therefore vital that a potential buyer engage a local bilingual lawyer who is experienced at handling inbound investments and capable of relating complex legal issues in both the local language and English. This will facilitate any necessary liaison with the acquirer's U.S. attorneys or in-house counsel.

A difference in languages can create a potential for misinterpretation of "agreed-upon" matters, and it is therefore recommended that a letter of intent be issued prior to the detailed drafting of legal agreements. This is particularly important if contingent payments are involved under an earn-out arrangement where interpretative differences may not otherwise arise for a year or more after the deal is closed.

Inevitably, the need for clarity slows the acquisition process. Yet language is rarely the main reason for delays in closing a deal. With the exception of U.K. companies and larger continental European corporations such as Nestlé, BSN, ABB, and Siemens, for whom acquisitions and divestitures are a regular occurrence, this activity is unfamiliar territory for most European business executives. As a result, they tend to tread carefully and slowly. Furthermore, some sellers are suspicious of the intentions of a large U.S. multinational seeking to buy their companies. In such cases, gaining the trust and cooperation of a seller may well necessitate nurturing a relationship over a number of months before a final offer can be made.

A final practical note: it is advisable to consider the impact of national holidays and vacations when establishing a transaction timetable. Europeans tend to hold public holidays sacrosanct, particularly religious holidays. Spain, for instance, recognizes 18 public holidays on its corporate calendar. Moreover, four weeks of vacation annually is standard in Europe, and five, or even six, weeks is not uncommon. And in some sectors on the Continent, such as manufacturing firms, businesses close for the entire month of August, when all employees go on holiday.

CHAPTER 19

VALUATION AND FINANCING ISSUES IN CROSS-BORDER TRANSACTIONS

Undoubtedly, two of the most important aspects of any acquisition are the determination of the value of the target company and the manner in which its acquisition is to be financed. Valuation and financing become even more significant issues when the proposed transaction involves a company based in a foreign country, where valuation conventions and the local financing environment may be vastly different from those in the United States, presenting a plethora of risks and opportunities to the U.S. acquirer.

This chapter does not attempt to address all of the issues that impact valuation and financing aspects of cross-border acquisitions. Instead, the discussion develops the principles dealt with earlier in a domestic context, adding an international dimension to the equation.

Tax and accounting issues related to the valuation and financing of cross-border acquisitions by U.S. corporations are dealt with in Chapter 21. Although some mention here of those issues is unavoidable, this chapter's focus is the corporate-finance aspects of cross-border transactions.

VALUATION ISSUES

The Importance of Valuations in Cross-Border Acquisitions

In any acquisition it is important for the buyer not only to determine the value of a prospective acquisition candidate, but also to understand the goals and needs of the seller, including the seller's perception of its company's value. Such an understanding will enhance the likelihood of a successful deal, because the buyer will be more likely to price and structure a mutually acceptable offer. However, unlike what happens in a domestic U.S. acquisition, where the buyer and the seller (or their respective advisers) usually adopt broadly similar valuation approaches to valuing a target company, the owners of a foreign target—because of differences in capital markets and other factors—frequently adopt valuation conventions entirely different from the U.S. approach in determining their "asking price."

The range of commonly applied valuation techniques varies from country to country. In locales with relatively well-developed stock markets, including Japan, the United Kingdom, Australia, and Canada, valuation methods typically focus on multiple analysis and discounted cash flow techniques, both of which rely on data derived from comparable public companies. In contrast, in countries with limited public equity arenas, such as Spain, Italy, Norway, and the Netherlands, market-based valuation methods are less common. Instead, valuations in these countries are determined through a variety of approaches based on the net assets of the target company or the capitalization of its profits. In countries such as Germany, where debt has traditionally represented the major source of financing, valuations are often based on the company's balance sheet—adjusted if necessary for differences between book and market values. In Eastern Europe, where the concept of profit measurement is in the nascent stage, valuations have traditionally been asset based.

Two issues arise from the differences in generally accepted valuation approaches between an acquiring company and its prospective target. First, from its own perspective, how does the U.S. acquirer determine the valuation of the target? Second, how does the U.S. acquirer develop an understanding of the prospective seller's perception of the target company's value? The answers to these two questions will provide the U.S. buyer with most of the information necessary for it to frame a mutually acceptable offer.

Valuing the Target from the U.S. Acquirer's Perspective

With the exception of companies involved in industries such as oil and gas, cellular communications, and cable television, a U.S. acquirer usually attempts to establish a value for its overseas target by applying a discount rate, derived from a cost of capital model, such as the capital asset pricing model, to the target company's projected cash flows. This is known as discounted cash flow analysis. A second approach is multiple analysis, which uses the relationship between either announced transaction values or the public market value of public companies in the host country and their operating performance to estimate the value of a private target company. With discounted cash flow analysis and multiple analysis, the U.S. acquirer will have to consider whether the public equity markets in the host country are sufficiently liquid, and include a large enough group of comparable countries to provide reliable data.

In countries such as Germany and Spain, where a significant proportion of public company equity is owned or controlled by a relatively small group of financial institutions, shares are usually held for the long term, resulting in relatively low daily trading volumes. In fragmented sectors, where participants are generally smaller companies whose equity is usually controlled by a founder, shares of the public companies may be thinly traded. In such cases, the stock-market quoted price of the shares may not reflect accurately the company's intrinsic value. In contrast, sectors undergoing consolidation may consist of one or two large companies engaged in activities comparable to the target; to rely on such a small population of comparable companies for valuation purposes could produce misleading results.

Where local host country markets may not be viewed as a reliable source of valuation reference data, the U.S. acquirer may opt to derive a discount rate by using data from other U.S. companies operating within the same industry as the target. Multinational U.S. corporations with major operations in the country in which the target operates can generally provide better indicators of industry risk characteristics for estimating the cost of equity than purely domestic U.S. concerns.

However, economic conditions, market structures, and competitive factors—all of which affect share-price volatility—may be substantially different in the target company's operating environment than in the United States. Therefore, any valuation of a foreign target that is conducted using domestic market data should be interpreted with extreme caution, because the discount rate and multiples derived from comparable U.S. companies may not fully reflect the risks within the local operating environment in the host country.

A further complication is that unless the target company is being marketed actively, it is unlikely that projections required for discounted cash flow analysis (typically for a five-year period) will be available to the prospective acquirer. Although it is true that most small and medium-sized companies outside the United States prepare budgets for the current fiscal year and that some forecast results for the next fiscal year, only the larger and more sophisticated companies project beyond a one-year horizon.

It is theoretically possible for the prospective acquirer to compile high-level projections using some basic assumptions. This approach is to be discouraged, however; when discounted cash flow analysis is applied, a small variance in the projections can have a major impact on the estimated terminal value of the target, which usually represents a significant proportion of its estimated value.

If a discounted cash flow valuation is not possible owing to a lack of reliable projections and comparable public companies, the U.S. buyer should attempt to focus on comparable company multiple analysis. However, like the discounted cash flow method, multiple analysis also depends on the existence of both liquid capital markets and comparable public companies. A buyer should also attempt to derive valuation multiples from representative sector transactions in the target's industry. By comparing the prices paid in recent transactions to the underlying performance of the acquired companies, it may be possible to derive transaction multiple ranges (e.g., price to sales, price to operating income, etc.) for use in valuing the target. However, this latter technique is predicated on the availability of the necessary transaction data, which is frequently not disclosed in many countries.

Valuing the Target from the Foreign Seller's Perspective

An understanding of a seller's likely approach to valuing the target business makes it possible for a prospective buyer to estimate the offer the seller may be willing to accept. It also enables the buyer to assess how closely the seller's value correlates with the value of the business to the buyer. Clearly, if the seller's perception of value is thought to be significantly greater than the buyer's, much time and effort can be saved by addressing the pricing issue at the outset.

Where the pricing gap is not so large as to be considered a "deal breaker," the U.S. acquirer is advised to concentrate on gaining the seller's confidence before discussing proposed terms. On the other hand, if the buyer considers the company to have greater value than the seller appears to be demanding, the buyer will be in the enviable position of framing an offer that satisfies the seller's expectations without the risk of overpaying.

When applying local valuation methodologies to determine the target company's worth from the seller's perspective, a U.S. corporation is likely to encounter a number of problems. Not the least of these is the difficulty in understanding and interpreting local financial statements (assuming that the prospective buyer has been fortunate enough to obtain them at an early stage in the process).

The United States, arguably, has the world's most developed set of accounting standards, with recommended accounting treatments set out in detailed prescriptive form. Most countries have less developed standards and permit much greater choice, resulting in greater inconsistency in accounting treatments. Such inconsistencies, which potentially affect all forms of valuation approaches based on reference companies, should be taken into account and adjusted for in the development of comparable company data.

Other problems relate to the availability of sufficiently detailed and timely financial information about the target company and other comparable companies. The availability and quality of such data vary from country to country. For instance, like the United States, Canada and the United Kingdom require public companies to report a significant amount of audited financial information to their respective stock exchange authorities. In many countries, however, disclosure of such detailed information is not required.

Pricing and Earn-Outs

In cross-border acquisitions, where the target may be located thousands of miles from the United States, an acquirer often relies on the continued involvement of the former proprietor in the management of the business for a transition period. Typically, this transition period lasts two or three years after the acquisition. In such situations, it can be beneficial to both the acquirer and the seller to include an earn-out, or contingent deferred-payment component, in the structure of the deal.

An earn-out is designed to motivate a seller to maximize the performance of the business for a specified period of time following a sale, by making part of the purchase price dependent on a future performance variable such as profits or sales. The earn-out consideration is calculated through use of a formula related to predetermined growth rates or absolute targets. An earn-out structure is particularly appropriate in cross-border acquisitions, because it protects an acquirer from overpaying for a business over which the acquirer may have little direct influence in the critical first years following the acquisition.

Thus, the fixed element of the sales price under an earn-out arrangement is typically below the value that the acquirer would ascribe to the target company if it were to make a single payment at completion. However, the earn-out element, when added to the fixed component, allows the seller to achieve a higher total price than the single payment value. Usually, the price an acquirer would be willing to pay outright falls somewhere between the fixed amount and the most likely total price under the earn-out. In other words, the earn-out is a useful way to bridge the gap between buyer's and seller's expectations while maximizing the likelihood of the foreign target company's performing well during the early years following the acquisition.

FINANCING ISSUES

The financing issues relative to cross-border acquisitions are considered from the perspective of a U.S.-resident acquirer and are addressed in the following three sections. Capital structure and financial market issues are discussed under the heading "Funding Issues," and "Foreign Exchange Risks" examines the currency risks arising from investing in an entity domiciled in a foreign jurisdiction and how these can be mitigated. Finally, an overview of some of the tax-related matters that impact the financing decision are discussed under "Tax Issues."

Funding Issues

In an acquisition, the two forms of consideration generally available to a vendor are equity and cash. Equity typically consists of stock in the acquiring entity which may or may not be listed on a stock exchange outside the country in which the acquirer is resident ("the home country"). Cash may be provided from the existing funds of the acquiring entity, or alternatively, it might be borrowed from one or more of a number of potential sources. Another variation on the cash alternative is a vendor note or earn-out consideration, both of which represent a right to receive cash in the future.

Equity Consideration. Foreign vendors are generally reluctant to accept stock in the acquiring entity, whether public or private. As many vendors of the mid to late 1980s will confirm, a public company's equity can be subject to significant market fluctuations, changes in investor sentiment, and other factors largely unrelated to the underlying value of the business being acquired. A foreign vendor wishing to invest in the acquiring entity can purchase stock in the public market using its own cash proceeds. A possible exception to this reluctance to accept stock in the acquiring company arises when the stock being offered is quoted in the public equity market of the country in which the target is resident ("the host country"). This stock is referred to worldwide as "Euroequity." Because the acquirer is less well known in the host market than in the home market, its Euroequity may trade at a discount to its price in the home market. Under such conditions, the use of equity will make an overseas acquisition more expensive than a domestic acquisition. The option of using locally listed equity to effect an acquisition is a luxury available only to the largest multinationals; of the thousands of public companies in the United States, only 60 or so have a listing on the London Stock Exchange. It is rare for an acquirer to pay for an acquisition in the form of unquoted or private company stock unless a buy-back provision provides an exit for the vendor.

The use of Euroequity to finance an acquisition may be appropriate where the acquirer is an established global organization seeking to strengthen its presence in the host country equity market through a major issue. This can be important if subsequent acquisitions are planned. Generally, continental European investors, like Japanese investors, have a longer-term investment horizon than U.S. companies and therefore tend to hold stocks longer than their U.S. counterparts. This provides stability in the equity market, reducing share price volatility. One way of issuing equity while paying the vendor in cash is to arrange for an institutional placing of the Euroequity in the host country. However, institutional investors tend to have a shorter investment horizon than private investors and may reduce the stabilizing influence of international stockholders. The costs associated with a Euroequity listing can be significant, including fees for underwriters, stockbrokers, accountants, and lawyers. Further, it will also be important to continue to educate the investing community about the issuer through expensive and time-consuming road shows and the retention of investor relations firms.

Cash Consideration.   When the transaction involves a domestic or foreign target company, surplus or idle cash is the cheapest form of finance, because its opportunity cost, that is, its yield, is lower than both the cost of borrowing and the return demanded on equity investments. The opportunity cost of using cash currently required for the operation of the business is equal to the marginal cost of borrowing; it is still cheaper than the cost of equity.

Debt Consideration.   There are many possible forms of debt financing available to the U.S. acquirer, including revolving credit facilities, senior and subordinated term loans, public debt securities, unquoted debt securities, and commercial paper. These are discussed in the context of domestic acquisitions in Chapters 00.

The following discussion addresses some of the acquisition financing considerations related specifically to cross-border acquisitions.

Sources for Borrowing Funds.   An acquirer should attempt to minimize the cost of borrowing by raising funds in the market that offers the lowest interest costs. This does not necessarily restrict a U.S. acquirer to a choice of either the United States or the host country, although in practice only the larger companies will have the ability to borrow in markets where they have no operations. A currency swap would permit a U.S.-based acquirer, for instance, to borrow from a bank in the United Kingdom to fund a French acquisition. Alternatively, a Eurobond issue may enable a highly regarded U.S. acquirer to raise funds in the host country capital market in an efficient manner.

Where possible, an acquirer should aim to exploit existing banking relationships. If the acquirer's principal bank has operations in the host country, it is logical for the buyer to approach its own banker before considering other sources; an established relationship, combined with an understanding of the acquirer's business, will likely result in the quickest response and often the most favorable terms. Furthermore, a global banking relationship will facilitate subsequent cross-border transactions. If, however, the acquirer's U.S. bankers do not have representation in the host country or at least a relationship with a major bank in the host country, the U.S. buyer may wish to raise the funds through a local bank in the host country.

The attractiveness of borrowing from a local bank in the host country will depend in part, at least, on the size of the intended transaction and the sophistication of the local banking environment. An obvious candidate to provide the necessary funding is the target company's existing bank, due to its ongoing relationship with the target and its knowledge of the target's operations. Borrowing from the target's bank in local currency will obviate the need for a currency swap transaction. However, notwithstanding the local relationship, it is likely that guarantees will be sought from the U.S. parent company. Introducing a third-party local bank will likely entail a slower response to the funding request than either of the two alternatives mentioned above, as the bank will need to become familiar with the acquirer and the target before it can make a credit assessment.

Short-term versus Long-term Loans.   The decision as to whether to finance a cross-border acquisition with short-term or long-term borrowings is essentially the same as for a domestic acquisition in the United States. In an international acquisition, however, for which the decisions concerning where to borrow and for how long are interrelated, it is necessary to consider the yield curves of the debt markets in the various jurisdictions in which the acquisition financing might be raised. The yield curve represents the relationship between the yields on debt instruments and their maturity structure. A normal upward-sloping yield curve reflects the fact that longer-term funds are more expensive than shorter-term funds. Different countries' yield curves show different gradients, reflecting differing expectations regarding their economic prospects. Therefore, whereas short-term interest rates in country A might exceed those in country B, owing to different yield curve gradients, the opposite might be true for long-term interest rates.

Covenants and Collateral.   A potential drawback of using term loans to finance a cross-border acquisition is that because of possible difficulties of perfecting a lien, a U.S. bank may require that the loans are secured by the assets of the U.S. company, and sometimes by those of the target company as well. Furthermore, because of the remoteness of the target company's assets and uncertainty about their value in the local market, a U.S. lender will frequently ascribe lower security values to those assets, limiting the extent to which the acquirer can leverage the transaction. Another possible problem with term loans, particularly senior term loans, is that a U.S. bank may impose strict financing and operating covenants on the foreign company. Such restrictions may have a detrimental impact on the morale of local operating management, particularly where the seller continues to manage a business that has hitherto been unleveraged. The acquirer should negotiate covenant terms that take into account all seasonal or cyclical influences impacting the target company's profits and cash flows, including taxes, staff bonuses, and significant equipment purchases.

Availability of Mezzanine Finance and Subordinated Debt.   Mezzanine financing is largely a U.S. concept. At the time of this writing, approximately 70 percent of the total below-investment-grade Eurodebt derives from issues by U.S. companies, with 20 percent representing issues by U.K. and Australian companies. The balance comprises the sovereign debt of several Latin American nations. Subordinated term loans may be available in some situations; however, it is generally considered extremely difficult to raise subordinated financing in the United States for foreign acquisitions, where the operation on whose performance the loan decision is based happens to be thousands of miles away. In many countries with less developed financial markets, the concepts of mezzanine financing and cash flow lending do not exist, and local borrowing is constrained by the target company's balance sheet.

Contingent Consideration (Earn-Outs).   In cross-border acquisitions in which the target company may be located thousands of miles from the United States, the acquirer is frequently dependent on the continued involvement of the selling proprietor in the management of the business for a period of time (typically two or three years) following its acquisition. In such situations, it is often beneficial to include an earn-out, or contingent deferred payment, in the deal structure. An earn-out is designed to motivate a seller to maximize the performance of the business during a specified period following the transaction, by making part of the consideration dependent on a performance variable such as operating profits or sales. The earn-out consideration is calculated by using a formula related to either predetermined growth rates or income levels targets. An earn-out structure is particularly appropriate in cross-border acquisitions, because it enables an acquirer to avoid the risk of overpaying while motivating the seller to ensure that the company continues to perform following its acquisition.

Recent Developments.   The globalization of the world's capital markets and the growth of the investment community in recent years have resulted in the development of a panoply of sophisticated alternatives for determining the most appropriate means of financing a cross-border acquisition. For example, in 1992 the HSBC Holdings, the parent of the Hong Kong and Shanghai Bank, completed the first-stage funding of its £3.6 billion ($6.5 billion) acquisition of the United Kingdom's Midland Bank in an innovative manner, involving a rare use of the bond market. HSBC Holdings' £448 million ($800 million), 10-year subordinated Eurobond issue provided a number of subsidiary benefits, including the avoidance of excessive dilution of shareholders' funds. Because of the nature of Eurobonds as internationally traded bearer instruments, it was possible to effect a considerably wider distribution than would have been possible with a domestic sterling issue in the United Kingdom. For a large company like HSBC Holdings, the existence of international demand for its paper can have the benefit of ensuring efficient global pricing while reinforcing demand in the home market.

Foreign Exchange Risks

There are three potential risks associated with the foreign exchange aspects of cross-border acquisitions:

1. *Risk associated with the timing of payment of purchase consideration.*
Where acquisition financing is to be raised in the home country, there is a risk that the host currency will appreciate against the home currency between the date of finalizing the transaction price and settlement. This exposure to exchange rate fluctuations is increased where the price includes deferred consideration.

There are several approaches to dealing with this potential exposure. The first and most effective means of eliminating the exposure is to denominate the transaction in the home currency. In other words, the foreign vendor incurs the potential exposure rather than the U.S. acquirer. For obvious reasons, this is not a popular solution from a vendor's perspective. A second approach, which like the first does not involve a "hedge," is that the acquirer and vendor share the effect of any exchange rate movements between the date on which the price is set and settlement, by adjusting the transaction price immediately prior to settlement. Here any risk, and indeed any potential benefit, is shared by both parties.

There are several hedging mechanisms that help to limit or even eliminate the risk of foreign currency markets changing the deal price. The most commonly applied hedges are forward purchase contracts and currency options. A forward purchase contract might, for example, involve the acquirer's entering into an agreement with a bank to purchase £20 million at a predetermined (or "forward") rate of $1.60 = £1, in three months' time (the estimated closing date for the transaction), for the acquisition of a company based in

the United Kingdom. Assuming that the current exchange rate is
$1.50, giving a dollar purchase price of $30 million, the forward
contract limits the maximum price, three months hence, to $32
million (i.e., £20 million × $1.6), irrespective of exchange rate
movements. The disadvantage of a forward contract is that the acquirer is contractually obligated to purchase the foreign currency
(in this case £20 million). For a variety of reasons, the transaction
might not take place, leaving the acquirer with a large amount of
currency to dispose of in the foreign exchange markets. Not surprisingly, there is a cost to doing so, in the form of commission on
the conversion of the funds back into dollars.

An alternative approach to hedging that avoids the contractual
commitment to purchase the foreign currency is the use of foreign
currency options. This approach can be applied to the situation
described above. For a fee a bank will enter into an agreement with
the acquirer, giving the acquirer the option to purchase £20 million
at the predetermined rate of $1.60 = £1. Unlike a forward contract,
however, by using a currency option the acquirer is not obligated
to purchase the sterling and may choose not to do so if, for example,
the transaction did not proceed or the dollar appreciated against
sterling, making the purchase of sterling in the spot market (i.e., at
the then prevailing exchange rate) a cheaper alternative. The drawback of a currency option is its cost, which can run to several
hundred basis points.

2. *Exposure to exchange rate fluctuations on the acquired entity's continuing cash flows.*

After the transaction has been completed, the acquirer may be
anticipating receipts of annual income from its foreign subsidiary
in the form of dividends or a management charge (or both). The
amount of such receipts in dollars will depend on the exchange rate
between the dollar and the local currency at the time of the re-
mittance. If the remittances are anticipated to be significant
amounts, the parent could be exposed to material losses on the
conversion. As previously described, the two main hedging alternatives available to the U.S. parent are the use of the forward agreement or a currency option. In this case, however, in regard to the
example above, the parent would be seeking to fix the rate at which
the foreign currency is sold, rather than bought. If the dollar weak-
ens against sterling, the parent would exercise the currency option

at the predetermined rate; if, however, the dollar strengthens relative to sterling, the parent would choose not to exercise its option, but would instead sell the sterling in the spot market.

If the acquisition is financed through borrowings by the parent in the host country, the exposure to exchange rate fluctuations will be based on the anticipated difference between the anticipated interest and loan repayments, on one hand, and the expected dividend or management charge on the other. Therefore, given that the payments and receipts are in the same currency, any exchange rate exposure will be limited to the net receipt or payment.

3. *Asset value risk (erosion of investment).*

There is a risk that the acquired entity will decline in value owing to the depreciation of the host country currency relative to that of the home country. This risk might affect not only the U.S. parent but also U.S. institutions that advanced the funds to finance the acquisition. For example, a U.S. acquirer might have paid FFr 75 million, borrowed from its U.S. bankers, to acquire a French company five years ago when the exchange rate was FFr 5 = $1 (i.e., a cost of $15 million). If the current exchange rate is FFr 4 = $1, ignoring other factors, the value of the company (and potentially, the bank's collateral) would have fallen by 20 percent in terms of U.S. dollars (to $12 million). In such cases, the lender will probably require guarantees from the parent company.

Of course, the movement of exchange rates does not mean that the parent company has incurred a realized loss, unless the subsidiary is sold and the proceeds are converted into dollars. Even if the subsidiary is sold, there are many factors besides exchange rate movements that will influence the value of the company, including the company's performance, M & A market environment, and the conditions in the industry in which it operates. Therefore, it is generally not considered appropriate to hedge against the effects of such potential currency erosion unless there is a clear intention to "exit" from the investment at a predetermined future time. In such cases, borrowing in the host country to finance the acquisition will achieve at least a partial hedge against such currency fluctuations by creating an equivalent liability in the host country currency. For example, such an approach might be beneficial in the following case: A U.S. company invests in an overseas joint venture with a foreign company, and the joint venture agreement provides an option for the local company to buy out the U.S. company after a specified period of time. By borrowing in the host country under a maturity structure that matches the buyout time horizon, the U.S. company can substantially reduce its exposure to the foreign currency.

The hedging techniques described above will not be available in every case. Although hedging between the U.S. dollar and the major foreign currencies, including the German deutsche mark, the Japanese yen, the U.K. pound, and the French and the Swiss franc, is offered by most major banks, forward contracts and currency options may not be available between the dollar and the currencies of many smaller and developing countries. The rapid increase in the pace of cross-border activity of United States companies in Latin America and Eastern Europe—as a consequence of extensive privatization programs—may result in an acquirer incurring full exposure not only to exchange rate movements but to greater political, economic, and market risks. Accordingly, such risks should be fully reflected in the purchase price. For acquisitions in those developed countries that are not major players in world currency markets, it is sometimes possible to achieve at least a partial hedge by executing forward contracts or currency options in one of the major currencies whose movements are correlated to fluctuations in the host country's exchange rate movement. For example, a U.S. acquirer of a company in New Zealand might use an option to buy Australian dollars to hedge the risk that the U.S. dollar will depreciate against the New Zealand dollar during the time between determination of the purchase price and settlement.

Costs of hedging can be substantial. Accordingly, some multinationals do not employ the techniques described above to mitigate the effects of exchange rate movements, but instead "take their chances" with the global currency markets. However, such companies are in the minority, and most treasurers would agree that some form of hedging is preferable to none. The lessons of the currency market turmoil experienced in the autumn of 1992 should be taken seriously; in a matter of days the dollar/sterling exchange rate fell from $1.90 to $1.55, a decline in the pound of over 20 percent. Although a U.S. acquirer contemplating a sterling-denominated U.K. acquisition would have actually benefited from the rate movement, the example serves to illustrate the volatility of currency markets and the attendant risks to a cross-border acquirer.

Tax Issues

When an acquirer is deciding on the form and source of financing for an international acquisition, tax considerations can be a key determinant of the costs associated with the various alternatives. The tax aspects of international transactions are explored more fully in Chapter 21. This discussion merely serves to raise some of the tax-related issues associated with the financing aspects of cross-border acquisition.

In addressing financing options for a cross-border acquisition, the principal tax-related issues revolve around the deductibility of interest on borrowings for local tax purposes, the deductibility of issuing costs, and the effect of withholding taxes. Subject to the funding and foreign exchange issues discussed above, from a tax perspective the choice of borrowing (internal versus external) and source will be determined by the maxim that interest should be paid in the highest taxing jurisdiction and received in the lowest.

Deductibility of Interest on Borrowings.   The ability of a U.S. acquirer to obtain tax relief for interest payments on local borrowings will be dictated by the host country's desire to encourage foreign investment. One particular mechanism for regulating the use of debt financing in acquisitions by foreign corporations is to set a debt-to-equity threshold, above which interest payments on debt cannot be deducted for tax purposes. Such restrictions are termed "thin capitalization" rules. Thresholds imposed by thin capitalization rules can vary markedly from country to country. For instance, in Australia thin capitalization rules deny a deduction of interest paid to nonresidents for tax purposes on foreign debt, to the extent that the foreign debt-to-foreign equity ratio exceeds 3:1 (6:1 for financial institutions). By contrast, interest incurred on acquisition borrowings is fully deductible for Irish tax purposes. Where an acquisition is to be financed substantially through borrowings, it may be possible to avoid the thin capitalization rules in some countries, such as Australia, by establishing a local acquisition vehicle as the borrowing entity, thereby attracting interest deduction for the full amount of the borrowings. However, it should be noted that antiavoidance provisions are likely to deny relief where back-to-back loans are established between the local lender, the acquisition vehicle, and the foreign parent.

Deductibility of Issuing Costs.   Although the deductibility of issuing costs for tax purposes is unlikely to be the principal determinant of the source of funding in a cross-border acquisition, in large acquisitions funding costs for different types and sources of funding may vary by substantial amounts owing to different tax treatments. For example, in Australia, the noninterest costs incurred in borrowing money for business purposes, including underwriting costs, legal fees, and brokering costs, may be written off over the term of the borrowing, subject to a maximum period of five years. In the United Kingdom, the incidental costs of issuing debt are also deductible against trading profits for tax purposes, whereas the costs of an equity issue are deductible in neither the United Kingdom nor Australia.

Effect of Withholding Taxes.   Many countries impose withholding tax on interest payments to a nonresident lender. In Belgium and Australia the rate is 10 percent, and the United Kingdom and Canada withhold at the rate of 25 percent. Other countries, such as Denmark, the Netherlands, and South Africa, do not apply withholding tax to interest payments. In a number of countries, including Belgium, the United Kingdom, Italy, and New Zealand, the withholding rate can be reduced substantially for lenders residing in countries with which the host country has a double taxation treaty—sometimes to zero. In other countries, such as Australia, the existence of a double taxation treaty does not reduce the withholding tax on interest payments. If an acquisition is contemplated in a jurisdiction where withholding taxes are not applied or can be substantially reduced or avoided owing to the existence of double taxation treaties, subject to funding and exchange risk issues, it could be beneficial to fund the acquisition outside the host country. Conversely, if withholding taxes cannot be mitigated, local borrowing in the target country may represent the most cost-effective source of funds.

Other Tax Issues.   The attractiveness to a foreign seller of deferred consideration under an earn-out arrangement will vary, depending on the local tax treatment in the host country. For example, in an acquisition of a U.K. company, where the purchase price depends on the future performance of the acquired business, a vendor will be deemed to have received consideration in the form of a right to receive an uncertain future amount. A value will be ascribed to this "right to receive" for U.K. tax purposes. Provided that the deferred consideration, when finally received, is in the form of shares or loan notes, the U.K. Inland Revenue will be willing to apply concessions that treat the gain as not being realized until the shares or loan notes are subsequently disposed of for cash. Therefore, it is important that the acquirer consider the tax position not only of the acquiring entity but also of the vendor when making a financing decision.

Of all the areas that can impact the success or failure of a cross-border acquisition, taxation is, arguably, the area where the most opportunities and pitfalls exist for the acquirer. It is therefore critical to obtain professional tax advice before determining the transaction financing structure.

CHAPTER 20

DUE DILIGENCE

Cross-border transactions present an additional set of due diligence issues that do not arise when the acquirer and the target are located in the same country. For acquisitions within the same country, the acquirer and the intended target fall under the same general rules of their political and economic systems. They operate under the same laws and accounting and tax standards, and even within the same cultural value system. But when the companies are located in different countries, new issues arise, because the political system within a particular country establishes the rules of the game for conducting business there. The acquirer and its advisers must have a good understanding of the nature and influence of those rules before focusing the due diligence process primarily on fundamental business issues.

In a given cross-border transaction, the "country risk" of the host country (i.e., the country where the intended target is located) must be assessed. At first glance, the concept of risk might be thought to apply only to lesser developed countries where the greatest danger to a foreign investor would be political instability. Risk factors do include, but are not limited to, political instability. There are a number of areas that can have an impact on the due diligence process. These include, in addition to the stability of a country's political system, its receptiveness to foreign investment and the degree of influence of the government on business operations in general.

In cases where the political and economic systems are significantly different, the need for risk assessment is clear. For example, a U.S. company evaluating the potential acquisition of a firm based in the People's Republic of China would be immediately aware of the importance of the country-risk assessment in the due diligence process.

Although China has made itself more amenable to foreign investment since the late 1970s, a number of country-specific issues must be resolved before an investment decision can be made. Other countries for which risk assessment forms a part of the due diligence process may be less obvious, because the countries in question may appear to have similar political systems. But when the host country's political system appears to be similar to the acquirer's political system in form, those similarities may mask profound differences in government-business relations.

For example, if the host country is operating under a democratic political system, it might reasonably be assumed that the political system generally acts to foster a free-market business environment. Upon conducting due diligence, however, the acquirer may learn that the host country has designated certain industries or markets for internal growth, and may therefore impose trade barriers or restrictive foreign-investment or technology-transfer policies for those industries. Japan is a good example of a country where the political similarities mask major differences in business culture.

Host government intrusion into business may take several forms, all of which must be factored into the due diligence process. Some forms of intrusion are not specifically aimed at foreign-controlled businesses; they may equally affect joint ventures or local firms that have licensing agreements, although a large multinational firm may often become a more visible target for enforcement. Some examples of these types of impediments include requiring the construction of certain facilities by the investing firm, or mandating a certain percentage of local content in the manufacturing process. In addition, host countries may also have stringent requirements concerning the use of local nationals in management positions, which can affect the way the acquiring company ultimately conducts its business in the host country.

More severe measures may be aimed at foreign companies to protect local firms, such as special taxes that are not levied against domestically owned firms. Other measures may be carried out to give certain national groups an advantage. In Malaysia, for example, legislation provides for ethnic Malays to own increasingly large percentages of the national wealth; at the same time, Malaysian citizens of Chinese or Indian ancestry and foreigners are permitted to own less. Sometimes, a host country may make life extremely difficult for a foreign acquirer through legal measures, such as requiring special permits or overstringent documentation. In extreme cases, the government may encourage a boycott of a foreign firm's products.

Occasionally, a government will undertake measures that are effectively designed to make it all but impossible for foreign firms to operate profitably; eventually, they will be driven from doing business in the host country. Although a host country may do this for nationalistic reasons or to clear the market for its own entrepreneurs, the end result for the foreign investor is the same. These measures, often referred to as "creeping expropriation," may include severe controls on foreign-owned businesses with respect to remitting profits to the home country. They may also include the imposition of such heavy taxes or other special charges against foreign businesses that it makes profitable operation impossible.

The final level of interference is expropriation or nationalization. Although international law calls for fair and prompt compensation for an expropriated firm, negotiating those terms is usually difficult. Most cases of expropriation occur in developing countries, but there have been exceptions. Following the 1981 election of Socialist President François Mitterrand, France scheduled the nationalization of some of its industries. Historically, Latin American countries have been the most likely to seize control of foreign holdings.

It is, of course, impossible to predict accurately every conceivable outcome under every possible political regime. However, the acquirer must be keenly aware of the dynamics of the political system when performing the country-risk assessment. Political systems are dynamic, and in some cases, those dynamics may cause relatively sudden changes in the business environment. For example, in 1979

Iran's business climate became untenable for American investment almost overnight, whereas a decade later the former Soviet Union began to lay out the red carpet almost as quickly. In today's world, an acquirer would be myopic if it based its country-risk assessment on *only* the existing political climate.

In assessing risk, companies can visit the host country themselves, but this is probably the least effective method. It is difficult to become an instant expert on the workings of another society, and the host country's government can effectively manage the visit so as to encourage investment. In fact, the due diligence process on a cross-border transaction can be intimidating—even for an experienced cross-border acquirer. The range and complexity of due diligence issues, especially in country-risk assessment, are different in each case. Therefore, acquirers that would not even consider seeking outside advice in a domestic transaction should seriously consider seeking such advice in a cross-border transaction.

Advisers include the traditional transaction advisers that would be employed in domestic transactions, including commercial banks, investment banks, accounting firms, and attorneys. In addition, there are companies that specialize in risk management, whose resources would be particularly helpful. In choosing an adviser, it is imperative to determine whether the candidate has a strong operating presence in the intended host country. That local market experience is the key value-added component.

Once the acquirer has thoroughly evaluated the host country–risk issues and is comfortable with the rules of the game of doing business there, due diligence can then focus on the traditional business issues outlined in Chapter 4. Even then, those issues must be evaluated within the context of the risk issues of the host country that have been uncovered. Finally, the acquirer must be careful not to base its evaluation of due diligence issues solely on the value system of its own country. It must approach the evaluation process with sensitivity and respect toward the host country's cultural norms and values.

CHAPTER 21

INTERNATIONAL TAX PLANNING FOR CROSS-BORDER MERGERS AND ACQUISITIONS

An often overlooked principle in tax planning for an international merger or acquisition is that the number of players is greater than the number of parties to the transaction. In addition to the parties, there are also the various taxing authorities that have jurisdiction over the parties. A merger or acquisition is not a zero-sum game in which an advantage for one party is gained only at the expense of another. Consequently, no matter how adverse their interests, the parties—individually or in concert—should ensure that their tax advisers pause to consider whether the combined tax burden of the parties has been minimized and deferred to the greatest possible extent. This will enable them to maximize the size of the pot over which they are negotiating.

Another principle in tax planning for an international merger or acquisition is that there should be an investigation of differences in treatment among different tax jurisdictions that can be exploited to produce multiple tax benefits. For example, the payer's tax jurisdiction may view a particular instrument as debt and may permit a payment made to be deducted as interest. On the other hand, the recipient's tax jurisdiction may view the instrument as equity and may permit the payment to be received as a dividend "tax free" as the result of a participation exemption or a foreign tax credit.

One jurisdiction may view a legal entity as a "flow-through" and subject the nonresident owner to no taxation or to only low withholding taxes, whereas another jurisdiction may view the same legal entity as a corporation on whose earning the owners are subject to tax only when repatriated. One jurisdiction may view the source of an item of income or expense differently than another jurisdiction. For example, a non-U.S. tax jurisdiction may view interest expense as fully deductible against the entity's profits, whereas the same entity may be simultaneously subject to U.S. tax for which the interest is allocable among the worldwide assets of the entity and its affiliates, with the result that a substantial portion of the interest expense is allocable to U.S.-source income and produces a second tax benefit.

Moreover, one jurisdiction may view the character of an item of income or expense differently than another jurisdiction. For example, a non-U.S. tax jurisdiction that does not permit interest expense to be deducted at all, or only under very limited circumstances, may view a transaction as a lease and may permit payments to be deducted as rent. The United States, however, may view the transaction as a financing and may permit the interest to be allocated among the worldwide assets of the payer and its affiliates, providing a second tax benefit for the portion of the interest allocated to U.S. operations. One jurisdiction may view a particular legal entity as subject to tax based on the location of its operations, but another may view the same legal entity as subject to tax based on the location of its "mind and management" or on where it is incorporated. This paves the way for differences in treatment of the source or character of an item of income or expense, as described above.

EXAMPLE OF TAX PLANNING

Tax planning for a cross-border acquisition in which the target's owners want continued participation might include the following considerations.

Target's Unrealized Gain or Loss

Does the target have unrealized gain or loss with respect to its assets? Can losses be triggered and used to offset current-year taxable income or carried back to obtain a refund of taxes for prior years? Can gains be deferred in a "tax free" transfer or by structuring the transaction as a transfer of target stock rather than target assets? Can losses be triggered while gains are deferred?

Target Owner(s) Unrealized Gain or Loss

Do the target's owners have unrealized gain or loss? Note that they are increasingly subjected to tax on their gains by the taxing jurisdiction in which their corporation operates, as well as by their home taxing jurisdiction. Note also that each taxing jurisdiction will probably denominate the tax basis in the shares in terms of its own currency, so that the amount of gain or loss may be substantially different, or there may even be a gain in one jurisdiction and a loss in the other. Can the owners obtain a tax benefit by triggering their losses? Can they avoid triggering their gains?

Target and Acquirer Tax Attributes

Does the target or the acquiring corporation have any tax attributes, such as tax loss carryovers? Will desirable tax attributes be eliminated by the transaction or restricted as a result of the change of ownership? Is it possible to restructure the transaction to preserve desirable tax attributes? Is it possible to "refresh" desirable tax attributes that will be eliminated or severely restricted? For example, a tax loss that will be severely restricted by the change of ownership might be "refreshened" if a gain asset is sold to an affiliate—the soon-to-be-limited tax loss can offset the gain, while the affiliate takes a stepped-up fair market value basis for its acquisition cost. Is it possible to eliminate undesirable tax attributes, such as the potential tax recapture of previous tax benefits?

Basis Step-ups and Other Incentives

Most tax jurisdictions will permit tax basis to be "stepped up" to reflect the acquisition cost. Many will accord various tax incentives, such as investment credits, accelerated depreciation, especially high first-year depreciation, and lifetime depreciation deductions in excess of cost. Usually such benefits can be obtained not only for cash acquisitions, but also for acquisitions for the issuance of debt or stock—provided that the issuance of stock or debt does not constitute a tax-free transaction. Is it possible to achieve such benefits? Do they outweigh any tax disadvantages for the transferrer(s), such as gain recognition? If the benefits are accorded by the home taxing jurisdiction of the acquiring corporation, but with no step-up in the jurisdiction where the operations are located, there may be a substantially higher tax in the jurisdiction of operations than in the home jurisdiction before foreign tax credit. In such cases, can the excess foreign tax credits be offset against tax liability on other foreign operations?

Some tax jurisdictions permit the asset tax basis to be stepped up where gain is recognized by shareholders. Occasionally, this occurs even where shareholders are protected from tax by their nonresident status or by tax treaties. Is such a "tax-free" step-up available?

Maximum Tax Benefit for Every Expenditure

Is every expenditure deductible everywhere? If not, can that expenditure be incurred by an affiliate in a tax jurisdiction where the expenditure will produce a tax benefit? For example, if intangibles cannot be amortized in the tax jurisdiction where the operations occur, can the intangibles be acquired by an affiliate in a jurisdiction where the intangibles are amortizable, with the affiliate licensing the intangible to the operating company? Are there opportunities for tax arbitrage where an affiliate might be accorded quicker depreciation of a tangible asset or receive a tax benefit at a higher rate?

Access Shares

Many tax jurisdictions integrate the taxation of corporations and their shareholders by exempting, partially or wholly, dividends received, according a deduction for dividends paid, or allowing the recipient a credit against its tax for all or part of the tax paid by the corporation. In an international business combination, the two sets of owners may be located predominantly in two different tax jurisdictions. Is it possible to structure the transaction so that each group will receive its dividends primarily from a subsidiary operating in the group's own tax jurisdiction in order to eliminate or to minimize the tax on its dividends? Can this be achieved while according each group the appropriate voting power at the holding company level?

Other Conduit Country Issues

The earnings of the acquired group's subsidiaries will first be channeled through their parent and then to the acquired group. For example, a German company may acquire a U.S.-based multinational group. As the earnings of the foreign subsidiaries pass through the United States, will they attract any U.S. income tax or U.S. dividend withholding taxes? Are there ways to avoid such intermediate-country tax? Are there opportunities for multiple tax benefits resulting from intermediate-country taxation?

For example, high-tax foreign operations of a U.S. subsidiary may present an opportunity for an interest expense double dip if the high-tax foreign operations are conducted as a branch of the U.S. subsidiary or a second-tier U.S. subsidiary or in a "flow-through" entity owned by the U.S. subsidiary. Interest expense incurred by the foreign operation can save foreign taxes at the high rate, while the United States views the interest expense as allocable to the worldwide assets of the U.S. group.

Assume the foreign operation generates $20 million of pretax income subject to a 70 percent tax rate, or tax of $14 million. If this is the only foreign operation under the U.S. subsidiary, the U.S. tax of the foreign income is only $6.8 million, and an unusual excess foreign tax credit of $7.2 million is generated.

Now consider what happens if the foreign operations incur interest expense of $10 million and 90 percent of the assets of the U.S. subsidiary, including its foreign operations, are viewed as U.S. assets. The foreign operations incur tax on only $10 million of net income, for a tax of $7 million—and a tax savings of $7 million resulting from the interest expense. At the same time, the United States allocates $9 million of the interest expense to U.S. assets for a U.S. tax savings of $3 million. Although the allocation means that the United States views the foreign-source net income as $19 million ($20 million from operations less only $1 million of interest expense allocated as foreign), the $7 million of foreign taxes is still sufficient to offset the U.S. tax of $6.4 million. Leaving the high-taxed foreign operations owned by the U.S. has provided an opportunity for an interest expense "double dip" where the $7 million foreign tax benefit and $3.4 million U.S. tax benefit have produced a total tax benefit of 104 percent of the interest expense.

Hybridization

There may be a number of reasons that a legal entity should be structured so that it is viewed as a flow-through entity by the taxing jurisdiction of the owners. For example, losses may be anticipated for a period of time and flow-through treatment may permit the owners to claim a tax benefit. Another example is the case in which owners qualify for foreign tax credits in their home tax jurisdictions for foreign income taxes they incur, but not for income taxes incurred by corporations from which they receive dividends. In such cases, flow-through treatment may enable them to claim a foreign tax credit for income taxes incurred by the flow-through entity.

Financing and Interest Expense Double Dips

Does the combination provide an opportunity to leverage the operations in any particular country at no or minimal tax cost? Can the owners also borrow against their stock? If the tax jurisdiction of either corporation or either of the owner groups imposes tax on unrepatriated earnings of foreign subsidiaries, can the two organizations be combined under a holding company located in a taxing jurisdiction that does not have such rules, while the diluted ownership of one or both owner groups permits them to escape current taxation on unrepatriated earnings? Will such a structure permit operations to be leveraged on an intercompany basis with the interest expense providing tax benefit, while the untaxed income is re-lent to operating subsidiaries?

Worldwide Integration

When two worldwide groups are involved in a business combination, there are likely to be many countries in which both groups have operations. Should their activities be combined in a single entity or group of entities linked by direct ownership, so that losses in the activities of one group can be offset by profits in the activities of the other group? What are the tax costs in achieving such a combination?

Is there any likelihood that either set of activities in a particular country will be sold in the future? If so, would it be possible to avoid taxable gains on the sale by keeping the activities that may be sold in a separate entity owned by a nonresident entity? Although each subsidiary of both groups is held by a nonresident entity, can a de facto onshore consolidation be achieved if, for example, the two subsidiaries form a partnership that can be unwound at no tax cost at the time a sale occurs?

Are tax problems created by "sandwiches," such as in cases in which a U.S.-based group acquires a U.K.-based group that has its own U.S. subsidiary? The U.S. subsidiary's earnings are subject to U.S. tax and, where they are repatriated to the United Kingdom, a U.S. dividend withholding tax is incurred. When the U.K. company distributes the earnings to the top U.S. company, they are subject to U.S. income tax, again with no credit for any U.S. taxes already incurred.

Reversing the Transaction

For any of the foregoing considerations, can a better result be achieved if the acquiring corporation is acquired instead by the other corporation? This might be advantageous if, for example, the acquiring corporation has unrealized losses that can be triggered or if it has advantageous tax attributes, such as tax loss carryovers, that might be extinguished if it is acquired.

EXAMPLE OF ADDITIONAL TAX PLANNING IN A CROSS-BORDER ACQUISITION WHERE TARGET OWNERS DO NOT WISH TO CONTINUE TO PARTICIPATE

Most of the tax planning considerations described above, in which target owners wish to continue to participate, will also apply when they do not. However, several comments are in order.

Asset Basis Step-Ups for Exit Gain Recognition

Greater flexibility is available when target shareholders are exiting. For example, if they have or recognize gain in their home country anyway and if their home tax jurisdiction is on a foreign tax credit system, would recognizing taxable gain with respect to the target's assets—in order to achieve a tax basis step-up—result in a greater foreign tax credit for the exiting target shareholders, so that they incur no greater tax than the minimum necessary?

Selling Foreign Operations Without Incurring Host or Home Country Taxes

Some home taxing jurisdictions permit shareholders to exit without incurring tax. For example, several continental European tax systems provide participation exemptions that may not only exempt profit repatriations but may also exempt exit gains. Other systems do not tax gains of foreign subsidiaries, so that a simple holding company structure may not only afford a mixing of high and low rate income for foreign tax credit purposes, but may also permit exit gains to remain untaxed.

Another example is the United States, where it is possible to avoid both foreign and U.S. income taxation upon disposition of foreign operations. "Disposition Planning Possible Under EC 1992 Merger Directive," by John Karls and Tom van den Hoven, in the January/February 1992 issue of the *Journal of International Taxation* (Warren, Gorham and Lamont) catalogs the way in which U.S. tax on disposition gains can be avoided. This can be achieved by using foreign tax credits, despite the fact that U.S. capital gains tax can be reduced only if the foreign tax jurisdiction in which the corporation operates taxes the U.S. shareholder. The article examines how the European Community 1992 Merger Directive increases the range of transactions in which the U.S. tax can be avoided. These techniques are aimed at converting capital gain to dividend income or gain, with respect to operating assets, so that regular foreign tax credits can be used. Although beyond the scope of this chapter, there are several techniques for avoiding U.S. capital gains tax even when the seller does not have sufficient foreign tax credits.

CONCLUSION

The parties to a cross-border merger or acquisition should retain the best international tax advisers available to ensure that their combined worldwide tax burden is minimized and deferred insofar as possible, and that opportunities for multiple tax benefits are seized.

CHAPTER 22

STRATEGIC PARTNERSHIPS AND CORPORATE VENTURE INVESTMENTS

In the past five to ten years, there has been an explosion in the number of joint ventures and other strategic alliances formed by American companies. Strategic alliances involve two or more companies that join, pooling risks, rewards, and resources, to achieve specific but sometimes different strategic goals. These alliances, ranging from full ownership control to contractual control only, are outlined in Table 22-1.

Industry sources estimate that the number of strategic alliances has grown from only 345 in the 1950s to more than 3,500 in 1991 alone.* The rapid growth in strategic alliances is perhaps best evidenced by a wave of joint ventures in the automobile and computer industries. As recently as a decade ago, it would have been viewed as "un-American" for a U.S. company to consider aligning itself with a Japanese firm to build cars. But today the marketplace boasts "Toyota Chevys" (Novas), "Chrysler-Mitsubishis" (minivan engines), and "Ford Mazdas" (Ford owns 25 percent of Mazda).

Throughout the global marketplace there have been dramatic changes since the 1970s. Companies that were once flush with cash

---

*"Slow Dancing with an Elephant," *Small Business Reports*, June 1992, p. 53

TABLE 22-1   Spectrum of strategic alliance alternatives

Full Ownership Control Only	*Partial Ownership and Contractual Control*	*Contractual Control*
Mergers (or acquisitions)	Operating joint ventures	Cooperative agreements
Internal ventures (and spin-offs to full business unit status)	Minority investments	R&D partnerships
		Cross-licensing or cross-distribution arrangements
		Joint activities

Katherine Rudie Harrigan, *Managing for Joint Venture Success* (Lexington, MA: D.C. Heath and Company, 1986).

now find that to remain competitive they must trim the fat from their operations and become leaner and meaner. Increasingly, they are recognizing the utility of strategic alliances.

The willingness of large companies to enter into alliances presents an opportunity for smaller firms seeking financing for growth. Small companies that are focused on niche applications of unique products are able to command high premiums from larger ones, which often have difficulties in reacting quickly to emerging markets and products.

Although this chapter discusses several of the alternatives listed in Table 22-1 as viable vehicles for financing growth, it focuses primarily on partial ownership alliances.

Which joint ventures or other strategic alliances represent viable options for companies seeking financing for growth? Before entering into a strategic alliance, one must first understand the risks involved. Katherine Rudie Harrigan, author of *Managing for Joint Venture Success*, has estimated that more than half of the cooperative ventures forged since 1975 were ill-conceived at birth: their objectives were unclear, owners' capabilities were poorly matched, or owners aspired to achieve more than was possible within the business in which their joint venture competed. Harrigan's conclusions are supported by her research, which indicates that more than 50 percent of joint ventures last four years or less.

For a company considering a strategic alliance as a vehicle for financing growth, it is important to note that alliances are more than a source of financing. Although it is certainly true that alliances can provide both an immediate and a longer-term source of funds, if the purpose of the alliance is to provide financing only, other more conventional sources should be explored first. Entering into an alliance is a strategic decision that involves ceding an element of control, but also provides the offsetting benefits of reduced risk, increased potential rewards, and/or reduced investment in resources. In fact, the reduction of future resources necessary to finance growth through leveraging a partner's development, operations, marketing, or distribution resources may greatly outweigh in benefit the immediate cash infusion provided by an alliance.

JOINT VENTURES

An operating joint venture may be defined as a separate entity (partnership or corporation) that has two or more companies as owners. The partners contribute capital to the joint venture in the form of cash, inventory, distribution networks, manufacturing processes, fixed assets, or intellectual property such as technology patents and trademarks.

When considering a joint venture as an alternative for financing growth, it is necessary to consider the positions of both potential venture partners. The company seeking financing is, presumably, a small or mid-sized firm, perhaps one without access to more traditional sources of funds. Conversely, the other partner is likely to be a larger company with greater access to and availability of cash. It is also likely to have the operational capacity, such as distribution networks or manufacturing capabilities, to support the product of the smaller player. Operational capacity is important—sometimes even more important than cash—to the smaller company seeking to expand.

When does it make sense to enter into an operating joint venture rather than into a minority equity investment?

Generally, an operating joint venture makes sense when the larger company is interested in a segment—but not all—of the smaller company's business. For example, a large company may be interested in a specific product line, market segment, customer application, or production operation of a smaller company. In such cases it may be logical to create a joint venture around the area of interest, with both companies maintaining ownership positions.

Another example of an appropriate situation for a joint venture involves a small company that has developed a technology or a capability outside the scope of its main business. For example, a manufacturing company may have developed software to control its production process. A computer hardware manufacturer may view the software as a viable product to market to other manufacturing companies. Thus, a joint venture could be created in which the larger computer company contributes cash and development and marketing assistance, and the smaller manufacturing company contributes its proprietary software.

Crystal Technologies Corporation, a union of Jones Engineering and Waste Systems, is an example of a joint venture that was used as a vehicle for financing growth. Jones Engineering, founded by a group of engineers, was a general engineering services company; its primary business was chemical-engineering consulting. Over the years, Jones Engineering expanded its scope and began to develop freeze crystallization technologies for its clients. Freeze crystallization is a physical process that separates the components of a liquid solution by freezing them and separating their crystals from the remaining liquid.

After several years of researching and developing the technology, Jones Engineering decided to analyze the potential of freeze crystallization as a stand-alone business. Market research convinced company management that the most profitable and easiest market entry for the technology would be in the field of hazardous waste.

Jones Engineering searched for hazardous waste companies with which to develop a strategic alliance and formed a joint venture with Waste Systems. Waste Systems provided the funding necessary to demonstrate the technology and to build the first commercial unit for hazardous-waste remediation activities. Jones Engineering contributed the technology.

The joint venture was a logical financing vehicle for the situation: Waste Systems was interested only in the freeze crystallization technology, not in Jones's consulting business. In addition, although Jones Engineering recognized that the freeze crystallization business had significant cash needs, the company had no such requirements for its core engineering-consulting business.

MINORITY EQUITY INVESTMENT

A minority equity investment occurs when one company buys less than a 50 percent equity interest in another company. The minority equity investment is frequently used by smaller companies to finance growth and is prevalent in high-technology industries. Large companies use this vehicle to spread out their research and development activities, as well as their investment risks. Large companies also use the minority equity investment vehicle as a way of obtaining interest in a product or service line that is complementary to their own business. This kind of investment is often accompanied by supporting production, distribution, and/or marketing agreements.

A minority equity investment generally makes sense when a large company is interested in all of a smaller company's businesses, or in situations where the area of interest is inextricably tied to the smaller company's total business. The minority equity investment is often an attractive alternative to creating a separate operating joint venture.

Minority equity investments often have structures that involve more than common stock ownership by the larger company. Traditional financing elements are also present in minority structures. Financing elements can include convertible preferred stock, convertible debentures, and debentures with warrants or options, as well as common-stock ownership.

LICENSING

In licensing, one company grants the right to another company to produce a particular product or service, or to use a proprietary process, technology, trademark, or other intellectual property. The licensee compensates the licensor—generally through cash payment—for these rights. Licensing, therefore, can be an attractive financing vehicle for a small company with a proprietary product or technology.

Generally, a licensee pays royalties to the licensor over time, as products are marketed or technology is used. However, it is prudent for the company seeking financing for growth to challenge this traditional arrangement, and seek a greater percentage of the royalty payments in advance. Ultimately, the licensor may find it advantageous to accept a lower overall royalty payment if the disbursement is skewed toward cash up front prior to licensing. License agreements can be structured as "exclusive" or "nonexclusive." An exclusive licensing arrangement allows the licensee the sole right to market or to use the product, whereas the nonexclusive arrangement may involve a number of licensees.

The following is an example of the use of a licensing agreement as a financing vehicle: Progressive Diagnostic Systems (PDS) was a technology-based company that had developed patents, trade secrets, and other proprietary technology relating to high-speed medical imaging. PDS had operated as a development corporation for five years but had not yet manufactured or sold products. The company was nearing the end of its second round of financing and needed additional financing to survive.

International Technologies Corporation (ITC) had developed a large installed base of medical diagnostic-imaging equipment in the United States. Both ITC and PDS believed that a program of mutual cooperation could significantly advance the development and exploitation of high-speed imaging technology, with the product to be manufactured by ITC as the technology progressed.

ITC made a significant up-front cash payment to its partner and also provided PDS with some R&D equipment. In addition, the agreement called for ITC to make royalty payments to PDS when products were manufactured and sold. The up-front cash payment provided PDS with the financing needed to continue development of the product; ITC's large cash payment was offset by reduced royalty payments when the product was manufactured.

APPROACH FOR CONSIDERING STRATEGIC ALLIANCES

The first step for a company considering a strategic alliance is to rigorously define its own company strategy. A thorough understanding of its own strategic core, as well as the elements of the business that must be protected from encroachment by competitors, is essential. An alliance represents a compromise in which a company gives up a measure of control or autonomy in order to obtain something of greater value.

The next critical step in the strategic review process is to determine the company's own strengths and weaknesses. An honest self-appraisal can help determine whether an alliance will yield beneficial results—and the type of alliance that makes the most sense—and can assist in identifying potential partners.

Consider, for example, Condor Computers, a manufacturer and marketer of portable computers. Condor had established a subsidiary several years earlier that was developing software to provide a valuable communication link with mainframe systems. The subsidiary was in urgent need of financing to sustain its prospects for growth.

Condor clearly understood its own strategic strengths and weaknesses. Its strengths included the development work completed to date on the integrated-system product, an established market presence in a number of industries, and the quality and performance of its portable computers. Condor's weaknesses included a lack of marketing strength necessary to promote a product that differed from its traditional line (a software versus a hardware product), a significant cash need at the subsidiary level, and insufficient field support for an integrated-system product.

Condor's careful analysis of its strategic position helped it to understand the viability of various strategic alliance possibilities. Condor identified a major computer hardware/software manufacturer as the most appropriate potential partner with the cash, operating capabilities, and marketing wherewithal necessary to compensate for its own weaknesses.

Finding a Strategic Partner

In some ways, successful strategic partnerships are like successful marriages: each partner's strengths should complement the other's weaknesses; each partner must contribute to the union, and through it, contribute to the other partner's well-being; and, to maximize the likelihood of long-term success, both partners should make equally valuable contributions. In narrowing the range of potential alliance partners whose strengths complement a company's weaknesses, it is important to consider categories of potential partners. When Condor began its search it considered U.S. computer hardware manufacturers, foreign computer manufacturers, computer software companies, direct competitors, and even a professional service company that was organized according to industry sectors.

After a partner category has been selected, the process of identifying and contacting the most appropriate partner begins. At this stage, a company should begin to analyze the mechanics, as well as the specifics, of the potential venture. Such analysis should include a preliminary financial analysis, market and competitor analysis, and analysis of the potential venture's impact on its parent companies. Appendix 22-1 at the end of this chapter provides a checklist of areas to consider when analyzing a joint venture or other strategic partnership.

Negotiating the Alliance Agreement

Once a potential partner has been identified and contacted, the process of negotiation begins. Negotiators should strive to complete a letter of intent and, eventually, a definitive agreement for the joint venture. It is important to remember that a win-win strategy must be employed in a strategic alliance, which may be different from strategies used in outright acquisitions. Appendix 22-2 provides an outline of the issues and sections in a typical definitive agreement.

A critical business issue to address during negotiations is the interaction between the venture and its parents. The alliance may either receive product from or supply product to its parents. In such cases, the interactions between the partners and the joint venture will involve transfer pricing issues. The mechanism for setting transfer prices should be determined during the negotiating stage.

Similarly, the procedures and charges for any administrative or operational function handled by one of the parents must be addressed during negotiations. If one partner is given responsibility for the accounting and personnel functions of the alliance, mechanisms for allocating overhead costs to the venture should be clearly defined.

Another key negotiating issue is that of capital contributions. Two points regarding contributions should be decided during negotiations: the initial value of contributions and the guidelines for ongoing contributions.

Initial contributions may appear in many forms: cash, machinery and equipment, land and buildings, technology, and/or management know-how. In general, fair market value is the determinant in setting the amount for capital contributions. However, setting the value of technology and management know-how is always difficult. The worth of such intangible contributions must be estimated and negotiated. Furthermore, U.S. companies should recognize the potential tax liabilities incurred when transferring technology whose value exceeds its tax basis—although with proper planning any potential tax liability may be avoided.

As negotiations proceed, the partners must collaborate with one another to develop a business plan for the joint venture. The development of such a business plan often involves the active participation of a number of task forces that analyze potential operations, financial, tax, and accounting matters, and personnel issues. In addition, each partner should conduct its own financial analyses.

One of the key business issues addressed during negotiations is control. It is important to differentiate between management control and ownership interest. Ownership interest relates to the value of the contributions from each partner. Although management control generally follows ownership interest, there are certainly situations in which a minority partner retains management control through a management agreement. Experience has shown that ventures are usually more successful and operate more efficiently when one parent has clear management control. This mitigates against 50-50 joint ventures without a definitive management agreement.

To ensure that the minority partner is involved in the fundamental decisions affecting the joint venture, the joint venture agreement usually grants blocking rights to that partner. Blocking rights cover areas or actions that require unanimous consent before the venture can proceed. These rights (outlined in Appendix 22-2 [12]) typically address selling or otherwise disposing of major assets, altering in any way the agreements that underlie the venture, the appointment and retention of key management personnel, and pledging the venture's material assets.

Other blocking rights involve borrowing beyond an agreed-upon limit and adopting the annual budget. They also address the issue of deviating materially from agreed-upon budgets, to guard against exceeding, to any measurable degree, the capital expenditure allocation. Blocking rights could also involve changing other authorized capital (to preclude the majority partner from unilaterally altering the venture's capital structure) and distributing income. The minority partner should insist upon having a voice in the distribution of profits.

Conflict resolution is another key business issue to discuss during negotiations. Establishment of blocking rights, as described, presents one way for the minority partner to exert some control over the process. But what happens when unanimous consent is not achieved regarding a matter of major importance? Most joint ventures have several mechanisms for resolving conflicts when consent of the joint venture board cannot be reached.

One effective mechanism is the coordinating committee. A coordinating committee, which is made up of senior members of both companies, has broader powers than the joint venture board. Its members are removed from the day-to-day operations of the joint venture and meet routinely—perhaps twice a year or more, as needed—to resolve conflicts. The coordinating committee's perspective is, presumably, broader than that of the joint venture board. Thus, the committee should be able to look past minor day-to-day issues to the larger picture. As an added benefit, the coordinating committee mechanism also provides an ideal way to keep the senior management of each partner informed of the joint venture's current status and operations.

Other conflict resolution mechanisms may be triggered if the coordinating committee is unable to resolve a conflict. One such mechanism is the "Chinese auction," in which one partner makes a bid to purchase the interests of the other. If the partner does not accept the would-be purchaser's bid, that partner is required to purchase from the first company at the bid price.

Arbitration is still another mechanism. Arbitration involves an objective arbitrator who reviews both sides of the conflict and then issues a resolution. If arbitration is to be used, decisions about how it will work must be made during negotiations. Such decisions include who the arbiter will be, where the arbitration will occur, and what circumstances will trigger this mechanism.

Because of the high percentage of joint ventures and other alliances that fail within the first four years, it is important during negotiations to consider the termination process. Clear identification of management responsibilities, streamlining the policy and operating decision making, and effective conflict-resolution mechanisms will go a long way toward preventing termination. If the joint venture does terminate, all partners should concentrate on cost minimization.

While it may be counterintuitive, one of the most important issues to focus on early in the process of pursuing an alliance are the exit strategies—what form the desired conclusion of the relationsihp will take, and what the escape valves are if expectations are not met. Although it is not often used, reverse business planning is one mechanism for achieving cost minimization. Reverse business planning examines the same factors as regular business planning: markets, product competition, and operations. The goal of reverse business planning is to identify strategies that will enable the partners to achieve the greatest overall economic value from a venture's liquidation. Such strategies may include selling portions of the venture back to the partners or other investors, and selling or otherwise disposing of assets and selling technologies that were developed during the alliance. Although termination can often lead to confrontation, it is important to remember that both parties are more likely to benefit if the liquidation is approached in a positive, constructive, and cost-minimizing way.

APPENDIX 22-1. STRATEGIC ALLIANCE CHECKLIST

1. Background
    a. Basic information
    b. Preliminary due diligence

2. Facilities
    a. Land and building
    b. Equipment and tooling
    c. Services and utilities
    d. Adequacy and future needs
    e. General evaluation

3. Purchasing and Traffic

4. Public Relations

5. Financial
    a. General
    b. Financial status
    c. Financial operations

6. Tax
    a. Legal form of venture
    b. Issues affecting characterization of entity for U.S. tax pur-
        poses
    c. Selection or creation of participating "parent" entities
    d. Capitalization
    e. Foreign income
    f. Constraints on transactions between parents and ventures
    g. Tax aspects of termination

7. Environmental
    a. General occupancy
    b. Present occupancy
    c. Previous occupancies
    d. Facilities and land
    e. Regulatory/enforcement actions

8. Legal

9. Markets and Marketing

10. Products and Services
    a. General information
    b. Competitive factors
    c. Technical aspects

11. Competition
    a. Competitors
    b. Competitive products
    c. Outlook

12. Management and Personnel
    a. Organization and management
    b. Compensation
    c. Labor
    d. Employment

13. Engineering and Research and Development
    a. Projects
    b. Activities

14. Manufacturing Operations
    a. Production
    b. General evaluation

APPENDIX 22-2.   OUTLINE OF A JOINT VENTURE AGREEMENT

1. General Information
   a. Date
   b. Names of partners
   c. Business description and location, or headquarters of partners
   d. Business description or purpose

2. Definitions of Terms
   a. Definition of major terms for accurate and clear understanding by the joint venture parties (e.g., *affiliate, board of directors, deadlock notice, GAAP, transfer price, investment costs,* etc.), are detailed in the Appendix.

3. Organization of Joint Venture Company
   a. Form of organization and state of jurisdiction. Include the Articles of Incorporation (if appropriate) and the bylaws in the Appendix.
   b. Name of joint venture company, principal place of business (e.g., local executive offices) and purpose (e.g., description of size and type of product and plant facilities)
   c. Names, locations, and business description of partners in joint venture, as well as each partner's percent interest in joint venture

4. Capitalization of Joint Venture
   a. Initial capital contributed by the joint venture partners (equity vs. loans with agreed-upon interest rate)
   b. Additional equity or capital contributions made by partners (e.g., required for continuation of joint venture and other types of contributions)
   c. Indebtedness (e.g., loans from sources other than joint venture partners, such as banks)
   d. Loans and/or guarantees from partners with agreed-upon interest rate
   e. Transfer of patents and technology, licensing of technology, etc.
   f. Transferability of common stock

    g. Nondissolution of joint venture

    h. Financing of the new company (e.g., start-up and ongoing operations)

5. Review and Term of Joint Venture

    a. Term or length of time for operating joint venture

    b. Extension of term

    c. Periodic review and review procedure

    d. Termination of joint venture

6. Joint Venture Partners' Interests

    a. Division of interests between joint venture partners

    b. Capital contributions of joint venture partners

    c. Failure-to-contribute clause

7. Management

    a. Powers, responsibilities, and procedures of stockholders, board of directors and operating management, officers, managers, etc.

    b. Stockholders—meetings (both annual and special), issues

    c. Board of directors—composition, number of members, constitution, responsibilities, frequency of meetings, action without meetings, telephone conference, voting, quorum, deadlock by board, actions requiring unanimous vote

    d. Operating management—composition, number of operating management members, responsibilities and authority, assignment of personnel, handling of unresolved issues (deadlock), names and titles of key executives

    e. Employment of personnel at joint venture

8. Relationship of Parties

    a. Parts, services, materials, installations provided by parents

    b. Products provided by parents

    c. Initial facilities

    d. Products description

    e. Engineering

    f. Manufacturing of product(s)

    g. Policies and procedures

        • warranties

        • R & D cost absorption

        • initial facilities

- change orders
- quality assurance procurement specifications
- proprietary information

h. Patents and technology
i. Confidentiality
j. Rights and third parties
k. Liabilities of company, indemnification
l. Performance bonds
m. Owner's right to review proprietary technology use
n. License of technology

9. Books and Records
   a. Fiscal year determination
   b. Maintenance, location, and inspection of books, records, and bank accounts
   c. Reserves
   d. Budget
   e. Annual financial reports
   f. Selection of auditors
   g. Tax returns
   h. Annual certification

10. Profits and Losses
    a. Distributable amount
    b. Distribution of cash flow
    c. Repayment of contribution loans
    d. Allocation

11. Allocation and Related Tax Provisions
    a. Contribution of property
    b. Recapture income
    c. Miscellaneous tax allocations
    d. Tax returns, tax credit, tax decisions not otherwise provided for
    e. Notice of tax audit
    f. Cost recovery
    g. Separate reporting
    h. Withholding
    i. Penalties

12. Blocking Rights and Deadlock

a. Fundamental issues
- additional capital for joint venture
- authorization of issuance of stock
- declaration or payment of dividends
- reinvestment of earnings in joint venture
- indebtedness
- corporate officers
- litigation
- guarantee, indemnity
- unusual contracts or commitments
- license agreement
- agreement/material transaction with one of joint owners
- policy change of any kind (e.g., manufacturing, sale of products, etc.)
- financial policy
- basic change in nature of business or product specification
- other material transactions
- amendments to joint venture agreement or certificate sale and/or transfer of all or part of joint venture partners' interests
- admittance of new member in joint venture
- increase in capacity, closure, or reduction of premises
- disposition of know-how, technology, or proprietary rights
- liquidation or merger of joint venture company
- confession of judgment against joint venture and/or its partners
- claim/liabilities of joint venture partners to arbitration
- act that makes it possible to do "business as usual"
- budgets for joint venture (e.g., including capital expenditures)

b. Procedure in event of deadlock

13. Adjustment of Joint Venture Partners' Interests
    a. Adjustment by agreement
    b. Adjustment upon departure, merger, or increase in capacity

14. Restrictions on Disposal of Stock
    a. Restrictions
    b. Transfers
    c. Assignees and new partners

    d. Right of first refusal
    e. Option to "put" or "call"
    f. Fair market value; terms of purchases or sales
    g. Effect on distributions and allocations

15. Termination of Joint Venture
    a. Date, if any determined
    b. Events causing termination
- end of term of joint venture and extensions
- written agreement by joint venture partners
- written notice by joint venture partner (against partner who has defaulted)
- change in control of a joint venture partner
- bankruptcy or receivership placement of a joint venture partner
- nonrenewal of technology exchange/license agreement
- court decree

    c. Rights and obligations
- terms for owner buyout
- assignment of interest (corporate)
- right of first refusal
- sale of joint venture
- liquidation (and liquidator)
- survival rights of technology
- implementation of grants, transfers, and conveyance
- release, discharge, and indemnification
- continuing obligations

16. Product Liability
    a. Insurance, additional insureds
    b. Claims administration for design and manufacturing, marketing, and combined claims
    c. Primary and excess coverage premium costs

17. Force Majeure

18. Confidentiality

19. Closing
    a. Terms of closing (date, place, transferred material, etc.)
    b. Conditions to the obligations of each partner

    c. Certificate from each parent, consents

    d. Attorney's opinion from each parent

    e. Approvals of information transfer (e.g., government, etc.)

    f. Delay of closing date, termination

20. Representations and Warranties (for all parents of the new joint venture company)

    a. Organization and standing

    b. Authority

    c. Absence of conflict

    d. Absence of required consents and contractual restrictions

    e. Acting on its own

    f. Property transfers to joint venture

    g. Disclosure

    h. Survival of representations and warranties

21. Miscellaneous Provisions

    a. Public announcements

    b. Governing law, consent to jurisdiction

    c. Arbitration/conflict resolution

    d. Section headings

    e. Partner covenant, interest

    f. Counterparts

    g. Further assurances

    h. Currency

    i. Governing language

    j. Assignments

    k. Entire agreement, amendments

    l. Severability

    m. Legal action and fees

    n. Expenses

    o. No waiver of rights

    p. References and inclusions

    q. Investment representation

    r. Estopped certificates

    s. Secrecy obligation

    t. Waiver of partition

    u. Exhibits

INDEX